Exploring
the North Coast

Exploring the North Coast

*from the Golden Gate
to the Oregon Border*

by Mike Hayden

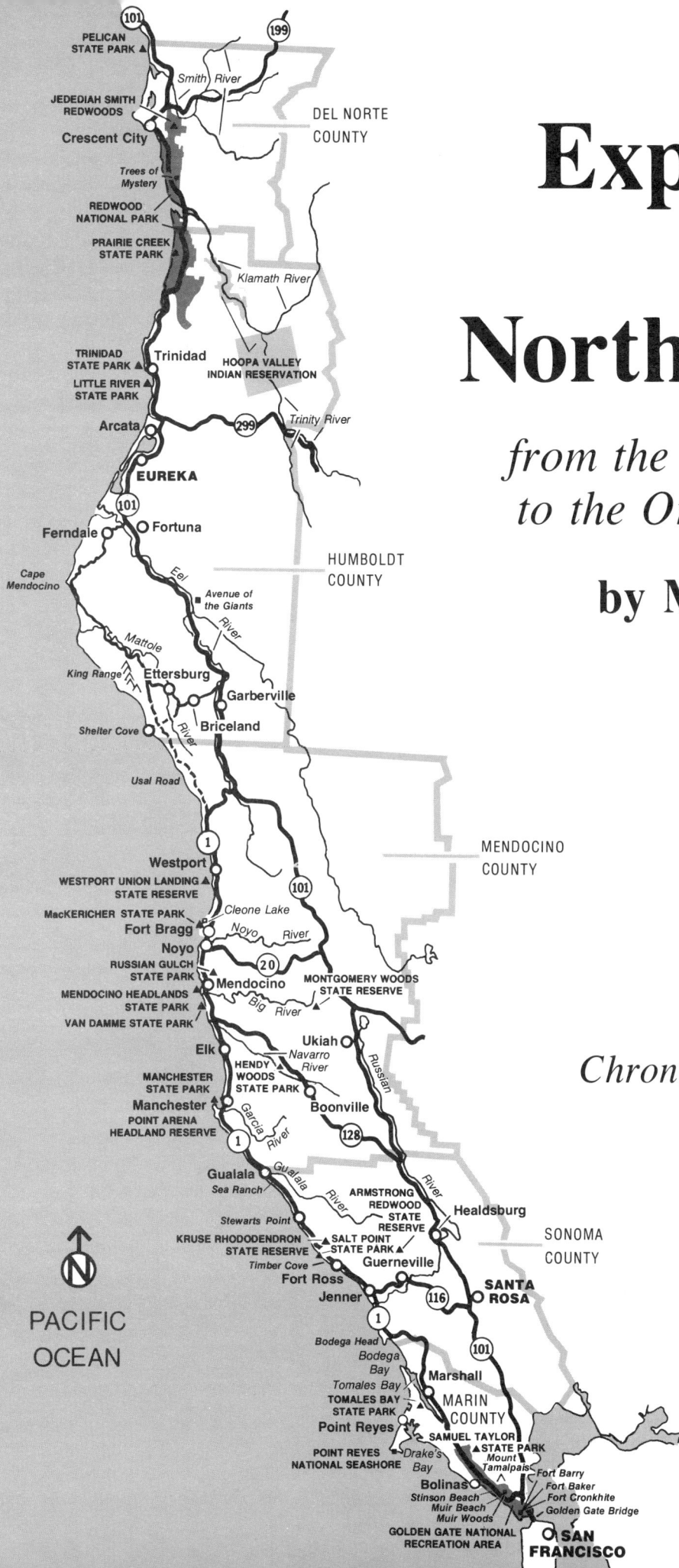

Chronicle Books

PACIFIC
OCEAN

Map labels:

PELICAN STATE PARK

JEDEDIAH SMITH REDWOODS

Crescent City

Smith River

DEL NORTE COUNTY

Trees of Mystery

REDWOOD NATIONAL PARK

PRAIRIE CREEK STATE PARK

Klamath River

TRINIDAD STATE PARK

Trinidad

LITTLE RIVER STATE PARK

HOOPA VALLEY INDIAN RESERVATION

Trinity River

Arcata

EUREKA

Ferndale

Fortuna

HUMBOLDT COUNTY

Cape Mendocino

Eel River

Avenue of the Giants

Mattole

King Range

Ettersburg

Garberville

Shelter Cove

Briceland

Usal Road

Westport

WESTPORT UNION LANDING STATE RESERVE

MENDOCINO COUNTY

MacKERICHER STATE PARK

Cleone Lake

Fort Bragg

Noyo River

Noyo

RUSSIAN GULCH STATE PARK

Mendocino

MONTGOMERY WOODS STATE RESERVE

MENDOCINO HEADLANDS STATE PARK

Big River

VAN DAMME STATE PARK

Elk

Ukiah

Navarro River

HENDY WOODS STATE PARK

Russian River

MANCHESTER STATE PARK

Boonville

Manchester

POINT ARENA HEADLAND RESERVE

Garcia River

Gualala

Sea Ranch

Gualala River

ARMSTRONG REDWOOD STATE RESERVE

Healdsburg

Stewarts Point

KRUSE RHODODENDRON STATE RESERVE

SALT POINT STATE PARK

SONOMA COUNTY

Timber Cove

Fort Ross

Guerneville

Jenner

SANTA ROSA

Bodega Head

Bodega Bay

Tomales Bay

Marshall

TOMALES BAY STATE PARK

MARIN COUNTY

Point Reyes

SAMUEL TAYLOR STATE PARK

Mount Tamalpais

POINT REYES NATIONAL SEASHORE

Drake's Bay

Bolinas

Fort Barry

Fort Baker

Fort Cronkhite

Stinson Beach

Muir Beach

Muir Woods

Golden Gate Bridge

GOLDEN GATE NATIONAL RECREATION AREA

SAN FRANCISCO

This book is dedicated to Oregos,
who dwells in a rock at
the mouth of the Klamath River

They had what the world has lost. They have it now. What the world has lost, the world must have again lest it die. Not many years are left to have or have not, to recapture the lost ingredient. . . . What, in our human world, is this power to live? It is the ancient, lost reverence and passion for human personality, joined with the ancient, lost reverence and passion for the earth and its web of life.

From Indians of the Americas
by John Collier
Commissioner of Indian Affairs, 1933-1945

Library of Congress Cataloging in Publication Data

Hayden, Mike.
    Exploring the north coast.

    Rev. ed. of: Exploring the north coast from
the Golden Gate to the Oregon border. c1976
    Bibliography: p. 154
    Includes index.
    1. California, Northern—Description and
travel—Tours. 2. Coasts—California, Northern
—Guide-books. I. Title.
F859.3.H37   1982   917.94'1045   81-21733
ISBN 0-87701-253-9   AACR2

Chronicle Books
870 Market Street
San Francisco, Ca. 94102

Cover photography by Baron Wolman
Cover design by Michael Fennelly

Contents

The North Coast: An Overview

The North Coast is shaped for adventure. Exploring its solitary sweeps of forest, pasture, and seashore affords a rare excitement in any season. The land is rugged, windblown, and fog-damp. Settlement is sparse. Some of the lonely shoreline drives are bold undertakings. On these stretches you rollercoast from timbered gulch to craggy headland, and wheel along the brink of knife-edged cliffs where Pacific waves explode with thunderous eruptions of surf and spray.

Here and there, a dim side road or tortuous foot path winds down to an isolated beach. Other byways lead off in an opposite direction to hidden places in the coastal mountains.

The term North Coast is often meant to include all of the redwoods and the interior Coast Ranges. The coastal redwoods form a belt of forest fifteen to thirty-five miles wide. The mountains of the interior Coast Ranges stretch sixty miles inland to the Central Valley. Another book or two this size would be needed to cover these highlands. This guide will help you to know the slender coastal shelf which runs between the western wall of the Coast Ranges and five-hundred miles of Pacific shoreline.

Across the Golden Gate from San Francisco tower the Marin Headlands. The book will begin here and guide you along the Northern California Coast to Pelican Beach on the Oregon line. The redwoods will be examined wherever these remarkable trees are found growing close to the ocean.

A mild, damp climate prevails everywhere along the North Coast but we will pass through a great diversity of natural settings. Foggy Point Reyes, where sea lions gather, is a world of its own. The precipitous Jenner Coast, with its Russian fort, offers sheep-dotted pastoral seascapes. The craggy Mendocino Coast, beloved of artists, naturalists, and history buffs, is more accessible and perhaps the most well-known area on the North Coast.

North of Westport, the pavement veers east to avoid the Primitive Coast. Here the coastal shelf is interrupted by the sheer slopes of the King Range. Beyond Rockport, you leave State Highway 1 to continue north across these mountains on a sketchy network of paved and unpaved roads. Salt spray mists your windshield as you round a desolate, wave-lapped causeway at windy Cape Mendocino. Across the Eel River, U.S. Highway 101 leads to Eureka, a bustling outpost of population and progress. North of Eureka the highway follows the Redwood Coast with its skyscraper trees, giant ferns, agate beaches, freshwater lagoons, swift salmon rivers, and herds of Roosevelt elk.

On this four-hundred-mile drive, you slow down for fewer than a dozen towns with more than six hundred permanent residents. Only Fort Bragg, Eureka, Arcata, and Crescent City have traffic lights. Eureka's 24,000 souls make it the largest California city north of the state capital. The sleepy fishing villages, rural trading centers, and antiquated logging towns invite an adventure into the past. Ferndale is filled with Victorian dwellings which antedate the horseless carriage. The pride of Elk, Little River, and Mendocino City are their handsome old inns. Point Arena's moldering wharf recalls the town's heyday as a port for whalers and lumber schooners. Crescent City has a lighthouse museum that you may walk to at low tide.

Perhaps the oldest home in California is the redwood shanty with a circular doorway that stands on the bluff at Requa overlooking the Klamath River estuary. Nobody is quite sure how many generations of a Yurok Indian family have lived there. Some of the coastal tribes were totally exterminated by the settlers, but others were never really defeated. Descendants of the Yurok, Karuk, and Hupa still reside near the banks of the Klamath.

The traveler who wishes to step back in time should know about the Salmon Festival, held each year in June at Klamath township. Here braves and maidens in 200-year-old costumes laden with seashells perform the sacred dances. Homage is paid to the spirit of the Four Winds and to the spirit, Oregos, who brings the salmon in. Select events such as the Salmon Festival and the Paul Bunyan Days at Fort Bragg will be described in later chapters. A complete, annually revised list of special events may be obtained by writing to the Redwood Empire Association, 360 Post Street, San Francisco, California 94102. Enclose 75 cents for delivery.

The North Coast remained a wilderness for three centuries after the Portuguese ship's pilot Ferrelo sighted Cape Mendocino in 1543. Picture this wild land as it was then with its treacherous reefs, enigmatic Indians, dismal swamps, impassable mountains, and dark forests of brooding redwoods. Early mariners rarely put ashore because of the lack of sheltered harbors. Yet even before much was known about it, the North Coast inspired rivalry among the Great Powers. Historians speculate that Drake's landing at Point Reyes in 1579 first persuaded the Spanish to extend their missions and presidios northward from Mexico. And James Monroe had in mind the Russian outposts at Fort Ross and Salmon Creek when he warned the European powers to stay clear of the Americas.

Early exploration by land was a chronicle of misfortune. In 1828, the mountain man Jedediah Smith nearly starved to death while blazing a trail up the Redwood Coast. A survivor of Josiah Gregg's ill-fated trek from Weaverville to Humboldt Bay cursed the redwoods as being "a miserable forest prison." Settlement, when it finally came in the 1850s, was sparked by the Gold Rush.

The earliest towns, such as Trinidad and Eureka, got started as waterfront pack stations for the northern mines. Soon interest switched to toppling the giant redwoods. Then as now the logging industry was plagued by fire, floods, and depressions in the lumber

Surf smelt run in summer off numerous beaches on the North Coast. Sport fishermen take them with a type of net that was used for centuries by the Coast Indians.

market. But life was made more difficult still by the logistics required to move the enormous logs to sawmills and dispatch the lumber by sea to San Francisco. There was a frightful loss of men and ships in winter storms.

At one time on the Mendocino coast, every cove and inlet "large enough for a dog to turn around in" was pressed into service as a shipping point. Wondrous systems of slings, trolleys, and chutes were improvised to load the schooners waiting as much as a quarter of a mile offshore. But now very little timber cutting occurs near the seashore. Except on a portion of the Redwood Coast, all the prime stands have been denuded. Here and there in a coastal village you may still see a small sawmill with its conical slash burner belching thick smoke. But more typical are the huge sprawling complexes of semi-automated plants located in the larger towns.

Still, a strong remnant of the frontier spirit persists on the North Coast. It must; life can be hard here. The lumber market, upon which most of the North Coast economy depends, suffers recurrent slumps. Added to the economic instability is the natural harshness of the coastal environment. In 1964, for example, twin disasters hit the coast: Eureka was isolated by a ruinous flood and Crescent City's business district was destroyed by a monstrous tidal wave.

Industry other than logging on the North Coast is small but picturesque. The scattered stock farms with their weathered barns, cypress windbreaks, and rustic fences add charm to the countryside. Crescent City grows most of the Easter lily bulbs marketed in this country. A large commercial fishing fleet crowds Noyo's interesting harbor. And salmon-fishing partyboats operate on a regular schedule through summer.

Adventure beckons the coastal sport fisherman every month of the year. In winter a hardy clan of diehards brave storm-battered roads to fish creeks and rivers for the migratory steelhead rainbow trout. In spring, when poppies and lavender sea daisies deck the headlands, a series of daylight minus tides uncover clam and abalone beds.

The prospect for hunters, on the other hand, brings to fore the scarcity of public land on the North Coast. The outer Coast Ranges abound with Columbia blacktail deer. Flocks of migratory bandtail pigeons feed on berries in the river canyons. On country lanes, you see Valley quail. Yet much of the land is posted to hunters. One exception is the Jackson State Forest near Fort Bragg. This 52,000-acre preserve of second-growth timber is laced with 15 miles of trails. Use permits are issued at forest headquarters, 802 North Main Street in Fort Bragg, (707) 937-7581. A map at

Ranch near Elk as seen from the Shoreline Highway.
Row of cypress on the left provides a buffer against
the northwest winds which prevail during summer.

headquarters shows the trail system, locations of campsites, and the areas open to licensed hunters during the deer season. Hunting for deer and upland game is also permitted in the 54,000-acre King Range National Conservation Area, which is administered by the federal Bureau of Land Management. The King Range is one of the few places on the North Coast that invite backpacking. One trail runs eleven miles along the crest of the range.

Altogether, there are 418 miles of seashore on the North Coast, not including the protected shorelines of Bolinas Lagoon, Bodega Harbor, Tomales Bay, and Humboldt Bay. Approximately 150 miles of the frontage is public land, of which two-thirds is open beach and one-third steep rocky headlands. Until recent years, the private frontage was almost exclusively the domain of sheep ranches, dairy farms, and timber companies. Now some choice stretches of seashore are fronted by recreational subdivisions. For

the most part, these are still lonely, unspoiled places. Few houses were built before the vacation home boom was hit by recession, inflation, and legislation enacted to protect the fragile shoreline ecology.

As of 1981, twenty-three state parks and beaches exist on California's northern coastline; twelve have campgrounds. Some of these preserves are being enlarged and improved with money provided from the 1974 Park Bond Act and the Bagley Conservation Fund (a spin-off from the surplus that resulted when California adopted the income withholding tax). Also, funds have been appropriated to create at least six new parks on the North Coast.

The rest of the public frontage is largely accounted for by the 46-mile-long Redwood National Park, the federal King Range Conservation Area, the 64,000-acre Point Reyes National Seashore, and the Golden Gate National Recreation Area, which takes in 22 miles of the Marin Coast.

*Visitors at Fort Ross Historic Park approach the red-
wood stockade on old by-passed portion of Highway 1.
Russian colonists occupied the fort from 1812 to 1841.*

Whither Goes the North Coast?

The great westward migration to California in the decade following World War II was slow to have an impact on the North Coast. The ports of Fort Bragg, Eureka, and Crescent City experienced only modest growth while scores of lesser towns fell into decline. But an unprecedented demand for building materials caused lumber production to soar in the 1950s. At the same time, however, competition by giant corporations for a fast-shrinking supply of mature timber caused many small sawmills to close. Employment sagged with increasing automation of the larger mills.

The rugged character of the North Coast frustrated efforts to lure new industry, so civic leaders began to place more emphasis on promoting tourism. The red carpet was laid out for vacation-home developers. Although many lots were sold, few houses were built because the boom that developed in the ocean frontage north of the Golden Gate was largely of a speculative nature. However, by 1970 the trend began to cause concern for the coastal ecology.

A study of the entire California coast by the U.S. Corps of Army Engineers showed that 86 percent of the shoreline had suffered "significant erosion." Much, if not most, of the damage could be traced to housing and industrial projects on San Francisco Bay and the South Coast. But even if physical damage were not a threat, public access to the beaches would still be a crucial issue. A portent of what could happen on the North Coast lies in the fate of Maine's scenic coast. Here private development preempted the beaches so thoroughly in the 1960s that by the end of the decade only thirteen miles of Maine's 3,478-mile coastline were left in the public domain for sightseeing and recreation.

As in Maine, local government on the California coast was too preoccupied with building a tax base to be effective in controlling development. Also as in Maine, a powerful lobby representing land companies, oil interests, public utilities, and the building trades were successful in defeating every coast-management act that came before the state legislature. Therefore, when Proposition 20 (otherwise known as the Coastal Initiative) won a place on the California ballot of November 1972, it was regarded by many conservationists as "the last chance to save the coast."

Proposition 20 provided for the establishment of a California Coastal Zone Commission and six regional bodies composed of eighty-four persons, of which fifty percent would be nominated by local government. The commission would have the authority to regulate development within one thousand yards of the seashore pending submission of a coastal conservation plan to the 1976 state legislature.

The great achievement of the Coastal Zone Commission was 443-page master plan that called for the purchase of numerous beaches, wildlife habitats, and scenic areas designated as "high priority" lands. Funding was to be provided by a bond issue put before the voters. The plan included measures to preserve coastal crop and grazing lands. It proposed that new industry and subdivisions be confined to locations near existing developed areas. Also, the plan urged appointment of a permanent Coastal Commission, which would work with local governments to implement the master plan.

The plan drew a mixed reception from the legislature in 1976. Voters in that year approved a proposition that made $110 million available for acquisition of coastal beaches and parks. But a bill to create a permanent Coastal Commission was enacted in Sacramento only after heated debate and much wheeling and dealing. The bill was a compromise that permitted city and county governments to implement Commission policies largely on their own terms.

In 1981 the future of the Coastal Commission appeared very uncertain. Opposition from special interests was unrelenting. The legislature was deluged with bills that would strip the Commission of its authority or abolish it entirely. The Commission had saved considerable farm land from subdivision and secured public access to many beaches. But it had suffered major defeats trying to curb unwise housing and industrial developments on the populated South Coast.

So whither the largely unspoiled North Coast? Its fate still seems to hang on how the voters and their representatives in Sacramento decide the seashore should be managed. The issue was fairly stated when the Coastal Commission, in a report to the legislature, asked:

> Shall the coast be abused, degraded, its remaining splendor eroded, or shall it be used intelligently, with its majesty and productivity protected for future generations?

From spring through autumn, a weekend congestion of visitors is apt to develop at the more popular recreation areas on the Marin-Sonoma Coast. However, campgrounds in the coastal parks north of Point Arena are rarely filled to capacity except during the major holidays. The remoteness of these parks, the chill ocean temperatures, and the ubiquitous coastal fog explain the modest attendance there even in summer.

The lure of the northern beaches is the treasure they hold. Some yield clams, perch, and surfsmelt. Some abound with driftwood, seashells, or semiprecious stones. On several beaches glass fishing floats from the Orient often turn up following a major storm. All along the coast are beaches and rocky places where abalone

On a quiet afternoon in Spring a curtain of cool, clean coastal fog drifts inshore to cast a spell of enchantment on this dilapidated old fish pier at Bodega Harbor.

are taken and where people gather to observe the wondrous variety of marine life that dwells in tide pools.

Marin, Humboldt, and Del Norte Counties have beaches which stretch for miles. More typical on the Sonoma-Mendocino Coast are small intimate crescents of sand tucked away in cliff-edged coves and stream inlets. You may find the water warm enough for swimming at Stinson Beach and Tomales Bay in Marin County and at Humboldt's Big Lagoon. Elsewhere, the dangerous surf and frigid water temperatures disqualify most beaches for swimming. Off Russian Gulch State Park in Mendocino, the water temperature climbs from the low 40s in April to a high of 65 degrees after Labor Day.

The prevailing northwest wind and strong currents produce an upwelling of cold water that discourages swimming and generates the fog which veils the coast most days in summer. In July the ambient temperature along the seashore may be ten to twenty degrees cooler that it is a mile inland. Just the reverse may be true in January. Therefore, the state parks located on forest-fringed coastal rivers a short drive inland from the fog belt are more attractive to swimmers and sun worshippers.

This book will describe preserves of azalea, rhododendron, and virgin redwoods where the only improvements are trails. Elaborate trail systems are a major attraction of the coastal parks too. All the larger parks have self-guiding trails with signs to identify such native flora as the lowland fir, red elderberry, and Sitka spruce. And in the redwoods at Prairie Creek is a quarter-mile trail designed for use by blind people. The trail has guide rails with signal bells keyed to a braille text which describes the points of interest. Another recent innovation, which is available now in nine North Coast state parks, is the low-fee campground reserved for use by people on cross-country hikes and bicycle tours. And the California Parks Department is working with other state, federal, and private agencies to establish a bicycle route that will run along the entire coast from Mexico to the Oregon line.

All along the North Coast the sun is most likely to win its daily battle with the coastal fog in early spring. Memorial Day draws the largest number of visitors, but the balmiest weather comes in September. Toward the end of February, a "false summer" lasting a week or more sometimes occurs.

Except in the vicinity of Fort Bragg and Mendocino City, motor lodges are not overly abundant on Coast Highway 1. But a surprising number of obscure little villages located on or near the Marin-Sonoma Coast have gourmet restaurants. Despite this cosmopolitan touch, adventuresome travelers should take heed: Some roads which leave Highway 1 to span the outer Coast Ranges are too steep for

Native cypress and exotic eucalyptus frame this view of Bodega Harbor where Highway 1 climbs a knoll on Mount Roscoe. Across the harbor rises Bodega Head.

trailers. The unpaved byways are recommended only for four-wheel vehicles during winter. An adventure to avoid is running low on gas after dark. Most filling stations on Highway 1 keep bankers' hours.

Some inconvenience may be anticipated touring the North Coast, especially north of Fort Bragg to Cape Mendocino. Here a name on the map which conjures up a settlement large enough to support a motel or garage may turn out to be a ranch or deserted crossroads. Westport, the largest trading center, is only one step removed from being a ghost town. The traveler is constantly reminded that much of the North Coast is less populous today than it was a century ago. Scores of thriving ports and bustling lumber towns have vanished without a trace. What remains is a nostalgic backwash filled with enchantment for hikers, beachcombers, and road explorers who delight in forgotten places.

*To find the access road to Muir Beach, you look for
a dim country lane that is shaded by Bishop pines.
Migratory monarch butterflies winter in these pines.*

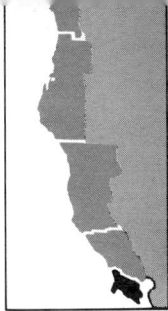

The Audubon Coast:
Marin County

The foggy side of the mountainous Marin Peninsula comprises 130 miles of coast and bayshore, two-thirds of which are fronted by Point Reyes National Seashore and the Golden Gate National Recreation Area. This verdant coast, with its mild climate and sheltered tidal flats, provides a habitat for one of the nation's most diversified populations of birdlife.

Of interest to hungry travelers, including those on day-long outings from San Francisco, are the excellent restaurants to be found at Olema, Inverness, and back in the hills at Lagunitas. Advance reservations are required on weekends. Inverness, Marshall, and Dillon Beach have motor lodges. There is a vehicle park at Olema with sites for tents, trailers, and motor homes. Resorts at Marshall and Dillon Beach afford the only roadside camping near the seashore.

Golden Gate to Bolinas

From San Francisco, the most direct approach to coastal Marin is by way of the Golden Gate Bridge. Across the mile-wide Golden Gate Strait, the U.S. 101 freeway climbs a grade on the towering Marin Headlands. The first turn-off leads to a vista point which commands a sweeping view of San Francisco Bay.

Until recent years, most of the isolated beaches and lofty sea meadows of the Marin Headlands were off-limits to the public. The precipitous ocean frontage belonged to the Army; the back country was taken up by private ranches. When old Forts Baker, Barry, and Cronkhite were declared surplus, the state began buying land for Marin Headlands State Park. But very soon a subdivider moved in to build an "instant city" named Marincello. This project was hardly under way when the entire headlands fell within the boundaries of the new Golden Gate National Recreation Area. Now all but a few acres of the Marin Headlands have been acquired for management as a public preserve.

The best time to visit the headlands is a mild day in spring when the upper slopes are sprinkled with wildflowers. Take the exit off U.S. 101 a short distance north of the vista point and turn left at the foot of the off ramp. Pass under the freeway, turn left, and then turn right through the open gate onto the Conzelman Road. About one-eighth of a mile west of the freeway, you will come to a gated road that is marked Kirby Cove. From here you may hike one mile down to a sheltered picnic area and small beach on the Golden Gate Strait.

About a half mile farther on the Conzelman Road, near the junction with the McCullough Road, is the trailhead for the first leg of the new Pacific Coast Trail. Eventually this footpath will be extended up the coast to link with trails in the Point Reyes National Seashore. Hikers who explore the trails and old ranch roads that lace the back country should beware of ticks and poison oak.

The Conzelman Road terminates at Rodeo Lagoon adjacent to Cronkhite Beach. This is a favorite spot for fishermen, rockhounds, and birdwatchers. The National Park Service maintains a Visitor Center here where you may purchase a map showing the trails open to horse and bicycle riders as well as hikers.

Leaving Rodeo Lagoon, the Bunker Road bears east to approach the freeway interchange by way of the Barry-Baker Tunnel. Shortly after you arrive back on U.S. 101, you will pass through the Waldo Tunnel and descend to Marin City near the shore of Richardson Bay. Slightly north of Marin City you will pick up California Highway 1, also known as the Shoreline Highway, where it leaves U.S. 101 at the Stinson Beach exit. U.S. 101 continues north through a twenty-mile belt of suburbia where most of Marin County's 200,000 population is concentrated.

California 1 bends westward through a small shopping district at the foot of Mount Tamalpais. The road soon narrows to two lanes as it starts to climb a shoulder of Tamalpais between rows of pungent eucalyptus trees. In 1973, the state proposed to widen and straighten this portion of Highway 1 because the accident rate was three times the average for rural two-lane roads in California. However, the Marin Board of Supervisors vetoed the project because it would have cost too much and detracted from "one of the most pleasant drives in the entire United States."

At the top of the grade, Highway 1 meets the south end of the Panoramic Highway. This ridge route leads to the Muir Redwoods and campgrounds in Mount Tamalpais State Park. The latter preserve has over two hundred miles of trails, which are most enjoyable to hike from late winter through June. Trail maps are available at the Pan Toll Ranger Station.

Bypass the junction and continue along Highway 1. Shortly you will see the brushy Pacific slopes of the ridge plunge steeply to the seashore. Most days in summer the ocean is masked by coastal fog, but a salt tang in the breeze lets you know it's there.

In a quick succession of U-turns, the highway descends Green Gulch. In 1971, the millionaire rancher George Wheelwright III donated most of Green Gulch to the Nature Conservancy, a non-profit group which acquires land for public parks. On the floor of the ravine is an old ranch where a Zen group practices organic farming.

Near sea level the highway swings north across

Summer cottages strung along the waterfront at Bolinas village lean out over the lagoon on pilings. West of town is Agate Beach and the tide pools on Duxbury Reef.

Frank Valley. The turn-off here to Muir Beach is easy to miss. Look for a rural lane that is shaded by Bishop pines.

Muir Beach is a small wedge of white sand where Redwood Creek enters the sea between rocky outcroppings. Silver salmon migrate up the creek in winter to their ancestral spawning gravels in the Muir Woods. For years Muir Beach was the site of a summer resort, which was private. Later, as an underdeveloped state preserve, the beach achieved notoriety as a rendezvous for nude bathers. Complaints from residents of a neighboring subdivision then prompted daily patrols by a horse-mounted deputy sheriff. Now a popular picnic spot, the beach is administered by the Golden Gate National Recreation Area. The rough surf at Muir Beach prohibits swimming but is often rewarding for anglers. The breakers yield perch and an occasional striped bass. Poke poling for eels is good, too, in the rocky areas.

In Frank Valley the Shoreline Highway intercepts a road that follows Redwood Creek to the visitor center in Muir Woods National Monument. From this junction, the highway climbs the seaward slope of Tamalpais. At a point four hundred feet above the ocean, there is an exit to the Muir Beach Overlook. From here a trail leads to a promontory which affords a spectacular view of the Marin Headlands. In late December and January people come here to watch grey whales spouting as they swim south on their annual migration to breeding grounds off Mexico.

The Shoreline Highway climbs another hundred feet above the sea before it gradually loses elevation, dipping in and out of brushy gulches as it follows the coastline. From Muir Beach to the southern boundary of Stinson Beach, access to the seashore is difficult and at most points dangerous.

Just inside the southern Stinton Beach boundary is Gull Rock, a favorite destination for poke polers and rock fishermen. Nearby Rocky Point is another productive spot for fishing. The old ranch road that winds down to Rocky Point affords a pleasant hike in spring. You may leave your car near the gate where the highway crosses Webb Creek. The gate is locked but there's a stile open for pedestrians.

A little farther up the highway are pull-offs which will give you an aerial view of Stinson Beach. Before dropping to the village, California 1 is joined by the Panoramic Highway, which winds down from the Pan Toll Ranger Station. The village of Stinson Beach was named for an early settler at Point Reyes. The former Grand Hotel burned down in 1971 but there may still be a few dwellings that hark back to the stagecoach days. The town has restaurants and several motels. Clustered near the beach are shingled vacation cottages with names like "Snug Harbor," "Green Dragon," and Pirates' Lair."

The annual Dipsea Race is a tradition that dates back to 1904. On the first Sunday in June, hundreds of people par-

Stinson Beach draws up to half a million visitors a year because of its proximity to the Bay Area. However, the beach rarely suffers crowding on week days.

ticipate in a rugged cross-country marathon from Mill Valley over the mountain to Stinson Beach. The runners descend to the shore on a tortuous footpath known as the Dipsea Trail. Because the ocean is shallow off the gently sloping beach, it stays warm enough for swimming from late spring through early autumn. Fishing isn't too popular here except when a rare run of striped bass enters the surf.

An exclusive subdivision known as Seadrift occupies the slender sandspit which stretches north of the beach to enclose Bolinas Lagoon. Before Seadrift was developed, the owner of the spit offered to donate it to Marin County for use as a public park. The county refused this gift on the grounds that a park there would be too expensive to maintain. Now only the immediate shoreline is open to the public.

North of Stinson Beach, the slopes of Bolinas Ridge drop steeply to Bolinas Lagoon. Here California 1 hugs the shoreline, passing within a few feet of the high water mark. The brushy Pacific slopes of the ridge are serrated by deep gulches. These contain the remnants of a forest which produced 13 million board feet of redwood in the 1850s and 1860s. The lumber was hauled by ox teams to the lagoon, where it was transferred in flat bottom boats to vessels anchored in the outer bay.

Bolinas Ridge and the lower slopes of Mount Tamalpais are wintering grounds for monarch butterflies. On sunny days in late winter, these colorful migrants may be seen swarming on the willows which fringe the parking area at Stinson Beach.

Low tide on Bolinas Lagoon exposes vast mudflats which used to attract clam diggers before the lagoon was posted with pollution warnings. In recent years, Bolinas Lagoon has been the object of intensive study by state biologists and private scientific groups because it is one of the richest, least disturbed areas of tidal marsh on the Pacific Coast. Surveys show that about 67 percent of California's original salt marshes and tidal flats have been filled in or otherwise destroyed with devastating effect on the native wildlive.

The low-tide mudflats at Bolinas Lagoon, though no longer as attractive to clam diggers, are natural "food factories" that support a large population of often quite vocal harbor seals as well. The tidal zone teems with plankton, curstaceans, mollusks, and small fishes. Lush beds of eelgrass provide forage for the migratory black brant, a subspecies of Canada goose found only along the coast.

Water temperatures invite swimming at Stinson Beach from late spring through early fall. Lifeguards are posted in summer. The surf can be dangerous at times.

About 3.5 miles up the highway from Stinson Beach is the Audubon Canyon Ranch, which is open to the public on weekends and holidays from March through the Fourth of July. The canyon is laced with nature paths. One trail leads to a promontory point where you may gaze down on herons and egrets nesting in the tops of redwood trees.

The Audubon Wildlife Area, owned by the Audubon Society, covers the northern arm of Bolinas Lagoon. Western grebes, pintail ducks, and Arctic loons are some of the migratory waterfowl that winter here. Willets and sandpipers frequent the shoreline. The brown pelicans diving for fish are perhaps the most fun to watch. In 1969, the brown pelican was designated by the Department of Interior as an endangered species. It was feared the bird would become extinct on the Pacific Coast because of reproductive failure attributed to ocean pollution by DDT. But since DDT was banned in 1971, the pelican population has shown a remarkable recovery. The only nesting colony in

The Golden Gate National Recreation Area

The main reason Congress created the Golden Gate National Recreation Area (GGNRA) in 1972 was to provide a magnificent outdoor playground for an urban population anticipated to exceed 7 million people by 1990. The preserve encompasses 34,000 acres. It takes in almost all the parks and beaches that rim the San Francisco waterfront west of Fisherman's Wharf, including rockbound Alcatraz Island and the lovely Angel Island State Park.

However, four-fifths of the total acreage is located north of the Golden Gate on the Pacific slopes of Marin County. Here the Recreation Area embraces a rugged, largely undeveloped countryside which invites such activities as hiking, fishing, and nature study. Included are twenty-two miles of seashore, several state preserves, and many acres of recently acquired ranch property and surplus military lands. An outstanding attraction is the sprawling 6,000-acre Mount Tamalpais State Park, which contains within it the Muir Redwoods National Monument.

No transfer of state-owned parks and beaches to the administration of the National Recreation Area is contemplated at the present time. Some preserves, such as the bird sanctuary owned by the Audubon

Society, will remain in private hands (so long as their use is deemed compatible with management of the Recreation Area). Bolinas Mesa, the village at Stinson Beach, and a few small subdivisions were exluded from the federal jurisdiction by Congress.

The federal lands are laced with old ranch and logging roads. Some of these will be maintained to provide a network of foot trails. Campgrounds are in short supply. Mount Tamalpais Park has a few primitive sites and a group camp that are available by reservation. In the Marin Headlands there are group camps that are located near Rodeo Lagoon and at Kirby Cove. Also, there's a primitive backpack camp, which is on Tennessee Valley Creek. But most other facilities are limited to day use.

Inquiries about the recreation area or your comments on how it should be managed may be addressed to the Superintendent, Golden Gate National Recreation Area, National Park Service, Building 201, Fort Mason, California 94123.

Two excellent guides to the hiking and riding trails in the Golden Gate Recreation Area are *Paths of Gold* by Margot Patterson Doss, and *To Walk With a Quiet Mind,* by Nancy Olmsted.

California is located in the Channel Islands off Oxnard. Here 305 baby pelicans were counted in 1975—a heartening contrast to the single downy bird observed in 1970.

Less than a mile north of the Audubon Ranch, the Shoreline Highway intercepts the Fairfax-Bolinas Road. This lightly traveled byway winds up Bolinas Ridge to Alpine Lake in the beautiful highlands owned by the Marin Municipal Water District. Shore fishing is permitted at several reservoirs in the district. The many miles of hiking and riding trails here link up with the trail system in Mount Tamalpais State Park.

A little farther north on California 1 is the poorly marked junction with the road that approaches the village of Bolinas. After roughly two miles on Bolinas Road, turn

right on Mesa Road, which leads to the Point Reyes Bird Observatory. This privately funded banding station is located just inside the southern boundary of the Point Reyes National Seashore. Visitors are welcome except on Fridays. One-half mile beyond the station, the road terminates at the Palomarin Trailhead. From here it's a 2.5-mile hike to Bass Lake, which is trout water. Nearby Pelican and Crystal Lakes have bass and sunfish. From the lakes, the main trail continues for sixteen miles up the coast to link with other footpaths and the roadhead at Limantour Spit.

Returning to the Bolinas Road, it's a short drive to the village (summer population 800), which is situated at the opening of the lagoon to Bolinas Bay. This

The Ocean Parkway Road out of Bolinas affords this view from the mesa of Bolinas Bay. The name Bolinas is believed to have evolved from a Miwok Indian word.

Poke Poling

Poke poling is an unorthodox method of sport fishing that calls for a bamboo pole twelve to fifteen feet long with three feet of stiff, heavy wire projecting from the tip. The wire is fastened to the pole by a wrapping of fine brass wire and black neoprene electrician's tape. The end of the stiff wire is bent into a small loop so that a six-inch length of heavy monofilament leader with a 2/0 hook may be attached. The hook may be baited with shrimp, mussel, clam, or cut-bait such as anchovy or herring. The baited hook is poked into the rocky pools and crevasses that become exposed at low tide. With any luck, the fisherman can hook rockfish, surfperch, and blennies.

The two kinds of blennies found on the North Coast are rock and monkeyface eels. When hooked, these fish are prone to wrap themselves around rocks, so you may have to tug very hard to land one.

A skin diver's wet suit or chest-high waders with warm sweater and parka is the dress recommended for poke poling on the North Coast. A large cloth sack serves as a creel. Other accessories include a pair of fisherman's pliers, knife, bait holder, and hand towel. All these may be accommodated in a utility belt or small shoulder pack.

Some advice for beginners: Never turn your back on the sea, or an oversized wave might push you into the surf. Keep an eye on the tide so you won't get stranded on an offshore ledge. Also, handle blenny eels with caution. They are not true eels, and have sharp teeth and powerful jaws.

To prepare blennies for the pan, skin and fillet the fish. The strong flavor may be mitigated by simmering the fillets for a few minutes in water which contains a little vinegar. After draining the fillets, dip them in egg, roll them in crumbs, and fry them to a crisp in butter. Serve with lemon slices, tartar sauce or hollandaise.

---

compact cluster of peaked-roof dwellings would resemble a New England hamlet were it not for some purely California palm trees. During the Gold Rush sawmills and shipyards sparked a lively settlement here. Afterward, the village stagnated pleasantly for years as a summer colony, later to become the permanent retreat of some prominent artists and writers.

Excepting the 1906 earthquake, nothing much happened to mar the serenity of Bolinas until the winter of 1971. It was then that a huge oil slick moved in on Bolinas Beach when two tankers collided off the Golden Gate. Perhaps half the present population of Bolinas was drawn from the volunteers who flocked in from all over the San Francisco Bay Area to help clean up the oil spill and wash off the stranded oil-covered birds. Much to the annoyance of many long-time residents, the newcomers were fiercely "pro-ecology" and "anti-growth" with a strong bias against Sunday drivers. Some of the more youthful activists were suspected of tearing down signs and barricading the access roads to discourage visitors.

Wharf Road is lined with restaurants, craft shops, and summer bungalows which lean over the water on pilings. Lagoon specimens are on exhibit at the College of Marin Marine Station. Off Brighton Avenue, the Ocean-Parkway ascends the mesa to promontories overlooking the outer bay and Duxbury Reef. In 1853, four hundred passengers barely escaped drowning when the steamer *Lewis* foundered on this reef. Wrecks were so common here in the early days that some Bolinas residents made a living salvaging the cargoes.

On a minus tide fishermen and tide-pool watchers may wander out on Duxbury Reef as far as a half-mile from shore. The reef has been designated a state marine reserve. Hence, no specimens may be collected other than the game species listed under the section headed "Duxbury Reef Reserve" in the California Sport Fishing Regulations.

Access to Duxbury Reef is from Agate County Beach. To get here from Ocean-Parkway, turn right on Overlook Drive and then left on Elm Road. The beach (a good spot to cast for surfperch) is mostly rock with patches of coarse sand. Agates, glass fishing floats and other treasure are apt to turn up on this beach following a major storm.

Bear Valley Trail is former ranch road that affords an
easy 4½ mile hike from park headquarters to Drakes Bay.
Side trails approach vista points and overnight camps.

Point Reyes

North of Bolinas Lagoon the Shoreline Highway enters a long, slender valley where cattle graze. Here the seacoast is screened from the road by Inverness Ridge. Just off the pavement runs the San Andreas Fault, where a sudden shifting of the earth's crust triggered the 1906 earthquake. The damage in the valley was slight compared with the holocaust that resulted in San Francisco. A few homes and cow barns were shaken out of plumb. Some trees and fence lines were moved from one side of the highway to the other. Portions of the road were dislocated.

The fault line that slices up the valley divides the Point Reyes Peninsula from the mainland. There is constant movement along the fault. The peninsula is creeping up the coast at the rate of an inch or two each year. It is believed to have traveled 350 miles from the place it was first formed about 40 million years ago. Some credence is given to the theory that the peninsula originated as part of the Sierra Nevada. True or not, it's a fact that Point Reyes is the only place on the North Coast (other than Bodega Head) where the bedrock is composed of granite.

From Bolinas Lagoon nine miles up the valley to the vicinity of Olema, the highway approximates the boundary between the Point Reyes National Seashore and the Golden Gate Recreation Area. Hiking and riding trails marked with signs lead off the road into both areas.

The hamlet of Olema slumbers at the junction with the Sir Francis Drake Highway. Olema was settled in the 1850s, and it gained some importance as a rural trading center. But its glory faded quickly after the roads were paved. During the 1920s, it was a hangout for rum-runners and racketeers. Now Olema has a few stores, restaurants, and a privately operated park for tent and vehicle camping.

Heading southeast from Olema, the Drake Highway winds four miles up Bolinas Ridge to the second-growth redwoods in Samuel Taylor State Park. Just short of the park boundary a few cottages mark the site of Jewell, once a station on the narrow-gauge North Pacific Coast Railroad. Taylor Park has seventy-four campsites, many lovely trails, and a small swimming hole on Lagunitas Creek (which used to be known as Papermill Creek). Trout fishing is poor but visitors in winter may see silver salmon spawning in the shallows.

The first paper mill west of the Mississippi was located on the creek within the boundaries of the present park. It was built in 1856 by Samuel Penfield

Taylor, who produced a high quality bond paper from rags collected by Chinese in San Francisco. During the first few years of the mill's existence, it was powered by a water wheel. An historical marker indicates the site of the mill.

Another road out of Olema approaches Bear Valley, where an old ranch at the foot of Inverness Ridge serves as headquarters for the National Seashore. The visitor center here provides a map of Point Reyes listing the points of interest.

A glance at this map shows that the Point Reyes Peninsula is shaped to form a triangle. Bolinas, Point Reyes, and Tomales Point occupy the corners. Inverness Ridge ranges up the side of the triangle which abuts Olema and Tomales Bay. The ridge marks a boundary between two micro-climates. The protected shore of Tomales Bay gets lots of sunshine. But on the windy western side of the ridge, when it isn't raining, it's apt to be fogging.

Most of the Point Reyes National Seashore is primitive or nearly so. The boundaries encompass seventy miles of coastline and 65,000 acres of beaches, salt marshes, sand dunes, bluffs, bays, lakes, prairie, brushy uplands, and coniferous forest. The National Seashore provides a habitat for several hundred kinds of birds and about seventy species of mammals, including rabbits, foxes, badgers, bobcats, and Columbia blacktail deer. Abundant but rarely seen is the shy *Aplodontia,* the mountain beaver, which feeds on berries in the uplands.

Grizzly bears were numerous at Point Reyes when the Mexican governor awarded a large tract of land on the peninsula to James Berry in 1836. Berry, an Irishman, was deeded the grant on St. Patrick's Day. In the 1860s, the greater part of the peninsula, then known as Rancho Punta de los Reyes, was acquired by three men who subdivided the land for lease to dairy farmers. These were the brothers Oscar L. and James McMillan Shafter, both prominent jurists, and Charles W. Howard, who headed a water company. This group later obtained the Rancho Tomales y Baulenes for which Bolinas is named. The two properties were consolidated into a single vast estate which reached southward all the way to the summit of Mount Tamalpais. Eventually, many of the leaseholds were sold outright to the farmers who worked them.

Point Reyes was the first important dairy area in California. Before 1865, only rough horse trails crossed the mountains to coastal Marin, so dairy shipments to San Francisco were made by schooner. Exports were limited to butter and cheese until improvement of the roads in the 1920s made possible the delivery of Grade A milk.

The ranchers at Point Reyes enjoyed a slow-paced, almost feudal way of life isolated from mainland concerns until the San Francisco Bay Area was rocked by a population explosion in the late 1940s. During that decade a rise in property taxes threatened to make their huge ranches obsolete. Elsewhere in Marin, dairymen found a way to minimize the tax bite by crowding a large number of cows onto a relatively small amount of land. Instead of growing hay, they purchased their feed from farmers in the Central Valley and as far away as Nevada.

Thus the squires at Point Reyes with their huge acreages were in trouble before land developers and conservationists squared off to fight for the peninsula in the late 1950s.

On September 13, 1962, President Kennedy signed the bill creating the Point Reyes National Seashore. This was a red letter day for the conservationists, or so it seemed before the price of land on the peninsula threatened to go out of sight. Within a few months, the $19-million appropriated for the park was exhausted. Seven years later most of Point Reyes remained in

The first national seashore on the Pacific Coast, Point Reyes was formally established as a unit of the National Park System in 1972. It encompasses 100 square miles.

private hands. Surveyors were staking out tracts for subdivision. Loggers were cutting down the Douglas firs on Inverness Ridge. An economy-minded Washington was deaf to pleas for additional funds to complete the National Seashore. Instead, the Interior Department proposed to sell or lease to private interests the land it had already bought. Included were nine thousand acres on Inverness Ridge wanted for development of a luxury "second home" tract, replete with shopping centers and a polo field.

In October 1969, conservation forces mustered a last-ditch petition drive to save the National Seashore. A month later the issue was decided when the White House announced it favored additional funds. The following year enough money was appropriated for the Park Service to buy up almost all of the peninsula. The squires of Point Reyes made a bundle and some were even able to retain temporary grazing rights.

At present the National Seashore draws more than two million visitors a year even though the only facilities there are information centers and some picnic areas with benches, tables, and rest rooms. The Park Service anticipates improvements such as a boating camp on Tomales Bay. However, the master plan for Point Reyes calls for retaining most of the peninsula in its natural state.

Overnight camping is restricted to a few primitive clearings on the National Seashore's hundred-mile trail system. From headquarters it's an easy four-mile hike or bicycle ride through wooded Bear Valley to Drake's Bay. Here the shore is rimmed with white cliffs that are riddled with sea tunnels. Some secluded beaches are accessible just north of the junction between Coast and Bear Valley Trails. But visitors should take care not to be trapped by an incoming tide here. Plan these excursions with the help of a tide table, available at the visitor centers.

Horses are permitted on most trails (except the Bear Valley Trail during weekends and holidays). Stables with saddle stock for hire are located a short drive from the Bear Valley Visitor Center. The trail system includes some short self-guiding nature paths, one of which explores the San Andreas Rift Zone.

Park Rangers patrol the back country of Point Reyes on Morgan horses which are bred at the old Bear Valley Ranch for use in several national parks. Morgan horses are calm, friendly animals which do not shy easily. This strain was first bred in New England during the 1780s.

About a mile and a half up the Bear Valley Road from park headquarters are the Bear Valley Stables. From here, the Limantour Road winds eight miles over Inverness Ridge to approach the inviting white sand

Historians speculate the bluffs at Drakes Bay may be the ''white bancks and cliffes'' which reminded Sir Francis Drake of the chalk cliffs at Dover, England.

beach at Limantour Spit. On this drive, you may see some descendants of the exotic species of deer introduced into the area by local ranchers in the 1940s. The European fallow deer appear white from a distance and have large broad antlers resembling those of a moose. Also present are axis deer, originally imported to this country from the island of Ceylon. Buff-colored with white spots, these small, swift deer favor the uplands where cattle graze. In 1976, each species was estimated to number five hundred on the peninsula.

Limantour Spit is a slender, wave-built finger of sand named for a French trader who was shipwrecked here in 1841 while searching for the entrance to San Francisco Bay. The tidal marsh enclosed by the spit is Estero de Limantour, a state marine reserve (closed to fishing and clamming) which attracts a large variety of

birds. You may also see harbor seals frolicking in the shallows.

Returning to the Bear Valley road, you come out on the Drake Highway near Lagunitas Creek and follow the shoreline of Tomales Bay north to Inverness. This quiet summer colony, founded in the 1880s, includes a yacht club, several motels, and some restaurants, plain and fancy. The village was named Inverness because its mountain setting reminded an early settler of his native Scotland.

North of town, the Drake Highway leaves the bayshore to ascend a wooded pass; here you turn right on the Pierce Point Road. One mile from the junction is the turn-off to Tomales Bay State Park. The park drive curls down through a magnificent stand of Bishop pines to a little cove bound by craggy outcroppings.

The water off Hearts Desire Beach in Tomales Bay State Park usually stays warm enough for swimming through October. Wooded trails lead to attractive picnic sites.

Here is Hearts Desire Beach, a popular place to swim as late as November. In September, the water temperature may surpass eighty degrees.

From Hearts Desire, a nature path leads to Indian Beach where sun bathers pass the time fishing for perch. On a nearby bluff is a wooded picnic area rimmed with laurel and madrone. Wildlife in the park includes pygmy nuthatches and a large population of raccoons.

Two miles farther on the Pierce Point Road is the trailhead for Kehoe Beach. This cliff-bound shore is a nice place for a picnic when the weather is fair. During winter high tides, the surf sometimes uncovers artifacts from Miwok shell mounds. About the time that Drake is supposed to have visited Point Reyes, more than one hundred Miwok Indian villages existed on the peninsula. The Park Service requests that visitors bring any relics they might find to the museum at Bear Valley headquarters.

Four miles north of the Kehoe Access the road ends at a parking area. From here it's a short walk to windy McClure's Beach. Mainly fishermen and abalone

Backpacking

In 1970, a 37-year-old journalist from Santa Rosa named Don Engdahl backpacked the 1200-mile length of the California Coast from the Oregon line to Mexico. It was quite a challenge for a "desk-bound type" who had never backpacked before.

Engdahl's adventure got off to a good start. He was delighted by the gorgeous scenery and friendly people he saw on his trek along the seashore of Del Norte and Humboldt Counties. But about half-way down the lovely Mendocino Coast, he began to encounter barbed wire fences strung across the beaches.

In the vicinity of Fort Bragg, Engdahl was evicted from state-owned tideland by irate ranchers and summer-home dwellers. He was able to obtain special permission to pass through some subdivisions. But in the case of other properties where the beach was not accessible, he had no choice but to walk on the state highway.

Engdahl's experience points up the deceptive character of the North Coast. Although unspoiled and sparsely populated, much of it is off limits to the hiker. Very little of it enjoys the protection of official wilderness status. Only the Point Reyes National Seashore plus a few trails in the King Range, Redwood National Park, and the Golden Gate National Recreation Area provide opportunities for an overnight hike in primitive surroundings.

Overnight camping in the roadless area of Point Reyes is restricted to four designated clearings with a total of forty-two tent sites. Such is the popularity of these camps that reservations may be required as much as two months in advance. Reservations for a campsite may be made by phoning (415) 663-1092 or by writing the Superintendent, Point Reyes National Seashore.

Since the National Seashore was created, the Sierra Club and other groups have been at odds with the Park Service as to how much of the peninsula should be designated as wilderness. Initially, the Park Service proposed 5,000 acres; later it raised its offer to 10,000 acres. But the Sierra Club wanted more than 30,000 acres placed in the wilderness category. The argument for including at least half of Point Reyes in the National Wilderness system was based on a provision of the Wilderness Act which prohibits any development other than trails and rustic camps.

At stake was the natural setting of the peninsula. Its abundant flora and fauna could be damaged and even destroyed by overdevelopment of recreational facilities and other Park Service "improvements." Conservationists were wary of Park Service intentions because of the agency's spotty record in managing Yosemite Valley and other natural wonders. Moreover, in 1965 the Park Service had contemplated such development as rimming Drake's Bay with a clifftop highway. Drake's Estero was to be impounded to provide a fresh-water lake for watersports. Then the frontage at Limantour Spit would be paved to accommodate a complex of shops, restaurants, and parking lots.

Subsequently the Park Service came up with a new plan under which many portions of the National Seashore would be classified as "natural environmental areas." However, critics argued that the plan was a vague "statement of principle" which did not preclude such development as road building or even logging on the slopes of Inverness Ridge.

The designation of a federal wilderness area requires an act of Congress, and the designation cannot be revoked except by Congress. Recently a compromise was achieved whereby 25,000 acres of Point Reyes is now listed as official wilderness. The area includes the lovely fir forest atop Inverness Ridge. Ultimately, another 8,000 acres of the seashore will likely qualify as wilderness.

The concept of a Pacific Coast Trail is now something more than a dream, though it may not be fully realized before the turn of the century. In California, the present policy is to give priority to the development of short hiking and bicycling trails that are easily accessible to people in the cities.

The possibilities for backpacking in the King Range and within other preserves are covered in the chapters that deal with these areas. Some of the larger state parks on the North Coast, such as Salt Point and the Del Norte Redwoods, afford the potential for overnight hikes. But as yet camping in these preserves is restricted to designated sites accessible by road.

The Bear Valley Road out of Olema affords a pleasant drive through wooded pasture to the main visitor center and headquarters of the Point Reyes National Seashore.

The Point of Kings

Point Reyes became a landmark for the Manila Galleons a quarter century after it was sighted in 1542 by Juan Rodriguez Cabrillo, leader of the first European expedition to California. Laden with silk, spices, and precious metals, the Manila Galleons navigated the "Great Circle" route from the Philippines to Mexico for 250 years. The name Point Reyes, which means "Point of Kings," dates back to 1603. In that year, the merchant-explorer Sebastian Vizcaino sailed by the point on the day of the Three Holy Kings.

At least thirty ships of fifty tons or more and scores of smaller vessels were lost off Point Reyes between 1850 and 1950. The earliest wreck on record was that of the galleon *San Agustin*, commanded by the Portuguese navigator Sebastian Cermeno. Cermeno entered Drake's Bay in 1595. While he was on the beach supervising construction of an auxiliary launch, the larger vessel was wrecked by a storm. Historians who believe that Drake did land in Drake's Bay are unable to explain why Cermeno didn't report seeing the redwood fort or other evidence of Drake's visit in 1579.

Before Cermeno resumed his voyage south, he named the bay "La Bahia de San Francisco." It did not become known as Drake's Bay until centuries later, long after Portola's expedition stumbled on what is now known as San Francisco Bay.

hunters seek out this lonely shore. At the southern end of the beach where sea stacks tower are tide pools which become accessible during an extreme minus tide.

Northward from the roadhead stretches Tomales Point. This slender strip of historic ranchland was acquired by the government in 1973 from the Bahai Del Norte Land and Cattle Company for 2¾ million. Now a drift fence built across the peninsula marks the boundary of a 2,500-acre wild area where a small herd of tule elk is free to roam. The herd was relocated here from a state refuge in the Central Valley. Tule elk (also called dwarf elk) are not as large as the Roosevelt elk that frequented Point Reyes before the settlers came.

On returning to the Drake Highway, bear west from Inverness Ridge across brushy moors that glow with blue and yellow lupines in spring. There are no trees here except for scattered windbreaks of cypress. Typically, the sun is blotted out by high fog which may descend at any time to shroud the road in places. Distant objects assume strange configurations in the mist. A ghostly castle towering from afar proves on closer inspection to be a tall Victorian farmhouse with whitewashed barns and outbuildings clustered about.

Three miles beyond the Pierce Point cutoff the highway skirts the head of Schooner Bay in Drake's Estero. Sailing vessels used to load dairy products at the landing here. Now there's a commercial oyster farm where visitors are welcome.

A bit farther up the road is the first of two spurs which afford access to twelve miles of white sand on Point Reyes Beach. Most days the spectacular surf here is too rough for fishing. Swimming is prohibited everywhere on this side of the peninsula, including McClure's and Kehoe Beaches.

At the north end of Point Reyes Beach is Abbotts Lagoon (which is most easily approached from the Pierce Point Road). Normally Abbotts Lagoon is a freshwater lake, but it opens to the sea during winters of above average rainfall and becomes populated with perch and flounder. Some portions of the peninsula receive up to fifty-five inches of rain a year, three times the normal precipitation on adjoining areas of the coast.

The side road to Drake's Beach leaves the highway a little more than two miles from the north access to Point Reyes Beach. Bound by high cliffs on the lee side of the peninsula, Drake's Beach normally enjoys a moderate surf. People swim here, fish for surfperch, collect shells and driftwood, and hunt for littleneck clams in the rocky areas. Lifeguards are posted in summer. Further east along the shore of Drake's Bay is Drake's Estero. The tidal flats in the estero are difficult to approach without a boat but contain some of the most productive beds of gaper and Washington clams on the North Coast.

From the Drake's Beach turn-off, it's a four-mile drive on the Drake Highway to the tip of Point Reyes. The highway forks here. One spur (which is sometimes closed to the public) runs west to the Point Reyes Light Station. This station had guided mariners for 105 years when it was declared obsolete in 1975. It was replaced by an automated light that is linked to a computer in San Francisco.

From the former lightkeeper's residence, 311 steps lead down to the old tower perched on a rock 296 feet above the water. The original light is a vast complex of glass manufactured in Paris from hundreds of contiguous lenses. In 1867, it was shipped around the Horn and delivered by oxcart to its present site where it was placed in a cast iron housing forty feet tall. The tower which enclosed this installation was built to withstand winds that reach one hundred miles an hour during winter storms. The tower is open to visitors from 10 A.M. to 5 P.M. except when the stairway is socked in by fog or the wind exceeds 35 miles per hour.

At the foot of the five-hundred-foot cliffs off the lighthouse parking area is an isolated beach frequented by seals and sea lions.

The other fork of the Drake Highway descends east to a commercial fish landing on Chimney Rock. Roughly a mile down the road is a parking area from which a short, steep footpath approaches one of the finest vista points in the National Seashore. The view of Drake's Bay you obtain from this promontory may bring to mind a question that has intrigued local historians for decades.

It is recorded that in the spring of 1579 Sir Francis Drake beached his ship, the *Golden Hinde*, for repairs in a bay situated at 38°30' north latitude. The question is, was this bay the one now known as Drake's Bay at Point Reyes? Or was it San Francisco Bay? Or possibly Bolinas Bay? After years of scholarly debate, a piece of evidence came to light in 1936 which seemed to prove that the landing site was in Drake's Bay, either on the outer beach or inside Drake's Estero.

While hunting at Point Reyes in 1933, a chauffeur named William Caldeira found a rectangular brass plate near the swale known as Muddy Hollow. Caldeira pocketed the metal thinking he might find some use for it. He didn't, so a couple weeks later he tossed the plate away on a San Francisco Bay flat near Point San Quentin. In 1936, Beryle Shinn, a young department-store employee, found the brass plate on a hill overlooking Point San Quentin. Shinn decided the plate was just the right size to patch a hole on the floor of his car. But while removing tarnish from the metal, Shinn discovered some strange writing, including the word "Drake," on the surface of the plate.

A replica of this plate is on display at the Bear Valley headquarters of the National Seashore. The original belongs to the University of California at Berkeley. It was consigned to an honored place in the archives after expert examination seemed to prove it was "the plate of brasse" which Drake "had fast nailed

to a great and firme post" when he claimed the North Coast in the name of Queen Elizabeth.

One mystery remained. How did the brass plate travel from the flat where William Caldeira claimed he disposed of it to the hilltop where Beryle Shinn reported he found it? Skeptics were quick to seize upon this discrepancy but failed to make much of an impression in academic circles until a book entitled *The European Discovery of America* was published in 1974. In this two-volume work, Harvard professor Samuel Eliot Morrison suggested that the brass plate was a hoax perpetrated by a collegiate prankster. Morrison cited the findings of a metallurgist which showed the zinc content of the brass plate to be no more than seventy years old. Morrison's argument was promptly countered by James Holiday of the California Historical Society who pointed out that mineralized vegetable compounds on the plate had been found to date back to the time of Drake.

Late in 1974, the controversy was fueled anew by the discovery of an English sixpence dated 1567. This find by archeologist Charles Slaymaker at the site of a former Indian village near Novato tended to support the theory that Drake had careened his vessel somewhere on the north shore of San Francisco Bay.

Then word got around that Dr. Aubrey Neasham of California State University at Sacramento had unearthed the remains of an old fort in a meadow near Bolinas Lagoon. Early in 1975, Neasham and his co-worker, state archeologist William Pritchard, told the press they were convinced that this was the fort Drake built while his ship was beached for repairs. However, Neasham conceded that they still lacked "one hundred per cent proof." So rival groups of academicians seek fresh evidence to bolster their theories, and the debate rages on.

Perhaps the most convincing evidence that Drake landed at Drake's Bay is not the brass plate but the great sweep of white cliffs you can see from the overlook at Chimney Rock. Francis Fletcher, the chaplain of the *Golden Hinde,* wrote that one reason Drake named the shore he visited "Nova Albion" (New England) was "in respect of the white bancks" which reminded him of the cliffs at Dover. There are white cliffs on the south side of the Golden Gate and elsewhere on the coast at 38°30' north latitude. However, none compare in breadth and splendor with the crescent of sandstone bluffs which rim Drake's Bay.

Following Drake's return to England, a colonizing fleet was dispatched which was intercepted by the Spanish off Brazil. Thereafter, no organized attempt was made to settle the North Coast until the Russians came in 1811.

Tomales Bay

Tomales Bay is a shallow inlet sixteen miles long and averaging a mile wide. Geologists speak of it as a "drowned valley." It was flooded after the last Ice Age when rising sea waters invaded the north end of the Olema Valley.

The bay reaches inland to a point two miles north of Point Reyes Station. Here migratory steelhead rainbow trout and silver salmon enter Lagunitas Creek during the rainy season. The Whitehouse Pool is accessible to fishermen off the Drake Highway about a mile west of

Point Reyes Station. In 1959, this water yielded a trophy-sized silver salmon that weighed twenty-two pounds. Winter steelheading is apt to be good on the creek directly following a major storm. A fair number of silver salmon are taken by skiff fishermen trolling the upper bay in autumn.

Point Reyes Station (population 420) is a drowsy farm center that used to be an active seaport. Samuel Taylor shipped paper products from here by barge and schooner. The town prospered as the depot for Olema after the North

Rolling hills north of Tomales Bay provide lush graze for sheep and cattle. Antique fence on this dairy farm near Tomales village is made of redwood stakes.

Pacific Coast Railway was completed to Tomales village in 1875. Now the former locomotive roundhouse serves as a community center. In 1979 David and Cathy Mitchell won the Pulitzer Prize for reportage in the weekly *Point Reyes Light* (circ. 3,300) on the controversial group known as Synanon.

North from town, Highway 1 follows the east shore of Tomales Bay a dozen miles to Walker Creek. On this drive, we pass a number of tiny settlements such as Bivalve, Hamlet, and Ocean Roar. The largest village is Marshall, with a population of 50. Wealthy sportsmen used to come here by train to shoot ducks on the bay. They lodged at the Marshall Hotel, which was destroyed by fire in 1974. The restaurant was saved and remains in business. Synanon was formerly headquartered near Marshall.

The east shore is the windy side of the bay. There are few trees and no beaches, but the tidal flats, accessible at many points from the highway, are productive of littleneck clams. The same gravelly areas where littlenecks are found may yield a few native oysters. The latter, known as the Olympia oyster *(Ostrea lurida)*, grows no more than three inches in length and is extremely difficult to pry from rocks. These oysters cannot be grown commercially at Tomales Bay because the water remains too warm in

The lone facility in many North Coast villages consists of a general store with gas pumps, post office and telephone. Marshall also has a restaurant and boat works.

autumn for the oysters to "harden up" properly. The main source of native oysters you find in markets is lower Puget Sound at Olympia, Washington.

Still, aside from commercial fishing, the most significant industry on the bay is oyster farming. There are several landings on the highway where fresh oysters may be purchased. The oysters are not natives but giant Pacific oysters *(Ostrea gigas)*, which are imported as seed oysters from Japan. The young seedlings, or "spat," are planted on old shells or other material known as "cultch." If the "set" is successful, the young oysters may reach marketable size within two years.

The oyster pens at Tomales Bay are fenced with redwood stakes to keep out sharks and skates. The kinds of sharks normally found in the bay are not dangerous to people. However, in 1969 a swimmer diving for abalone off Tomales Point was severely bitten in the leg. The victim managed to drive the shark away with a solid punch in the nose.

When the village of Marshall was settled in the 1850s, the only evidence of Indian occupation nearby were large mounds of clam and oyster shells. The Coast Miwok had long since been rounded up for labor in the Missions, where many perished from disease. When the Missions were secularized in 1833, the Christian Indians were supposedly to receive half the land. Instead, some Californios and sharp Yankee sea captains obtained the lion's share of it.

The brushy slopes of Bolinas Ridge which curve to rim the east shore of the bay were encompassed by a land grant known as the Nicasio Rancho. In 1835, Governor Figueroa awarded twenty leagues, or about 100,000 acres, of this land to some Mission Indians. Twenty years later the grant was nullified on a technicality by the Federal Land Commission. Henry Wager Halleck acquired most of it. This was the same Halleck who served without distinction as Lincoln's military adviser during the Civil War.

For a time following the Bear Flag Revolt a law was in effect requiring all Indians to possess a certificate showing that they were employed by a white man. Any Indian found without this paper was liable to be shot as a horse thief. The Miwoks were on the brink of extinction before scholars got around to studying their culture.

Investigations of shell mounds at Tomales Bay have uncovered mortars, pestles, and other artifacts. A surprising find was a group of rare Ming porcelain fragments. Historians speculate that the porcelain may have been given to the Indians by Drake. A short walk from the Bear Valley headquarters of the National Seashore is *Kule*

Commercial oyster beds on Tomales Bay are fenced with redwood stakes to keep out sharks and bat rays. Fresh oysters are sold retail at two piers on the east shore.

Loklo, which is a replica of a Miwok village, built with willows and tule thatch by a team of archeologists.

Just north of Nick's Cove is Miller County Park. The facilities here include a small boat launching ramp, picnic area, and rest rooms. The park serves mainly as a fishing access. Fishermen who do not bring a boat may rent one at Marshall or Cypress Grove. A large marina adjoins the privately operated campground at Marconi.

Surfperch, flounder, and small halibut abound throughout Tomales Bay. These species may be taken bait fishing off piers (where a fee may be charged) at Marshall and other landings. Fish caught mainly from boats include sting rays, bay rays, and sharks up to three hundred pounds. Large halibut, averaging ten to fifteen pounds, may be hooked trolling near the mouth of the bay. However, the water here can be treacherous

for small boats. The surface may be flat calm when suddenly out of nowhere a huge "sneaker wave" may engulf the unwary fisherman, capsizing his boat and throwing him into the bay. In one year alone, thirteen persons were reported to have drowned this way.

A "sneaker wave" usually occurs at a low stage of the tide when the sand bar at the entrance to the bay lies close to the surface. A gentle ocean swell meets the bar and instantly explodes into a breaker. The ebb tide rushing from the bay may add to the height of the breaker. Fishermen who wander outside the bay in small craft should plan to return before the tide starts going out. Otherwise, rough water at the bar may force them to seek refuge at another harbor, such as Bodega.

The major commercial fishery on Tomales Bay is for Pacific herring when these school fish enter to spawn in winter. For years the demand for herring was

*Aging commercial fishing craft awaits restoration at
Marshall Boat Works. Close by is a large marina with
campground, store, restaurant and boat launching.*

Bay Clams

Included in this category of bi-valve mollusks is a variety of clams found on tidal flats of mud, sand, or gravel in sheltered bays and river estuaries. The most productive areas on the North Coast are Drake's Estero, Tomales Bay, Bodega Harbor, and the vast flats on Humboldt Bay.

Littleneck clams (*Protothaca staminea*) grow to two inches in width. They are generally found a few inches deep in coarse gravel where they are most easily collected with a hoe, rake, or garden trowel. Japanese littlenecks (*Tapes semidedussata*) frequent the same cobble patches at Tomales Bay as common littlenecks.

Most abundant on the sand bars located just inside the mouth of Tomales Bay are gaper clams (*Tresus nuttali*). Locally known as "bignecks," they average six to eight inches across. One taken in 1938 was reported to weigh twelve pounds. Dig for gapers where you spot a small geyser of water spurting several feet in the air. The siphon or "neck" of a gaper is so elastic it allows the clam to bury itself to a depth of three feet or more. Clammers who work the fine moist sand on Seal Island use metal tubes to keep the holes they dig from caving in. These tubes, which measure three feet in length and fourteen inches across, may be rented at Lawson's Landing.

Washington clams (*Saxidomus nattali*) are found in the same areas as gapers but not quite as deep. Look for their siphon holes in soft mud, such as is common on Humboldt Bay. To unearth the clam, push a three-foot rod with a two-inch right hook down the siphon hole and hook it under the clam so you can yank it to the surface. Washingtons grow to five inches.

Another "longneck" species, which grows to eight inches and has been reported to attain weights up to seventeen pounds, is the geoduck (*Panope generose*). Geoducks are not as common as gaper and Washington clams because they dwell in a slender intertidal zone which becomes accessible only during the most extreme minus tides. To find geoducks, look for the tip of the siphon projecting from a hole about the size of a silver dollar. The clam will retract its neck when you start poking around, but mark the spot and prepare to dig to China. Near Bolinas, two clammers had to dig a hole six feet deep to unearth a geoduck that weighed eleven pounds.

Peculiar to soupy mudflats is the soft-shell clam (*Mya arenaria*). A potato fork is recommended for taking this clam, which has a very thin shell. The species is not native to the Pacific Coast but was accidentally introduced with a shipment of Eastern oysters to San Francisco Bay. Other clams which may be found in bays as well as on coastwise beaches include basket cockles, rough piddocks, and bent-nosed clams.

Clams may be kept alive for several hours in a wet sack and for longer periods in a pail of sea water that is changed twice a day. Galvanized containers should not be used.

One fair-sized gaper clam makes a meal for two people. The necks are split, pounded, and fried. The edible portions inside the shell are used for chowder. A Dillon Beach recipe for clam fritters calls for one cup each of chopped clam and cracker crumbs, two eggs, salt, pepper, and a dash of baking powder. The mixture is dropped by tablespoons into hot fat, fried on both sides to a golden brown, and served with lemon. Good sources of information on the preparation of clams for the table are *The Fisherman's Wharf Cookbook*, *Sunset Seafood Cookbook*, and *The Art of Fish Cookery*, by Milo Miloradovich. A handy guide for the identification of clams is the booklet *Marine Bivalves of the California Coast*, a publication of the California Fish and Game Department. Tide tables for the current year are available at most bait shops and marinas.

It's important to identify the clams you dig because state angling regulations specify different size and bag limits for the various species. Except for restricted areas, there's no closed season for bay clams. However, during the mussel quarantine (which goes into effect every year beginning as early as March and extending through October) the Public Health Department advises that clams be cleaned thoroughly before cooking and that stomach contents and all dark parts of the clams be removed. Only the white meat is safe to eat before the quarantine is lifted.

confined to bait shops. Restrictive quotas limited exports to Japan where *kazanoko,* a delicacy made from herring roe, commanded high prices. But suddenly this market opened in 1973 with removal of the quotas, devaluation of the dollar, and the collapse of the Japanese herring industry (some say from overfishing). Then commercial trawlers from far and wide converged on Tomales Bay, threatening to wipe out the run of herring here in one season. A bill to protect California's herring industry was rushed through the state legislature, with the result that the annual catch of the fish became subject to strict controls. The importance of the lowly herring was impressed upon the legislature by Senator Peter Behr when he told his colleagues, "We've already lost our sardines through overfishing. If we lose our herrings as well, we will have lost another vital link in the food chain for salmon, striped bass, albacore, and other fish of great commercial importance."

Beyond the launching area at Miller Park the Shoreline Highway turns up the estuary of Walker Creek. This is a good creek to try for winter steelhead trout when the larger streams are high and muddy.

A couple of miles up Walker Creek the road climbs out of the gulch to Tomales village, an old dairy center. From the heart of town the Dillon Beach Road bears west to approach one of the finest clamming areas on the North Coast. It's a lonely four-mile drive over green hills that are dotted with sheep and cattle.

Dillon Beach is a summer colony named for an Irishman who settled here in 1867. It fronts the coast at the extreme south end of Bodega Bay. There's a general store and resort here with housekeeping cottages, campsites, boat rentals, and access to a sheltered swimming beach. You can cast for surfperch at Dillon Beach, and the rocky north shore of the resort affords good opportunities for poke poling.

An unpaved toll road out of Dillon Beach runs through the dunes to Lawson's Landing, which is situated just inside the mouth of Tomales Bay. Here, on days of minus tides from October through June, the resort operates a clam ferry to Seal Island and Old

Waterside view of Marshall Hotel which fell into the bay during 1906 earthquake and was recently destroyed by fire. Adjoining structure houses a seafood restaurant.

Flatfish

The order of flatfish *(Herterosomata)* is well represented on the North Coast. It includes sand dabs, flounder, sole, turbot, and halibut, all of which contribute to the commercial catch. The species most prized by sports fishermen is the California halibut *(Paralichthys californicus)*, for which the accepted record is a sixty-one-pound fish that measured five feet in length.

Halibut are occasionally hooked in the surf, but more often they are taken by trolling or drift fishing over sandy bottoms in water less than sixty feet deep. During the summer halibut averaging ten to fifteen pounds are caught off the bar at the mouth of Tomales Bay. The tackle used is much the same as for ocean salmon: a standard boat rod and star drag reel spooled with thirty pound test monofilament line. A fresh anchovy or herring on a size 4/0 hook is trolled slowly a few feet above the sand bottom. Spliced between the line and leader is a device that releases the sinker when the halibut takes the bait. About twelve ounces of lead is recommended for working the bar at Tomales Bay. But take note: The bar is not a safe place for small boats on an outgoing tide and usually gets too rough for fishing after the prevailing northwest winds pick up in the afternoon.

Shore fishing for flounder in the shallows of bays and estuaries is a sport the whole family can enjoy. The flounder most commonly taken with hook and line on the North Coast is the starry flounder *(Platichthys stelatus)*, which feeds on clams and small crabs. The best shore fishing occurs from November through early spring when the adult flounders enter shallow water to spawn. Starry flounder have been reported up to twenty pounds in weight, but two to three pounds is a respectable size.

At slack tide in a sheltered bay you might hook a flounder with a fly rod and enjoy tremendous sport. However, water conditions normally require tackle capable of casting sinkers one to four ounces in weight. For this tackle use a light saltwater spinning outfit with line of no less than twelve-pound breaking strength.

Terminal tackle consists of the standard saltwater leader for bottom fishing which may be purchased at any coastwise bait or sporting goods store. It is a three-foot length of stout monofilament with two dropper loops, spaced about fifteen inches apart. A plain brass swivel is attached at one end of the leader and a swivel with a snap for the sinker at the other end. Attach Numbers 4 or 6 snelled hooks to the dropper loops, bait up with shrimp or cut-bait, and you are ready to cast. It's important to reel in the slack after the sinker hits bottom so you can tell when you get a bite. When hooked a flounder resists by swimming backward and trying to bury itself in the mud.

The starry flounder is easily identified by its orange-tinted fins striped with black bars. The underside is white and the top a mottled black-brown which serves as protective coloration when the fish forages on a muddy bottom.

Another flatfish common in bays is the Pacific sand dab *(Citharichthys sordidus)*. Adult sand dabs, which average about eight inches long, are rarely taken in water less than sixty feet deep.

Most kinds of flatfish found off the North Coast are held in high esteem as tablefish. Restaurants on San Francisco's Fisherman's Wharf feature sand dabs as a delicacy. Starry flounder is often marketed as "sole" or "fillet of sole."

For a scrumptious meal, sprinkle salt and pepper on fresh-caught fillets of flounder, dust with flour, and fry *quickly* on both sides to a golden brown. Serve with lemon or tartar sauce.

Island. These clam-rich bars are exposed only at low tide. Most abundant are Washington and gaper clams. The latter, locally known as "bignecks," average four pounds in weight. All the equipment needed for clamming, as well as fishing tackle and crab nets, may be rented at the resort. For information on the tides and barge schedules, phone (707) 878-2443.

Clamming off Lawson's Landing is apt to be best on an extreme minus tide in March or April before the vacation crowds arrive. The landing includes small boat launching facilities. Scheduled partyboats leave in summer on blue water trips for salmon and bottomfish. Tomales Point, approached by boat from Lawson's Landing, is productive of abalone.

Coastal fog shrouds commercial fishing craft moored in Bodega Harbor. Note rear deck of vessel piled high with circular traps used for catching crabs.

The Abalone Coast: Sonoma County

The forty-mile Sonoma Coast provides only one safe harbor for small boats but is renowned for its historic sites, lovely pocket beaches, and the long stretches of rocky tide pool areas which afford the choicest abalone picking on the North Coast.

This rugged shore is only a shade more populated today than it was when the frontage was dotted with Miwok villages and the flag of Imperial Russia flew over Bodega and Fort Ross.

Travelers can camp by the sea at several coastal parks. Motor inns are located at Bodega Bay, Jenner, Ocean Cove, and Sea Ranch.

Bodega Bay

Juan Francisco de la Bodega y Cauadra sailed his schooner, *Sonora*, across Bodega Bay in 1775. Bodega's mission was to chart the coastline as part of a plan to extend the Spanish presidios northward. But in 1808 only Miwok Indians were present when the *Kodiak* arrived with a large complement of Russian artisans and Aleut hunters. This expedition was headed by Ivan Alexander Kuskoff, agent for the Russian-American Fur Company, which had been chartered by Catherine the Great in 1796. The firm was organized along the same lines as the Hudson Bay Company.

In 1809, Kuskoff sailed back to headquarters at Sitka, Alaska, with a cargo of grain and 1,453 otter skins. He returned to Bodega in 1811 to build Port Romanoff, Kuskoff, and the stockade at Fort Ross.

The Shoreline Highway loops inland north of Tomales Bay to avoid the stretch of precipitous coast which fronts Bodega Bay. On this drive, the pavement climbs and dips through lightly wooded pasture once farmed by the Russian colonists.

Five miles beyond Tomales, the road spans Americano Creek approximately where it was forded by an Indian trail. Two miles farther up the north bank is Valley Ford, a small farm center which grew up around an old trading post.

From Valley Ford, it's three miles to a junction with the Bodega Highway. A short distance up this road, Bodega village sits alone in a pleasant valley drained by Salmon Creek. The business district amounts to a garage, general store, doll museum, antique shop, and a restaurant housed in the old Potter School. Several wooden dwellings and a steepled church date back to more prosperous times when potatoes were grown in the valley. The tubers were much esteemed by early San Francisco residents, who knew them as "Bodega reds."

The ridge that rises a mile north of town is forested along its crest by a tree farm known as the Joy Redwoods. Visible from the church is a small lumber mill on the lower slopes. An Indian village stood here until the Russians built Kuskoff on the site in 1811. For thirty years, the colonists grew crops in the valley for export to fur posts in Alaska.

Reluctant to challenge the Russians in a military way, the Mexican administration brought other pressures to bear. Traders, trappers, and sailors who drifted into Yerba Buena were encouraged to take Mexican citizenship and homestead lands adjoining the Russian settlements. In 1834, a ship's deserter, James Dawson, built a sawmill on Salmon Creek a short way upstream from Kuskoff. Later Dawson went into partnership with another ex-sailor, Edwin McIntosh. The partners shared a house on the creek until 1839, when General Vallejo awarded the land to McIntosh. In a fit of anger, Dawson sawed the house down the middle and removed his half by ox team to a site on Americano Creek.

The Russians withdrew in 1841, and Bodega began to flourish as a shipping point for fish, cheese, and "Bodega reds." After the Russians evacuated Kuskoff it was acquired by Stephen Smith, a sea captain from Maryland who obtained Mexican citizenship and married the daughter of a Californio. Smith built an adobe mansion on the site of Kuskoff and in 1843 California's first steam-operated sawmill. A year later he gained title to Rancho Bodega, about 35,000 acres of land which stretched from Estero Americano to the Russian River. Smith began the coastal lumber trade when he purchased the bark *George Henry* to carry redwood planks to San Francisco. Previous to 1840, the settlements inside the Golden Gate imported most of their lumber from Hawaii, then known as the Sandwich Islands. Smith's estate was broken up in the 1850s following a dispute with squatters from the goldfields known as the "Bodega War."

Two miles up the Bodega Highway from Bodega village is a small park. The picnic facilities border a one-room schoolhouse built in 1856.

Four miles from Bodega by way of Highway 1 is Bodega Harbor. Enclosed by a sand spit and rocky headland, the harbor bears a resemblance to Bolinas Lagoon except that it's deeper and the narrow opening to the sea is protected by rock jetties. As many as five hundred commercial fishing boats crowd into the port during summer.

The village of Bodega Bay is perched on the lower slopes of Mount Roscoe which incline steeply into the harbor. No vestige of the Russian occupation remains. Rather the village has a New England look to it. The St. Teresa Church was built in 1862 and at least one home dates back to the 1850s. Some of the Gothic settings for Alfred Hitchcock's film *The Birds* were

Old Potter Schoolhouse at Bodega village is now an art gallery. Former Russian settlement of Kuskoff was situated on flat seen directly beyond the steepled church.

Rockfish Partyboats

Part of the excitement that goes with bottom fishing off a partyboat is never knowing what variety of fish will take the bait. It might be a wee tomcod or a big lingcod in the thirty to forty pound range. Or perhaps you'll catch an ugly cabezon, a pretty kelp greenling, or a ferocious wolf eel.

On most days, "rock cod" comprise the bulk of the catch. These are not true cod but members of the rockfish family Scorpaenidae. Over fifty species are found in California waters. They come in all colors and range up to thirty pounds in weight. Blue, black, copper, and canary rockfish are most commonly hooked on the shoals off Bodega Head, Tomales Point, and Fort Ross.

The partyboats leave at 7:00 a.m. or earlier and return around 2:00 p.m. when the prevailing winds begin to whip up a choppy sea. Advance reservations are usually required. Tackle may be rented at the boat landing. The basic gear consists of a short boat rod and star drag reel with 40 pound test monofilament line.

Bottom fishing is ordinarily done in water forty to fifty feet deep. The terminal rig consists of a stout leader three to four feet long with two dropper loops and a one to two pound sinker snapped to the end. Snelled hooks, size 2/0 or larger, are fastened to the droppers. Squid, shrimp, and fish chunks are the favorite baits and metal jigs are sometimes effective. A good jig for rockfish is a plain hook tied with a few strands of red or yellow thread.

All bottomfish caught off the North Coast are edible. Most are palatable. Only the roe of the cabezon is toxic. The flesh of a lingcod is green before it's cooked. Special care is advised when removing a hook from a bottomfish. Most varieties have razor-sharp spines and teeth.

A useful pocket book to take on a partyboat trip is the California Fish and Game publication *Offshore Fishes* by John E. Fitch. Of the 550 different kinds of fish that have been caught off the California Coast, this illustrated guide describes 27 of the most sought-after game species. A complete listing of the 52 kinds of rockfishes (with photographs) may be found in Fish Bulletin No. 104, *A Review of the Rockfishes of California* by Julius B. Phillips.

Charter boats to accommodate private parties are available for hire year round at Bodega Bay and most other fishing ports on the North Coast. During the summer scheduled partyboats operate out of Noyo Harbor at Fort Bragg, Eureka, Trinidad, and the Citizen's Dock at Crescent City.

All skippers of partyboats must be licensed and certified by the U.S. Coast Guard, which also requires periodic inspections to determine that boats are seaworthy. Marine radios are standard equipment and most commercial craft are outfitted with sonar, radar, direction finders, and other electronic gear needed to cope with most any emergency that might arise.

filmed at Bodega Bay in 1962. Strung out along Highway 1 are numerous fish landings plus a few stores, motels, and restaurants. A Coast Guard station shares the sand spit with Doran County Park. The latter has 141 sites for trailers and camper wagons. There's a small boat launching ramp here and across the harbor at Westside County Park (which has fifty spaces for RV's and trailers). Gaper and Washington clams are found on flats off the east bank of the sand spit. The east jetty is popular for fishing and skin diving.

Shortly after the Coastal Zone Conservation Com-mission was formed in 1972, it contracted with the Army Engineers and State Fish and Game Department to survey the remaining wetlands on the coast. This survey determined that the salt marshes, tidal flats, subtidal channels, and variegated shores at Bodega Harbor support an amazing diversity of wildlife. The list includes 77 kinds of birds, 33 species of mammals, 12 species of reptiles and amphibians, at least 75 kinds of fish, and 250 marine invertebrates, including 14 species of shrimps, 22 of crabs, and no less than 36 kinds of clams. A report on the survey published in 1975 recommended improved facilities for sport and commercial fishing craft. But it warned that the living marine resources of the harbor were probably receiving as much public use as they could stand without detrimental effects.

The peninsula which curves out to Bodega Head is occupied by Westside County Park, the University of California Marine Biological Reserve, and park land of Sonoma Coast State Beach. The laboratories at the Biological Reserve are engaged in such applied research as a project to develop techniques whereby New England lobsters may be farmed cheaply enough to become a viable industry in California. Wild lobsters found in water averaging fifty degrees require five to eight years to attain a legal catchable size of one pound in weight. Researchers have found that lobsters farmed in seventy-degree water will reach a mature size in little more than two years.

Bodega Head itself, a monolith of granite lying west of the San Andreas Fault is approached on the Big Flat Road. The road terminates atop the headland at a state picnic area. The spot overlooks a stretch of rocks and surf where agile anglers find precarious footholds to cast for perch and kelp greenling.

Bodega Head is uninhabited and largely unspoiled except for a massive excavation on the harbor side of the headland. This ninety-foot hole was dug to accommodate what was to have been the largest nuclear power plant of its kind in North America. Construction was halted following a stormy public hearing in 1962. Conservationists claimed that the project would desecrate a natural area of great beauty and scientific interest. Local fishermen feared that power lines would interfere with marine radio communications. Another crucial consideration was the proximity of the power site to the San Andreas Fault. Geologists and engineers disagreed as to the possible consequences of a major earthquake. Over the years, the big hole has filled with water to become what one observer described as "the world's most expensive duck pond."

Local conservationists hardly had time to celebrate their victory at Bodega Head before their quaint and quiet fishing village was invaded by vacation-home developers. At present there are two subdivisions at Bodega Bay, the largest of which is an eight-hundred-acre project with sixteen hundred lots known as "Bodega Harbor." This development of Brown and Kauffmann (an affiliate of Potlatch Forests) extends from the waterfront back into the rolling hills south of the harbor. The developers found it necessary to appear at fifty-seven public hearings before twenty-three different agencies before they sold their first homesite in 1971. Scarcely a dozen homes were built before the Coastal Zone Conservation Act was passed in 1972.

Since then the developers have argued with indifferent success that the principle of "vested rights" entitles them to an exemption from controls on home construction. At last report the whole matter was tied up in litigation which may take years to resolve. The population of Bodega Bay is listed in the 1970 census as three hundred persons. Should all the lots be occupied at "Bodega Harbor," the population would zoom to five thousand. This prospect moved one resident of the village to declare that "Bodega needs five thousand people like the Pacific Gas and Electric Company needs the San Andreas Fault."

"So who needs a 'running fence?'" This question became a burning issue around Bodega in 1972 after the Bulgarian-born artist Christo Javacheff announced his plan to "wrap" the Sonoma Coast.

Christo said he wanted to build a fence of nylon fabric that would stretch 22 miles from a farm near Petaluma to the seashore somewhere between Bodega and Dillon Beach. The nylon would be suspended by cable on nineteen hundred steel poles spaced at sixty foot intervals. The cost, estimated at a million dollars, would be borne by the artist. The fence would be removed after two weeks.

It seemed the "running fence" had no purpose but to provide an esthetic experience for the artist and his admirers, a group which includes such prestigious institutions as the Metropolitan Museum of Art. San Francisco art critic Alfred Frankenstein noted that Christo had "made a major art of wrapping—objects, people, even buildings—and reached a climax in that aspect of his work with the wrapping of a considerable stretch of seacoast in Australia."

In 1975, when the Coastal Zone Conservation Commission was asked to rule on the fence, the commissioners were deluged with phone calls and telegrams from Christo supporters. These included messages from the French ambassador to the United Nations and the president of the Rockerfeller Family Foundation. One letter claimed that when Christo "wrapped" 14,000 square feet of seashore at Newport, Rhode Island, "the marine life, especially the fish and sea gulls, actually liked it."

The Commission came out against Christo's plan on the grounds that the fence and the crowds it would attract would harm the environment. But finally in September of 1976, after seventeen public hearings and three court sessions, Christo's nylon "fence-to-the-sea" was erected. He accomplished it with the help of three hundred volunteers. The fence drew crowds of weekenders from the Bay Area, but the turnout was not as big as conservationists had feared or local merchants had hoped.

Sonoma Coast State Beach

On the shoreline drive from Bodega Bay to the Russian River you might easily overlook Sonoma Coast State Beach were this 2,200-acre preserve not very well marked. Along this stretch you will find not one state beach but a baker's dozen of them strung out along twelve miles of rocky coast. Only small portions of Carmet and Salmon Beaches are visible from the pavement. The other beaches lie hidden from the road in small coves at the foot of precipitous bluffs. Corkscrew paths lead down to them from trailheads marked with signs.

Summer fog is particularly thick on this rugged shore. There are few trees to stay the ocean breezes and the surf is much too cold and rough for swimming. This is primarily a fisherman's coast. It is seen to best advantage in spring when the bluffs are bright with wildflowers.

Park headquarters are located on Salmon Creek

Tall, shaggy sheep of the Romney strain thrive better on the coast than most fine wool breeds. Their long fleece is effective in shedding the heavy winter rains.

*Sea stacks dot the water off the 15 mile stretch of
bluffs and mini-beaches which front the Sonoma Coast
State Beach. Fishing and camping are popular here.*

Dip Netting for Surf Smelt

Surf smelt rarely exceed a foot in length but they are superb tablefish and fun to catch when a school moves inshore to spawn. The schools favor steep beaches of coarse sand where there is some seepage of fresh water. Smelt eggs are adhesive and cling to individual grains of sand. The runs may begin anytime from mid-March through June and recur at sporadic intervals through early fall.

A smelt run may occur at any stage of the tide except slack water. The presence of a school is usually advertised by an unusual concentration of gulls and other fish-eating birds. Of the several kinds of smelt netted off North Coast beaches, all are true smelt, members of the family Osmeridae. The common day smelt, *Hyposmesus*, grows to ten inches in length. The night smelt, *Spirinchus*, is caught mainly between dusk and midnight.

Hawaiian-type throw nets may be used to take smelt; however, the traditional A-frame dip net is more popular on the North Coast. It closely resembles the so-called "squaw net" used for centuries by the Coast Indians. Some tribes relied heavily on the smelt runs for food. The fish has a fine delicate flavor when dipped in batter and pan-fried the same as trout.

Maneuvering a clumsy A-frame in the surf is hard work. The trick is to intercept the smelt on an incoming breaker and then trap them by quickly pivoting the net towards shore.

Some resorts rent A-frame nets but few sporting goods stores carry them because most fishermen prefer to make their own. The mesh size and overall dimension of the nets is governed by state angling regulations. The regulations specify bag limits for day smelt, night smelt, and whitebait smelt.

Lagoon a mile north of Bodega Bay, just beyond the village of Salmon Creek (population 150). Steelhead trout enter this creek in winter but do not linger long in the lagoon, the only place on the stream open to fishing.

An access road leaves the highway south of the park headquarters for an improved one-hundred-site campground located in the dunes which front Salmon Creek Beach. This beach stretches more than a mile south to Mussel Rock on Bodega Head. In summer it affords good dip netting for surf smelt.

Just north of park headquarters is Miwok Beach, which is followed by Coleman Beach. Near here the Coleman Valley Road forks east through hilly sheep pasture where the Russian colonists once cultivated grapes. The road leads to Occidental, a small village renowned for its country-style Italian restaurants. The Union Hotel, now a restaurant, dates back to 1876.

North of Coleman Beach is Arched Rock Beach and then Carmet Beach, site of a summer subdivision. Next door is Schoolhouse Beach which adjoins Portuguese Beach, a good place to cast for perch and rockfish.

Duncan Rock interrupts the chain of beaches about mid-way between Salmon Creek and the Russian River. This is a treacherous area to fish. The ocean hereabouts is prone to generate an occasional giant "sneaker wave." At least twenty-one persons were reported lost in the vicinity of Duncan Rock before it was fenced and posted out of bounds to fishermen.

On the lee side of Duncan Rock is a little cove which served as a "doghole port" from 1862 until 1877. Lumber was brought here by tramway from Duncan Mills on the Russian River.

Skin divers work the rocky ledges off Wrights Beach during the abalone season. Surf netting is often good here for both day and night smelt. A campground with thirty sites for tents and camper wagons adjoins the beach.

Shell Beach is popular with rock fishermen. It's also a rewarding place to study tide pools.

Still more beaches may be approached from a side road which leaves Highway 1 just before it veers east to Bridgehaven on the Russian River. Blind Beach is tops for surf smelt. Goat Rock near the mouth of the Russian River affords shore fishing. A mile of beach frontage on the south side of the Russian River Lagoon draws crowds of steelhead fishermen in early winter. And accessible by boat from the south bank is a low, sandy state-owned isle on the river known as Penny Island. The river mouth becomes a hazardous area for small craft after the bar at the entrance to the lagoon is opened by winter rains. In spring, perch fishing is apt to be productive on the surfside of Goat Rock Beach.

Fly caster works the Northwood Pool near Guerneville for spring-run American shad. The same water yields steelhead to drift fishermen during the winter season.

The Russian River

A side trip up the Russian River Canyon offers a change of pace and respite from the coastal fog. Geologists speculate that the Russian may have emptied into San Francisco Bay before ancient upheavals changed its course. From its source in the Eastern Highlands, the river runs seventy-five miles towards the Bay only to execute a ninety-degree turn below Healdsburg in the direction of the sea. Unlike most North Coast streams, the Russian supports a strong flow of water throughout the dry season. Some of this water comes from the turbines of a powerhouse on the Eel River.

Just a few miles inland State Highway 116, the river road, enters the busiest summer playground on the North Coast. From Villa Grande to Mirabel a dozen miles upstream, the redwood-shaded banks are jam-packed with vacation cottages and resorts offering lodges, campsites, swimming beaches, and boating facilities. The River Inn serves lobster thermidor. Ramona's Place has hot dogs. Other restaurants feature French, German, Italian, Mexican, and Oriental cuisines. In a redwood glade near the crowded beach at Monte Rio, the venerable Bohemian Club provides a rustic retreat for celebrities and military brass.

The lower Russian River was a heavily populated place even before the Spanish discovered it. According to Alfred Kroeber, the Pomo Indians numbered between seven and eight thousand when their villages dotted the coast from Goat Rock to the Noyo River. By Kroeber's estimate, about one-third of this population lived in the Russian River Canyon.

The Russians explored the river but didn't settle on it. They called it Slavianka, which means Russian maiden.

In 1836, the Mexican governor awarded some land on the river near Mirabel to Juan Bautista Roger Cooper. A sea captain of English descent, Cooper made a business of obtaining land grants and selling them to his friends after he married a daughter of General Vallejo. At Rancho El Molino, he built the first sawmill on the Russian in 1837. But logging didn't amount to much here until lumbermen found a way to cope with the redwood giants. This happened in the 1850s. An ancient redwood felled on the river near Austin Creek was reported to measure twenty-three feet in diameter. One man hacked away at it for two years to produce 600,000 shingles.

The redwoods do not grow all the way to the mouth of the river. Where Highway 1 spans the estuary at

Bridgehaven the steep banks are brushy. From the junction at the north end of the bridge, Highway 116 runs three miles to Duncan Mills. The small resort village here is located near the site of a lumber mill built by Sam and Alex Duncan in 1860. The Duncan Mill made money despite heavy losses from floods. Seven million board feet were swept out to sea in the winter of 1862.

The first throngs of holiday visitors arrived on the Russian River in 1877. This was the year the narrow-gauge North Pacific Coast Railway was extended from Tomales to Duncan Mills by way of Occidental and Valley Ford. The old depot at Duncan Mills has been restored to serve as an office for a privately operated 125-site campground and resort.

The Moscow Road leaves Highway 116 at Duncan Mills to cross the river and follow the south bank to Monte Rio. Built in 1908, the Village Inn at Monte Rio still provides food and lodging for the traveler. The rooms are small, the floors uneven, the chairs antiquated, but the beds are comfortable and the menu is "international." Monte Rio has a water carnival on the Fourth of July.

The bridge at Duncan Mills marks the limit of tidewater and overlooks a favorite stretch of the Russian to fish for winter-run steelhead trout. Downstream are Duncan Hole, Freezeout Riffle, Lone Pine Pool, and Alligator Snag. Upstream are Watson's Log, Brown's Pool, and the Austin Creek Riffle. Brown's Pool is fronted by the Casini Ranch, a stock farm which includes a large attractive campground with boat launching and sites for tents and trailers.

The redwoods begin a mile upriver in the vicinity of Austin Creek. The resorts on Austin Creek have a quieter, more conservative aspect than those on the main river. A music camp sponsored by the City of Berkeley holds summer concerts here.

A paved road follows Austin Creek up the north wall of the canyon six miles to Cazadero, which means "hunting place" in Spanish. In winter Cazadero is the wettest spot in Sonoma County, with an average annual rainfall of 82.39 inches. The village became a logging and recreation center after a spur of the North Pacific Coast Railway was extended to it in 1885. A small sawmill operates in the heart of town. Standing on the edge of main street, you can watch green planks being edged and trimmed on a sorting table.

The Fort Ross and King Ridge Roads out of Cazadero afford a back country approach to the coast north of Jenner. Both roads are steep and single lane in places. Logging trucks use them on weekdays. The Fort Ross Road is paved but it's advisable to inquire locally before attempting the King Ridge route in a conventional car.

Six miles east of the Austin Creek turn-off on Highway 116 is the largest settlement in the resort area. George Guerne built a lumber mill here in 1860. (The tallest redwood felled near town was said to measure 367 feet.) The lumber was transported first by wagon and later by steam locomotive on a branch line of the San Francisco and North Pacific Railroad. Much valuable timber and most of Guerneville were destroyed by fire in 1923. Rail service was terminated in the early 1930s.

The summer population at Guerneville averages about five thousand but may swell to more than fifty thousand on holiday weekends. Perhaps half the nine hundred or so permanent residents are former "hippies" who've settled down to earn a living.

In the heyday of the counterculture large numbers of itinerant middle-class youths flocked to the lower Russian River area, partly because it is beautiful and partly because it has provided odd jobs in summer and cheap lodgings during the off-season.

In recent years many Russian River resorts have been upgraded, and attractive country inns have opened. The price of summer homes has soared. However, Guerneville remains a relaxed, unpretentious village that still bears more than a trace of the frontier look and spirit. Weekenders are lured to Guerneville in late May or June by the annual Russian River Rodeo and "Stumptown Parade." In September the town hosts the Russian River Jazz Festival.

The road forks at Guerneville. Highway 116 crosses the river and meanders south to Sebastopol, an apple growing center. The Westside Road follows the river through vineyards and orchards to Healdsburg on the Redwood Highway, which is U.S. 101.

A third road bears north for three miles to Armstrong Redwoods State Reserve. Near the park checking station, the Sweetwater Springs Road branches east to approach a mercury mine and the state forest lookout on Mount Jackson. The rough spur to the lookout is traveled on foot. The summit affords sweeping views of the Russian River Canyon and Santa Rosa Valley.

In the 1870s, Colonel James B. Armstrong operated one of the largest saw mills on the river. He owned so much land that he felt he could spare 440 acres of virgin redwood for an "arboretum and botanical garden." A state-owned preserve since 1934, the Armstrong Redwoods are laced with trails which include a self-guiding nature path. A

Thousand-year-old trees encircle the picnic grounds at Armstrong Redwoods State Reserve. A road leaves here for the Austin Recreation Area.

Anadromous Gamefish

The kinds of fish most prized by anglers on the North Coast all happen to be anadromous. They include such highly rated game species as the American shad, king or Chinook salmon, and the steelhead rainbow trout. Anadromous fish spend much if not most of their lives at sea but enter fresh water to spawn. The principles of osmosis determine that freshwater and saltwater fishes will have different lifestyles. Freshwater fish do not drink but absorb water through their gills. Saltwater fish drink and employ their gills to excrete salt. Anadromous fish such as the steelhead must be capable of adapting to either system.

Scientists can only speculate as to why some fish are anadromous. One theory has it that the steelhead rainbow used to be strictly a saltwater fish. Then, as the oceans warmed, the steelhead began to enter streams to find water that was the right temperature to incubate their eggs. Or, it could be that steelhead eggs deposited in shallow bays were less subject to predation than elsewhere in the ocean and in time these bays became rivers.

Another theory suggests that steelhead were forced up rivers as the oceans they inhabited began to dry up. Because these trout (like most freshwater fish) were prone to reproduce at a rate that depleted the food supply, some eventually found their way back to the ocean where food was more plentiful. They returned to their native streams only when driven by the urge to propagate. But whatever happened took place over eons of time when climates changed, mountains rose and fell, and the patterns of oceans and continents underwent drastic alterations.

Still a mystery is the steelhead trout's ability, after traveling hundreds of miles across the North Pacific, to find its way back to the stream where it was born. Many ichthyologists believe that anadromous fish possess a capacity to perceive direction in a manner completely unknown to humans.

Some anadromous fish, such as the king salmon, are caught mainly in salt water, while the steelhead fishery is based entirely on the rivers. Large numbers of American shad (originally introduced into California from the East Coast in 1871) migrate up several North Coast rivers, but few people fish for them near the ocean except on the Russian River.

Angling for spring shad on the Russian is most productive on pools and riffles in the resort area of the lower river. Here the shad (Alosa sapidissima) are apt to be most numerous in early May. These herring-like migrants are very game fish; they often make dazzling leaps above the surface when hooked on a fly or small spinner. Buck shad average two to three pounds in weight; roe shad range to eight pounds. Local stores on the Russian carry the preferred patterns of Numbers 4 and 6 wet flies. In general, the same tackle and techniques are recommended for shad as are used in fly fishing for winter-run steelhead.

Other anadromous fish caught in the Russian besides salmon, steelhead, and shad include an occasional sturgeon and striped bass.

A pocket guide with a wealth of practical information for anglers is the state publication Anadromous Fishes of California by Donald H. Fry, Jr.

---

forest amphitheater accommodates two thousand people for concerts, weddings, and theatricals. The tallest redwood in the preserve towers to 310 feet.

An attractive, cool picnic area ringed with tall trees is located just inside the northern boundary of the park. From here, a slender byway climbs steeply to enter the 4,300-acre Austin Creek State Recreation Area. The road leads to a rustic twenty-five-site campground at pond-sized Redwood Lake. Another camp, located off the access road, is for use by horse parties.

Most of the Austin Creek Recreation Area remains a wilderness for the enjoyment of hikers and horseback riders. The Pomo Indians used to collect acorns and hunt deer here. The country is all up and down, a patchwork quilt of fir forest, steep meadows, and lush streamside woodland. Fire danger is high in summer and no open fires are permitted. Overnight camping in the back country is restricted to a small site on Thompson Creek, reserved for use by organized groups.

A lush streamside woodland backed by towering redwoods gives canoeists on the Russian an illusion of wilderness. The trees hide scores of resorts and campgrounds.

You can enjoy the illusion of wilderness by taking a canoe trip, lasting one to five days, down the Russian River. Most resorts on the river rent canoes only for use in their immediate area, but W. C. Trowbridge, whose fleet of six hundred canoes is based at Healdsburg beach, specializes in trip rentals. You may choose your own launching site and the resort will send a car to pick you up down river at a prearranged time and place. For information write Trowbridge Canoes, P.O. Box 942, Healdsburg, CA 95448, or call (707) 433-7247. Much the same service is provided by Burke's Canoe Trips, based on the same river a mile north of Forestville, (707) 887-1222. Both outfits have been in business for more than thirty years.

Summer angling on the Russian is good in places for smallmouth black bass. The favorite baits are night-crawlers, lampreys, and crayfish. Trolling for silver salmon on the lower estuary and lagoon may turn hot for a brief spell any time from October through early December.

A small run of American shad usually begins in late April and continues through Memorial Day. Steelhead fishing in November and December is centered on the lagoon and estuary. Beach fishermen troll the tidal pools with wet flies and small wobbling plugs.

After December rains raise the river, the steelhead action shifts to pools and riffles upstream from the Duncan Bridge. These are worked by bait casters in chest-high waders. The wise steelhead enthusiast phones a local resort or bait shop for advice on water conditions before visiting the Russian. The river is prone to flood at least once every winter, inundating resorts and portions of Highway 116.

Winter Steelheading

It has been suggested that the steelhead rainbow *(Salmo gairdnerii gairdnerii)* and the Atlantic salmon *(Salmo salar)* originated from a common ancestor in the Arctic. Whether or not the theory is correct, there are only minor anatomical differences between the two species and these fish share a far-flung reputation as the gamest of all the salmons, trouts, and chars.

Winter-run steelheads may also qualify as the most elusive member of the family Salmonidae. They are notoriously hard to hook and often impossible to land. Their evasiveness, combined with the chilly weather and difficult water conditions, limits the appeal of winter steelheading to the most dedicated trout enthusiasts.

High muddy water renders the larger North Coast rivers unfishable for weeks following a major storm. And just when the Russian begins to clear, a flood control dam near Ukiah releases tons of silt into the stream. But a prolonged period of low clear water affords no better fishing. At such times only the practiced fly fisherman may have the luck to raise a steelhead.

Bait fishing is ideal when the river is milky green. Drift fishing with bait calls for a strong, limber 8.5- to 9.5-foot rod and heavy-duty spinning or level-wind reel spooled with ten pound test monofilament line. The bait may be a nightcrawler or the "strawberry" of fresh salmon roe. Cast the bait from the shallow side of the river towards the opposite bank and allow it to drift in the current with the sinker bouncing along the bottom. When your line points downriver, reel in and cast again. A variety of lures may be drifted in the same manner. The favorite offerings include spoons, weighted spinners, and "Cherry Bobber" type lures which imitate a cluster of salmon roe.

Steelhead on their upstream migration are believed to travel mostly at night. By day they rest near the bottom where the current provides well-oxygenated water. Steelhead are rarely found in slack water; nor do they favor the more turbulent riffles. Water that is too rough to wade is not likely to hold a steelhead. Favorite targets of drift fishermen are the slicks at the tail of a pool, the pockets screened by brush beneath an undercut bank, and any deep water where a submerged boulder or snag deflects the full force of the current.

Cold water dulls the appetite of a winter-run steelhead, so he will not strike unless the bait or lure is drifted in front of his nose. Often the fish will mouth the offering so gently that the inexperienced angler misses the strike. But if the hook is set, the steelie explodes with a powerful run that can strip a reel in seconds. When this happens, the angler has no recourse but to try to keep up with the fish by sprinting along the bank.

A favorite terminal rig consists of a three-way swivel with a six-inch dropper for the sinker and a twelve-inch leader for the bait or lure. Sinker weights from one-quarter ounce to two ounces are used, depending on the force of the current. The bait or lure must be weighted so it drifts close to the bottom without snagging. Hook sizes Numbers 4 to 1/0 are favored when using "strawberries" of fresh roe.

Other methods of catching winter steelhead include plunking, mooching, rafting, and float fishing. Plunking amounts to still fishing with a sinker heavy enough to anchor the bait. It may be the only way to hook a steelhead in water that's too high and roily for drift fishing. Mooching is effective on the tidal reaches of estuaries. A fly, spoon, or bait is trolled from a skiff which is allowed to drift with the wind or current. A few split-shot lead sinkers may be required to weight the line, depending on water conditions.

Rafting on large rivers, such as the Eel, is recommended only for the experienced. Float fishing is practiced on the Klamath where boats with guides are for hire.

The winter-run steelheads taken on North Coast streams average about five pounds in weight. Some ranging up to fifteen pounds are caught every year on the Russian. These sea trout tend to grow at a much faster rate than their land-locked cousins because the supply of natural fish foods is vastly more abundant in the ocean.

For a complete but easy-to-read exposition on winter steelheading, see *California Steelhead Fishing* by Jim Freeman. This paperback book contains information on all the productive steelhead waters of the North Coast.

This restoration of Russian Orthodox church at Fort Ross was destroyed by fire in 1970. The structure has since been rebuilt and the fort reopened to visitors.

The Mendocino Highlands range north from the Russian River to rim 180 miles of coastline. These are fold-fault mountains, probably less than a million years old, and heavy with sedimentary rocks such as shale and sandstone. In Pleistocene times, these mountains were uplifted from an inland sea which spread west from the Sierra Nevada to the lost continent of Salinia.

The coastal shelf shrinks to nothing between Russian Gulch and Fort Ross. Here the mountains rise directly from the sea. On this stretch, the road resembles the John Muir Trail more than a modern highway. Slides and washouts present a hazard in wet weather. But the route has been much improved since it was taken over by the state in the 1930s. Before that time, motorists were required to stop every mile or so to open a rancher's gate.

Sheep graze off the highway in places where climbing ropes are needed to approach the water. Most of the ocean frontage is private and posted. By contrast with the fierce topography, the climate is exceptionally mild. The so-called "banana belt" between Jenner and Anchor Bay enjoys fogless days.

The closest thing to a town on the whole 180-mile stretch is Stewarts Point, which supports a general store. Other facilities can be summed up quickly: Luxury motor inns are situated at Timber Cove, Ocean Cove, and Sea Ranch. There's camping at Salt Point State Park but no accommodations at Fort Ross. The nearest facilities south of the fort are on the Russian River estuary.

The resort at Bridge Haven has sites for trailers. One mile north of the bridge crossing, the weathered village of Jenner clings to a steep bank overlooking the lagoon. Here are motels, restaurants, and a resort with boats for rent. It's a short walk from the resort to Jenner Beach, which abounds with driftwood in spring.

From Jenner the highway climbs to a grassy shelf and then plunges into Russian Gulch. Access to the beach for surf casting and smelt netting is by permission.

We leave Russian Gulch on a series of massive switchbacks which crest on an exposed bench six hundred feet above the ocean. The Meyers Grade Road forks here to approach the junction of the Seaview and Fort Ross-Cazadero Roads on Campmeeting Ridge. These mountain roads provided a stage route to the Fort Ross area before there was a shoreline approach.

Highway 1 drops off the bench to follow the con-tours of the sheer-sided ocean bluffs. The road dips into timbered ravines and loops around naked shoulders where the roadbed was blasted from solid rock. After several miles of cliff-hugging, the pavement abruptly straightens on the coastal terrace occupied by Fort Ross. The name "Ross," or "Rossiya," is an archaic literary term for "Russians."

The road runs east of the redwood stockade which, after years of neglect, was reconstructed by the state in the 1950s. An old by-passed section of the highway provides a trail to the fort. Several fires in the early 1970s (believed to be set by arsonists) destroyed the chapel and severely damaged the stockade and north blockhouse. Since then, with help from local residents, Fort Ross has been sufficiently restored so that visitors can imagine how the settlement looked when the Russians occupied it.

The original stockade enclosed nine buildings, including a military barracks. About sixty dwellings were scattered outside the fort. The population averaged around 250 people. The colony was self-sufficient, or nearly so. Wheat, potatoes, and leaf crops were grown for local consumption and export to the Russian settlements in Alaska. Besides a tannery, there were blacksmith, carpentry, cooperage, and brick-making shops. The stables had a capacity of two hundred cows. A small shipyard was located in Fort Ross Cove.

The fort was built in 1812, the same year Napoleon invaded Russia. Before that time the site was occupied by Mad-shui-nai, a Pomo Indian village which Ivan Kuskoff leased for trade goods. Kuskoff chose the spot partly because it was easily defended from attack by land or sea.

Fort Ross was probably stronger than any of the California presidios. All the principal structures were built of heavy redwood timbers, skillfully mortised at the corners. The stockade was fourteen feet tall and armed with forty French cannon that had been left in Russia in the wake of Napoleon's defeat.

The Russian-American Fur Company's announced purpose in California was confined to trade, farming, and otter hunting. Neither Kuskoff nor any of the commanders who succeeded him made territorial claims. When the authorities in San Francisco questioned the need for a fort, Kuskoff replied that it was merely a "fence" for protection against the Indians.

In 1821, the Czar issued an edict closing the ports north of San Francisco to all but Russian ships. This declaration upset the British and Americans in the Oregon Territory. But after President Monroe delivered his historic message to Congress in 1823, the Czar did not attempt to enforce his *ukase.* In fact, the California colonies enjoyed no priority at Saint Petersburg, which was preoccupied with affairs in Europe and the Middle East. Even so, Fort Ross was not evacuated until 1841.

The decision to leave was influenced by General Vallejo's containment policy as well as Anglo-American pressures. The Mexicans flatly rejected a Russian offer to buy Marin and Sonoma. Besides, the colony had experienced crop failures, grizzly bears were killing the cattle, and fur exports had ceased with the virtual extermination of the sea otter.

The Russians sold most of their possessions at Fort Ross to the Swiss immigrant John A. Sutter. At least one of the cannon was used to arm Sutter's private redoubt at "New Helvetia" on the site of Sacramento.

The Pomos reclaimed Fort Ross and fought a battle with white settlers who tried to eject them. After the Indians were removed, the property passed through a number of hands before it was deeded to the state in 1906. The Commander's house was variously used as warehouse, bar, and hotel. The stockade served as a pig pen. Horses were stabled in the Russian chapel before it was shattered by the 1906 earthquake.

The 446-acre historical park takes in a small beach and picnic area at Fort Ross Cove. Bottom fishing is excellent in and around the cove. Small boats may be launched from the beach on calm days. The Northwest Cape shields the cove from the prevailing winds but affords no protection from storms which blow in from the southwest.

Before leaving Fort Ross, a note about the otters: Aleut and Pomo hunters based at Fort Ross had harpooned sea otters from skin boats known as *bairdarkas,* and the animal was believed to be extinct after 1833. But in 1938 a herd of one hundred otters was sighted off Monterey. Thirty-four years later, an aerial census tallied more than a thousand otters off the Central California Coast. This come-back of the otter has triggered a conflict between conservationists and commercial divers. State biologists argue that unless the otter population is controlled, it could wipe out the commercial harvesting of abalone and other shellfish. An adult otter may eat as much as fifteen pounds of shellfish a day. But conservationists want to see the

Fort Ross Cove provides shelter for commercial fishing boats when a strong wind blows from the northwest. Small skiffs may be launched at the cove on calm days.

Abalone

The rugged seashore between Fort Ross and Stewarts Point is California's "Gold Coast" for abalone hunters. The good pickings are not limited to skin divers. Some productive beds may be approached by waders on extreme minus tides. The minus tides in spring are favored by waders because they occur in the daylight hours. Both waders and divers must wear rubber wet suits for insulation against the frigid ocean temperatures.

In the last century abalone were so abundant on the North Coast that they were used to feed construction gangs who built the logging railroads. Large quantities of dried abalone were exported to China.

The abalone is a giant marine snail *(Haliotis)* which uses its broad foot to obtain a powerful grip on rock surfaces. Iron pry bars are used to dislodge them. The mound-like shell has a coarse exterior but is lined inside with mother-of-pearl which was in great demand for jewelry manufacture during the 1870s.

Abalone grow more slowly off the North Coast than in waters south of Monterey. For this reason, no commercial diving is permitted here and the use of self-contained underwater breathing apparatus, or SCUBA, is restricted to fish spearing or rock-scallop collecting.

Angling regulations specify the months in which abalone may be taken during the spring and fall. The law requires that abalone hunters carry a measuring device. There are minimum size limits (as well as bag limits) for all seven kinds of abalone found in California waters. Most prized is the red abalone *(Haliotis rufescens)* which has been reported to twelve inches in diameter and nine pounds in weight.

The regulations are very precise when it comes to the shape, length, and thickness of the iron bars used to take abalone. The present specifications are intended to reduce the number of undersized abalone killed through improper handling. This loss results from cuts inflicted by poorly designed abalone irons and by improper use of irons. The results of laboratory experiments suggest that up to 90 percent of undersized abalone injured by pry irons fail to survive after they are returned to the ocean.

The Fish and Game Department advises fishermen to slide the pry iron under the abalone at a fifteen to twenty degree angle, *keeping the tip of the iron against the rock.* He should then *lift up* on the iron after it is under the abalone. A "short" abalone should be put back on the bottom with its *foot down*, preferably in a crevice where it will not be exposed to such predators as bat rays and sunflower starfish.

The edible portion of the abalone is the foot. This is trimmed, sliced into thin steaks, and tenderized by pounding. Gourmets have perfected some elaborate recipes but the simplest way to prepare abalone is by frying. Dip the steaks in egg, roll in cracker meal, and sauté briefly in a hot skillet. Serve with hollandaise or sauce made of butter, lemon juice and minced parsley.

range of sea otters expanded. They fear the present concentration off Monterey could be destroyed overnight by an oil spill.

Two miles up the road from Fort Ross is Timber Cove where pine trees are scattered over an expensive subdivision. The Timber Inn (also expensive) features Japanese sunken baths, rooms without television, and a piece of sculpture by the late Benjamin Bufano which towers eight stories tall.

At one time or another, Timber Cove and just above every cove on the Sonoma-Mendocino Coast served as a "doghole port" for schooners carrying lumber and produce to San Francisco. A steam-powered sawmill was built at Timber Cove in the 1860s. In 1879 the settlement included a hotel, schoolhouse, general store, and post office. At this time, all the larger landings, such as Fort Ross and Fisherman's Bay (near Stewarts Point), possessed a station of the Pacific Coast Telegraph Line.

About 1.5 miles north of Timber Cove is a new

sixty-acre county park at Stillwater Cove. On the headland north of the park, the privately operated Stillwater Cove Ranch provides overnight accommodations.

Next door to Stillwater Cove is Ocean Cove where there's a restaurant, motel, and fee access to fishing and skin diving.

Less than a mile north of Ocean Cove, the highway crosses the south boundary of Salt Point State Park. This 4,114-acre preserve encompasses almost six miles of seashore and reaches back into the highlands to a ridgetop which crests a thousand feet above the ocean. East of the highway, the park is a wilderness laced with hiking and riding trails that climb through open meadows and lush stands of Bishop pine and Douglas fir. One trail approaches a pygmy forest where dwarf redwoods grow.

The main access road to the seashore leads to a picnic area and primitive campground with thirty-one sites. Much of the shoreline is fronted by sheer

California Rose Bay grow to 20 feet high in the forest at Kruse Rhododendron State Reserve. Best time to see the shrubs in flower is April through early June.

Skin Diving

The stretches of Sonoma shore from Bodega to the Russian River and from Fort Ross to Stewarts Point comprise the most popular areas for skin diving on the North Coast. The water is clearer here than anywhere else on the California Coast north of Morro Bay. Most of the oceanside in these areas is accessible from public parks or from resorts and private ranches which may charge a trespass fee.

The state parks in the vicinity of Mendocino City also attract many skin divers, but north of Fort Bragg the water is more turbid as a result of fine sediments which emanate from the larger rivers.

Favorite areas on the Humboldt-Del Norte Coast include the North Jetty at Eureka, Trinidad Harbor, Patricks Point State Park, and the Crescent City Jetty to Point St. George.

The frigid ocean discourages diving without a wet suit. In winter, the surface temperature may range as low as forty-five degrees. Water conditions on the North Coast are most favorable for skin diving in September and October. These months afford the smoothest seas, the warmest temperatures, and the best visibility.

It has been estimated that divers on the North Coast spend thirty percent of their time gathering abalone and perhaps fifty percent spearfishing for lingcod, cabezon, greenling, halibut, and various kinds of rockfish. But in recent years the trend has been to devote less time to fishing in favor of nature study, underwater photography, and the exploration of such undersea wonders as the kelp forest off the bay at Van Damme State Park.

At present the California Parks and Recreation Department is working to develop a system of underwater parks and reserves. How these will be managed is still a question. But the general idea is to have qualified divers on the park staff who can explain to visitors "the ocean currents, the marine geology and biology, and how the ocean affects our entire lives."

sandstone cliffs. But good places to cast for rockfish and dive for abalone are to be found in the vicinity of Stump Beach Cove. The tide pool area at Gerstle Cove is a state reserve where no fish or other marine life may be taken.

The inshore area off Salt Point was one of the first places in California to be designated an "underwater park," where park rangers interpret for visitors the marine biology and geology. Plans were approved in 1976 to expand the trail system, add more picnic areas, and to build several hundred campsites for families when funds became available. In addition, the state intends to develop Salt Point as an ecology center where young people may come to study the park's abundance of natural and archaeological resources. The latter includes the former sites of several Pomo Indian villages.

Salt Point Park adjoins the Kruse Rhododendron State Reserve. This densely timbered area was part of the German Rancho, the northernmost Mexican land grant to be recognized by the U.S. Land Commission.

The reserve is approached on the Kruse Ranch Road, which leaves the highway 2.6 miles north of the main access to Salt Point. It's a short steep drive to the parking area where you may obtain a map showing the two miles of trails which wind through the reserve. The best time for a hike is in May, when the pink blossoms of the Coast rhododendron are in full flower. Struggling for light in a forest of fir and redwood, the subjungle of sinuous rhododendrons grow to heights of twenty feet.

About a mile east of the reserve the Kruse Ranch Road connects with the Seaview and Houser Ridge Roads at Plantation. A former stage stop, Plantation has a summer population of 200. The Seaview Road lives up to its name where it winds south through open meadows overlooking Salt Point State Park. The Houser Ridge Road drops into the rugged South Fork Canyon of the Gualala River. At Houser Bridge it links with the King Ridge Road out of Cazadero. The river here affords summer angling for pan-sized trout. Angling regulations specify that only artificial flies may be used.

It's a good idea not to attempt any of these back roads without local advice. Conditions vary from year to year depending on usage by logging trucks and the damage inflicted by winter rains. There are no service stations and public telephones are rare.

Large portions of the controversial "second home" development known as Sea Ranch remain lonely and unspoiled. The property was part of a rancho granted in 1852.

Five miles up the road from Kruse Rhododendron Reserve a ghostly collection of weathered shacks, sheds, barns, and frame houses marks the site of Stewarts Point. The pioneer lumberman Calvin Stewart settled here in 1857. About the time that Herbert Richardson bought the frontage in 1876, Stewarts Point became a busy "doghole port."

Now the only place of business is an old-fashioned store which includes a post office and gas pumps. This dwelling, painted red and yellow, used to be a wayside inn where stage passengers paid ten cents for a water-sized glass of whiskey. Third-generation descendants of Herbert Richardson operate the store and run cattle on their property, which stretches inland twenty-one miles. During the last quarter century, the official population of Stewarts Point has declined from 200 to 80.

West of the store is the bluff where planks and railroad ties were delivered to schooners in the coastwise trade by means of a wooden slip chute. The greased chute leaned down over the water, suspended from an A-frame which rested on a slender trestle. Perched precariously on the lower end of the chute was the "clapper-man," who operated a braking device. A brake was needed so that each piece of incoming timber could be received by the ship's crew and stacked aboard the deck in orderly fashion. Accidents were common in rough weather when the pitch of a vessel made it difficult for crewmen to seize the heavy timbers at the right instant.

To approach the loading area a skipper had to thread his way through treacherous shoals and sea stacks. Then came the tricky business of maneuvering the ship so it was exactly positioned to receive lumber. Any slight miscalculation could cause the schooner to pile up on the reefs. Among the vessels which foundered in heavy weather at Stewarts Point were the *Portia* in 1899 and the *SS Albion* in 1913. The trans-Pacific freighter *Kenkoko Maru* ran aground off the point in 1951.

A side road out of Stewarts Point climbs five miles east to a junction with the Tin Barn and Skaggs Springs Roads on Huckleberry Heights. The forty-acre Kashia Indian Rancheria near the crossroads is inhabited by about fifteen Pomo Indian families. Conditions here are said to be superior to some of the more isolated rancherias in the northern Coast Ranges. Electricity was not hooked up in the modest homes here until the

1960s. More recently, a pipeline was completed so the community no longer has to truck in drinking water. The only convenient place to buy groceries is Stewarts Point. The county elementary school is unique in that it's staffed and managed by Indians. But the high school serving the area is at Healdsburg—a forty-mile drive by way of the steep and winding Skaggs Spring Road. Employment opportunities are limited mostly to seasonal work provided by local resorts, ranches, and logging contractors.

Stewarts Point was built on the site of a Pomo village known as Danaga. Here the women and children resided in cone-shaped shelters of bark. The men lived apart in sweathouses that were built low and partially underground. A dome-like framework of poles thatched with grass served as the ceremony lodge.

The Pomos were famed for their basketwork, now nearly a lost art. Baskets were used to boil water and cook a cereal made from acorn flour. The ceremonial baskets were decorated with shells and feathers.

Women held positions of leadership in some of the villages. The marriage ceremony involved an exchange of gifts. For money the Pomos used the shells of gaper clams. The shells were ground to a circular shape with sandstone and strung on cords of fiber obtained from the wild iris. Value of the money was determined by the thickness, diameter, and polish of the clam disks.

An important aspect of the Pomo religion was reverence for the land. Apathy and demoralization set in among the Pomos when they were forcibly removed to obscure worthless plots of land, barely large enough to provide living space. The Kashia Rancheria was typical of these small reservations in that it contained no improvements when it was created in 1917. The Pomos who settled here were required to dwell in brush shelters and hike several miles for water during the dry season. The policy of creating such small, isolated reservations was adopted in 1853 following failure of Congress to act on the "Eighteen Unratified Treaties." By signing these documents, the leaders of 139 tribes gave up their rights to California. In exchange, they were promised cattle, provisions, and large tracts of land, most of which they never received. Congress took a dim view of these treaties after an official California delegation argued that the lands deeded to the Indians were rich in gold. So the treaties were consigned to the archives and locked from public view

The settlement at Stewarts Point includes many relics of the years when schooners called to take on lumber. Now the only place of business is a general store.

until 1905. Litigation to obtain reimbursement for the lost lands began in 1928. A partial payment was made in 1950.

Final settlement was authorized in 1968, with compensation based on the going price of land in 1852—determined to be 47 cents an acre. However, deducted from the total amount was the most of previous hand-outs to the Indians down to the last needle and thread. Also deducted were all expenditures by the Bureau of Indian Affairs, including money spent in the early days to forcibly evict Indians from their ancestral homes. If the settlement is accepted by the Indians and the government distributes the money, the compensation will work out to less than a thousand dollars per Indian. Quite a few, if not all, Indians on the North Coast seem to share the view expressed by the late mayor of San Francisco George Moscone, when he declared in 1972 that the 47-cents-an-acre settlement was made "in the worst tradition of white America."

The outlook of Indians on the North Coast appears more hopeful now, although many still live in poverty. A few of the younger generation are moving on from high school to college. But, as most reservation Indians see it, the problem is to achieve a place in the economy without losing their cultural identity and links with the land.

The late Senator Robert F. Kennedy, on a nation-wide tour of Indian reservations, flew by helicopter to Stewarts Point to visit the tiny Kashia Rancheria in 1968. For a time in the early 1970s, the Mohawk activist Richard Oakes and his Pomo wife, Anne, lived in the rancheria. Oakes, a steelworker from Rhode

Island, led the 1969 Indian "invasion" of Alcatraz Island. The group Oakes represented wanted the government to return the island to the Indians for a cultural center. Later, Oakes was arrested for collecting a one-dollar toll from motorists on the Skaggs Springs Road. The Indian community imposed the toll to protest the county's move to obtain three acres of the Kashia Rancheria for purposes of widening the road.

The tortuous Skaggs Springs Road was built in stagecoach days by Chinese labor. For several miles, it closely follows the Wheatfield Fork of the Gualala River. Only artificial flies may be used on this wooded trout water. The road crosses many streams, including Tobacco, Wild Cattle, and Little Strawberry Creeks, before it approaches Skaggs Springs near the confluence of Black Sulphur and Little Warm Springs Creeks. A spa built here in 1864 was fashionable up to the turn of the century.

Instead of returning to Stewarts Point, the back-road explorer may complete a loop through the highlands on the Annapolis Road. This ridge route leaves the Skaggs Springs Road about two miles east of the junction at Huckleberry Heights. It's an eight mile drive to the rustic post office at Annapolis. Five miles farther, the road joins Highway 1 near Black Point. The bridge at Valley Crossing marks the lower limit of summer trout fishing on the Gualala River.

Near Black Point the expensive "second home" development known as Sea Ranch begins. This Castle & Cooke venture encompasses 5,200 acres of the old German Rancho which was granted to Ernest Rufus, a captain in John Sutter's Indian Company. The development stretches fourteen miles north almost to the Gualala River and ranges east across the highway into the somber green forest of the highlands.

Forest and meadows have been subdivided into 5,200 lots; 1,750 of these have been developed for sale at prices ranging to $110,000. Protective covenants govern the design of homes and provide that half the land be retained in its natural state. All utilities are underground. The facilities for property owners and their guests include an air strip, golf course, tennis courts, stables, and heated swimming pool.

Almost all the homes are rendered in a strikingly severe version of Bauhaus architecture variously described as "brute force," "vertical box," and "grain-elevator modern." Quite a few of these dwellings (which are intended to "harmonize" with the coastal setting) have won architectural awards and been featured in magazines such as *Sunset.*

About 330 of these "second homes" were built

Summer Trout Fishing

With so many free-flowing creeks and rivers on the North Coast, the trout enthusiast might anticipate a wealth of summer angling. However, in summer the lower reaches of many coastal streams become too low and warm for good fishing.

The headwaters of such rivers as the Gualala, Noyo, and Big River support trout which rarely run larger than "pan-size." These waters serve as nurseries for baby steelhead, which may remain in fresh water for as long as two years before going to sea.

Studies have shown that stocking coastal streams with hatchery-reared "catchable-sized" trout is harmful to the steelhead and a waste of money. So the only waters stocked by the state on the North Coast are land-locked freshwater lagoons, such as Cleone Lake at MacKerricher State Park near Fort Bragg.

The seaward migration of juvenile steelhead peaks in April and May. For this reason the summer trout season opens on the first Saturday preceding Memorial Day, a month later than the trout opener for the rest of Northern California. The idea is to restrict the take of young steelhead so a sufficient number of these fish will have a chance to grow big in saltwater and return in two or three years to propagate in their native streams.

At one time steelhead were plentiful in Pacific Coast streams as far south as Northern Mexico. However, pollution and water diversions have virtually wiped out the runs on the South Coast. Few good streams remain on the Central Coast and since 1940 there's been a sixty-six percent decline in the numbers of steelhead which migrate up the rivers of the North Coast. Here the most serious pollution is caused by silt, slash, and bark washed down from the sites of logging operations. Silt smothers the eggs of steelhead and salmon. Piles of slash deny the fish access to the nursery streams. Tannic acid from bark renders some creeks incapable of supporting any kind of fish life.

A female steelhead twenty-four inches long can produce five thousand eggs. About eighty percent will hatch under favorable conditions, and perhaps one hundred fifty fish will live to go to sea. With luck, five of these trout will survive the perils of the ocean and return to propagate. This fearsome rate of attrition in the context of a shrinking habitat and heavy fishing pressure explains why so many North Coast streams are subject to special closures and reduced creel limits during summer.

before construction was halted as the result of a dispute between the developer and the Coastal Zone Conservation Commission. Although widely praised for the respect given to open space, natural values, and "good taste," Sea Ranch has been a source of bitter controversy since the project was begun in the 1960s. As a private playground of affluent upper-middle-class persons, the development denies public access to miles of lovely seashore which is state property below the high-tide mark. Also, many critics question the environmental impact should Sea Ranch be permitted to reach its full potential of 15,000 homes. By conservative estimate, this would allow for 50,000 residents—a population that would dwarf all existing cities on the North Coast.

Claiming "vested rights" to home construction, the developers of Sea Ranch rejected a proposal by the North Central Coast Regional Commission that would have permitted a yearly quota of perhaps fifty homes to be built if certain conditions were met. The first condition was the granting of an easement to provide public access to the seashore. Second, the commission wanted a few of the estimated 100,000 trees planted by the developers thinned so that motorists on Highway 1 might at least obtain a glimpse of the shore. A third condition called for the monitoring of septic-tank systems for possible polluting effects on the ocean. The matter has since gone to the courts where, as in the case of the Bodega Harbor litigation, it may linger for years.

In 1981 a federal tribunal upheld the Coastal Commission's authority to require access to the coast. Barring a successful appeal to the U.S. Supreme Court it appears Sea Ranch will have to provide public pathways to its beaches.

Facilities at Sea Ranch presently open to the public include a restaurant and plush motor lodge. Next door to Sea Ranch is the 150-acre Gualala County Park, which offers hiking, fishing, and overnight camping. The preserve extends along the south bank of the Gualala River to the ocean.

There's no telling the age of this redwood fence near Point Arena. Redwood has the highest rating of any softwood for durability and resistance to termites.

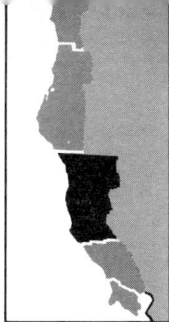

The Enchanted Coast: Mendocino County

Drifting fog, pygmy forests, lonely lighthouses, fern canyons, Gothic mansions, roaring caves, antique inns, dark rivers, brooding mountains, salt-damp headlands, and scores of ghost ports lend enchantment to Mendocino's 120 miles of coast.

Campgrounds, inns, and other accommodations are largely concentrated between Gualala and Fort Bragg. Vacancies may be hard to find on Memorial Day weekend and some other holidays.

Point Arena

Scholars have grown old and grey trying to trace the origins of such colorful place names as Tamalpais, Tomales, Marin, Sonoma, and Mendocino. In many instances, their efforts have produced more questions than answers. A prize example is the Gualala River, which marks a boundary between Sonoma and Mendocino Counties.

Years ago, Alfred Kroeber and other prominent anthropologists decided that "Gualala" was the Spanish version of the Pomo word *walali*, which means "where the waters meet." But Erwin Gudde in *California Place Names* mentions a Pomo chief whose name was spelled by a Spanish padre as "Valli-ela." On old maps, the river variously appears as "Walalla," "Wal Hollow," and "Arroyo Valale."

Local histories record that Ernest Rufus, the grantee of the German Rancho, named the river "Valhalla," or "Walhalla," the home of slain heroes in Germanic mythology. The name seems fitting because the Gualala is a beautiful stream, shaded near the coast by brooding redwoods.

The Gualala is a favorite of the hardy clan who fly fish for winter steelhead. Because the stream is small by comparison with the Russian, it clears much faster after a storm. The steelheading tradition goes back to the days when Jack London and his cronies would drive up in a horse-drawn buggy to work the Donkey, Snag, and Switchville holes.

The village of Gualala, a short way north of the Highway 1 bridge crossing, began its career as a lumber port in the 1860s. Here the wooden slip chute was soon replaced by the vastly more efficient wire chute. It was necessary to rig the wire chute for each loading operation. First, a light line was fired across the deck of the waiting schooner by a small cannon on the bluff. The ship's crew used the line to pull a heavier rope out to the schooner. The rope was used to winch out a wire cable. The end of the cable was attached to a mooring buoy anchored off the far side of the vessel. Then the cable was lifted above the deck and suspended from the rigging.

At the captain's signal, the cable was stretched tight by a donkey engine on the bluff. Loading began after a carriage block, or "traveler," was mounted on the taut wire. The carriage block was lowered to the ship by gravity and winched back by the donkey engine. A whole wagonful of lumber could be delivered on one trip by means of a sling suspended from the block. Passengers could be transferred by rigging the block with a seat similar to those used on ski lifts. The era of the wire chute ended when improved roads in the 1930s enabled mill owners to ship more cheaply by truck.

The last sawmill at Gualala shut down in the 1960s, but the town has grown as an art center and tourist stop. There are several stores, restaurants, and a motor lodge. The quaint Gualala Hotel, built in 1903, affords a sumptuous cuisine and lodgings in twenty-nine rooms decorated in late-Victorian bordello style.

An old stage road out of Gualala (County Road 502) runs up Iverson Ridge to link with the Ten Mile Cutoff, a back-road approach to Point Arena. You take this road south of town to approach the Gualala River Road (County Road 501). This forest spur approaches some fine steelhead water and a privately operated campground in the redwoods with 140 sites for tents and camper wagons. The camp includes a swimming beach. The Gualala Redwood Company, which owns much of the river frontage, provides points of access for winter steelhead fishermen.

Between Gualala and Iverson Point numerous fingers of forest stretch down from the highlands to fringe the coastal bluffs and headlands. The shoreline drive is wonderfully scenic but affords few opportunities for camping or fishing. One exception is Anchor Bay, four miles north of Gualala. There's a resort here with campsites and access to Fish Rock Beach. Small boats may be launched from the beach in calm weather. Just offshore is Fish Rock where sea lions gather. You can hear them barking when the wind is right.

Five miles farther on, the highway is joined by the north end of the Iverson Ridge Road. Opposite the junction is Iverson Point, where a lumber settlement is alleged to have fallen into the ocean during the 1906 earthquake.

Just south of the junction is Walker Gulch, named for "Long" Walker, one of the fastest axemen on the coast. Walker would spend a week chopping overcuts and undercuts without felling a tree. On Saturday afternoon, he would drop one tree which would cause the other trees he had worked on to topple like a row of dominoes. Some loggers deplored the "Walker drive" as being wasteful of timber. The accepted practice was to prepare a clearing layered with brush so the tree wouldn't shatter when it hit the ground.

After a big redwood was felled, trimming and

For 100 years, the main business of Gualala was lumber. Now the last mill has gone but this former stage stop still provides food and lodging for the traveler.

debarking could take as long as a week. The logs were moved to a skid road with large metal jacks known as "jack screws." As many as eight yokes of oxen were used to haul logs to the mill. The "bull puncher," who managed the team, was among the best-paid men in the woods. Normally placid and slow moving, the oxen were prone to panic when there were yellow jackets about.

The more heavily used sections of skid roads were paved with small logs laid crosswise. These were greased or doused with water by the "sugler," who preceded the team. It was the task of the "dogger" to hammer chains under the logs when they gathered too much speed on a downgrade. The carnage was frightful when a "dogger" lost control and allowed the logs to override the team.

Point Arena lies five miles up the highway from Iverson Point. The mountains around this quiet farm center recede from the coast, leaving a broad expanse of rolling pasture that is dotted with dairy cattle. For some years, Point Arena was the largest, most active lumber port between San Francisco and Eureka. It was also a whaling station and regular port of call for passenger steamers. The town sprang up around a solitary store built in 1859. Now Point Arena has some restaurants and motels and, north of town, a large privately operated campground.

Port Street winds down a stream gully to Point Arena Cove. Here a moldering wharf and abandoned Coast Guard station stand as memorials to the colorful past. Commercial salmon boats use the landing in summer. In winter the harbor is deserted for lack of protection against storms that blow in from the southwest. Fishing off the pier is sometimes excellent for perch and rockfish.

The tranquillity of the village was shaken in 1971 when the Pacific Gas and Electric Company applied to the Atomic Energy Commission for permission to build a nuclear power plant at Point Arena. Cost of the installation was estimated at $831 million. The nuclear plant was opposed by many residents because it meant the death of Point Arena Creek. Trout still swim in this little stream where it wanders through town lending charm to numerous gardens and backyards. But the strongest challenge to the project was mounted by the same conservationists who had frustrated the power company's plans to build a nuclear plant at Bodega Head.

Sierra Club lawyer David E. Pesonen (who figured prominently in the controversy at Bodega) highlighted the fact that the proposed nuclear site at Point Arena was only 4.5 miles from the San Andreas Fault. Pesonen cited an eye-witness description of how the

*On a quiet afternoon in February, fly casters fish the
Gualala River for steelhead rainbow trout. This
stretch of the river is known as the Miner Bend Hole.*

Point Arena lighthouse had swung back and forth
during the 1906 earthquake. The tower, built to
withstand hurricane winds, was so severely damaged it
had to be reconstructed from the ground up.

PG & E executives warned that, if the Point Arena
project was not completed on schedule, the north half
of the state might suffer power shortages and even
brownouts. The company said that studies had shown
the nuclear plant could withstand earthquakes. However, early in 1973, following an adverse report on the
site by the U.S. Geological Survey, the company
announced it would cancel the project.

One of the most significant fossil finds in recent
years was made in 1973 on the sandstone cliffs which
rim the seashore west of Point Arena. On a weekend
exploration, two University of California graduate
students, Bruce and Joann Welton, discovered the
skeleton of desmostylian—a marine mammal which
became extinct more than ten million years ago.
Paleontologists say the creature resembled a hippo-
potamus but was more closely related to the Stellar sea
cow, a species completely wiped out by Russian
trappers in 1768.

Three miles north of town, the Garcia River enters
the sea. The stream was named for Rafael Garcia, a
soldier of the San Francisco Company and brother-in-
law to Stephen Smith of Rancho Bodega. Garcia
obtained a grant to the Point Arena area in 1844 but it
was never recognized.

One-half mile south of the Highway 1 bridge, an
unpaved lane leads to Miner Bend Hole, one of the
choicer spots on the river to fish for winter steelhead.
The tidewater may yield silver salmon as early as
October.

A familiar sight on the drive north from Bodega to Humboldt Bay. The North Coast has been sheep country since the Gold Rush produced a huge demand for mutton.

Winter Fly Fishing: Lore and Tradition

After the Gold Rush when some Westerners took to trout fishing for sport rather than food, an inclination developed to follow the English tradition of casting the dry fly. The Pacific salmon were largely ignored because these fish refused to rise for a fly. But, lured by tales of hundred-pound Chinook salmon, a stranger would now and then turn up to show the natives how to work a wet fly of the type used for Atlantic salmon.

Invariably such missionaries were disappointed to find that Chinook showed no more interest in wet flies than dry flies. But some visitors, such as the British author Rudyard Kipling, were rewarded for their efforts by hooking a remarkable trout which their hosts advised them was a "salmon-steelhead." So it happened that by 1880 the sporting quality of the Pacific steelhead had become known in Europe as well as on the East Coast.

In the 1890s winter fly fishing for steelhead became established as a sport on the Eel River Delta. Here the lumber kings of Eureka enjoyed the leisure to experiment with Atlantic salmon flies. Fishing from skiffs on quiet tidal pools, they found it was possible to effectively drift a wet fly down near the bottom where the steelhead were. Many new fly patterns were devised then that are still in use today. One of the favorites was the Carson fly, named for Sumner Carson, son of the lumber magnate who built the Victorian mansion which is Eureka's most popular tourist attraction.

But fly fishing on the Eel was productive only during the first half of the season, before winter rains had raised and roiled the river. No way was found to present a fly in the deep, swift water of storm-swollen coastal streams until enameled silk lines and silkworm gut leaders were made obsolete by new synthetics.

The development of a fast-sinking synthetic fly line proved a boon for skiff fishermen. But for shore fishermen there remained the challenge of how to cast a fly the long distances required to reach the deep water of the main current. This problem was solved by members of San Francisco's Golden Gate Casting Club when they perfected the "shooting head," a weight-forward fly line that measures only 28 to 32 feet. When backed by fairly stiff monofilament shooting line, the shooting head enables an expert to cast distances of a hundred feet or more.

The shooting head is used with a glass rod, 8.5 to 9.5 feet long, thick at the butt with a pronounced taper. The productive fly patterns vary with each coastal stream. The late Claude Kreider did well on the Gualala River with the colorful Skykomish Sunrise tied on a Number 4 hook.

Other requirements are chest-high waders and a warm parka, preferably with pockets to accommodate a pair of hand warmers. Freezing temperatures are not unknown on the North Coast when the fishing peaks in late December and January.

The best opportunities for winter fly fishing are found on the smaller coastal rivers which clear rapidly after a storm. The Gualala ranks Number One with fly casters on the North Coast.

Call ahead before driving to any of the stormy North Coast streams. To check the weather, call:

Russian River: Grant King Tackle Shop, Guerneville, (707) 869-2156

Gualala River: Gualala Hotel, Gualala, (707) 884-3441

Big River and Noyo River: Cooney's Sporting Goods, Fort Bragg, (707) 964-5630

Eel River and Van Dusen River: Grunert's Sporting Goods, Fortuna, (707) 725-2223, and Bucksport Sporting Goods, Eureka, (707) 442-9529

Klamath River: Steelhead Lodge, Klamath Glen, (707) 482-6494

Smith River: Saxton's Tackle Shop, Smith River, (707) 487-7231

The lumber enterprise which contributed most to Point Arena's former prosperity was the Garcia Mill, located eight miles upriver in a rugged canyon. Here the stream was impounded to provide storage for logs floated down from the back country.

When the mill was built in 1869, the owners had planned to deliver lumber to the schooner landing at Point Arena by railroad. The plan was dropped when a local rancher wanted too much money for the right-of-way.

The mill road was too steep for wagons. The river below the mill pond was too shallow to float the lumber. So the company built a wooden flume which ran to Flumeville, one and a half miles north of Point Arena. Here a system of rollers powered by a water wheel lifted the lumber from the flume and carried it up a forty-five-degree grade. From the hilltop, the lumber was carted down to the harbor on a steep road known as the Devil's Cutoff.

The Garcia Mill was destroyed by fire in 1894. Some years later, much of the cut-over land was burned, seeded with grass, and sold to ranchers.

The site of Flumeville was near the intersection of Highway 1 and the Lighthouse Road. The latter runs two miles to the coast, where the ocean area within a thousand feet of the high-tide mark falls within Point Arena Headlands Reserve. No fish or marine life of any kind may be taken here without a written permit from the Department of Fish and Game.

The original Point Arena lighthouse was built of brick in 1870. The present structure is 115 feet tall and has the most powerful light on the coast. On a clear night its 380,000 candlepower may be seen from twenty-one miles out at sea. Recently the light was automated and its foghorn replaced by various electronic devices.

Punta de Arena, which means sandy point in Spanish, was the scene of many shipwrecks before modern navigational aids were developed. Perhaps the worst disaster occurred on November 20, 1865, when ten vessels foundered during the night.

From Point Arena to Westport the countryside is decorated with cypress windbreaks which fence homes, fields, and portions of the highway. Several varieties of cypress grow on the North Coast but it takes an expert to tell them apart. The pygmy cypress, *Cupressus pygmaea*, is native only to coastal Mendocino.

Split-rail and grape-stake fences predominate over barbed wire on Mendocino ranches. So picturesque and variegated are these fences that some resident artists have made a career of sketching them.

Less than a mile north of the Garcia River, the Mountain View Road leaves the Shoreline Highway for a lonely run over the mountains to Boonville. The road is paved but has very steep grades.

Two miles farther, just beyond the hamlet of Manchester, the Kinney Road turns off to Manchester State Beach. This preserve takes in seven miles of beach and 650 acres of open meadow and sand dunes. The forty-eight-site campground is a windy, fog-damp place in summer, but in spring it's filled with wildflowers. The beach has driftwood and often affords good surf bottom fishing for perch. There are occasional runs of surf smelt.

One-half mile north of the Kinney Road, the highway crosses Brush Creek, and two miles farther is Alder Creek. Coastal streams of this small size provide the only steelhead water worth fishing directly following a major storm. The most effective bait is a "strawberry" of fresh salmon roe.

Shortly before the highway spans Alder Creek, an obscure drive forks in a northwesterly direction to approach the south bank of the stream. This spur terminates at an undeveloped state beach where driftwood abounds. The San Andreas Fault goes out to sea here.

A mile beyond Alder Creek is Irish Gulch, a vacation-home development with cottages for rent. Between here and Little River, the coast is precipitous and fronted mostly by sheep and cattle ranches.

From Irish Gulch, it's six miles to Elk Creek, which used to be a lively "doghole port" known as Elk River. Two miles farther is Greenwood Creek; the old lumber town of Greenwood here has been renamed Elk. The settlement (population 200) is strung out along the bluff which rims Greenwood Cove. There are a few antiquated stores, a cafe, some salt-box and Victorian homes, and two lovely old inns—the Harbor House and the Elk Cove Inn.

On Memorial Day weekend, the townspeople invite abalone hunters to cross their property to gain the cove in exchange for a donation to the Elk Volunteer Fire Department Building Fund.

Greenwood Cove is heavily studded with craggy islets and tall dome-shaped sea stacks. Steam schooners used to brave this navigator's nightmare to load lumber on the lee side of Wharf and Casket Rocks. The wire chute there operated for the last time in 1929.

Elk, or Greenwood as it was called then, was settled in the 1840s by the sons of Caleb Greenwood, who guided the first wagon train to cross the Sierra. Britt Greenwood led a rescue team to the aid of the stranded Donner Party. In the 1880s, the lumber baron Lorenzo E. White made Greenwood the seat of a logging empire that grew to encompass the Garcia Mill and its vast holdings.

To bring logs to Greenwood, the Elk Creek Railroad was built in 1890. The main line ran twenty-four miles to the upper reaches of Alder Creek and had several spurs. This railway, with its sudden curves, lofty trestles, and fantastic grades, was said to have claimed more lives than all other railroads on the coast combined. Between Greenwood and Elk River, the tracks were supported by a surf-splashed trestle which leaned against the sea cliffs.

Greenwood Creek hosts runs of salmon and steelhead after winter rains open the sand bar which landlocks this stream in summer.

The steep, winding Greenwood Road is paved all the way to Hendy Woods State Park near Philo.

The Navarro River

Six miles north of Elk the Shoreline Highway meets the desolate, wind-swept estuary of the Navarro River. A side road leaves near the south bank to approach the beach at the river mouth. This spur terminates at a long-established resort known as Navarro-by-the-Sea. In 1973, a sign posted at the parking area read:

> *Casual attire* is acceptable provided *it is clean.* *Bare feet, patches, torn undershirts, faded clothing, and untidy appearance NOT ACCEPTABLE.*

The Navarro River in May. This portion of the stream, located four miles inland from the Shoreline Highway, is known to winter steelhead fishermen as the "Jungle."

When the Navarro Beach Road was closed by a new owner in 1970, the Sierra Club initiated legal action which resulted in a landmark decision by the California Supreme Court. The court ruled that, since the road had been open to the public for more than five years, there had been "implied dedication" of the route for public access.

The valley of the Navarro reaches deep into the Coast Range. The main river is fifty miles long. The

name Navarro is probably a Spanish version of an Indian word.

Across the Highway 1 bridge, turn east on State Highway 128, the river road. The redwoods begin two miles inland. For some distance, the river frontage is posted by the Masonite Corporation and patrolled by company guards. Farther up the road are some primitive campgrounds which the corporation has cleared for public use.

Eight miles from the bridge on Highway 128 is the Paul M. Dimmick Wayside Camp. This preserve is the smallest unit in the state-park system to provide camping. Contained within twelve acres of river frontage are twenty-eight improved campsites shaded by cottonwoods, tanbark oaks, and some very large second-growth redwoods.

Between the Dimmick camp and the tidewater, winter steelhead fishermen gather at such places as "The Jungle," "Hop Flat," and the Pepperwood Hole. Some pools may be approached only by boat. A favorite offering for steelhead on the Navarro is a single salmon egg on a Number 10 hook. The stream is usually too murky for fly fishing because of serious erosion of the watershed by a century of logging.

One effect of poor logging practice is damage to the small tributaries which provide spawning gravels for

Sign shows depth of water on Highway 128 when Navarro River spilled its banks during heavy rains of December 1964. Worse flooding occurred on rivers farther north.

trout and salmon. In the 1960s, the Fish and Game Department found it necessary to rehabilitate twenty-five feeder streams on the Navarro. Some were so choked with silt and logging debris that no fish could live in them. Tampering with streams in ways harmful to fishlife has long been prohibited by law. But logging is a messy business which disturbs the soil and creates piles of slash. Too often, logging contractors find it cheaper to pay the fine than clean up the debris.

In 1974, a Mendocino contractor was fined $625 by the Big River Justice Court after pleading no contest to charges of water pollution and illegal alteration of Tramway Creek, a tributary of Big River. The contractor was performing work for the Louisiana Pacific Company when he bulldozed a road up the center of the stream and denuded the banks of vegetation. Louisiana Pacific paid another contractor $30,000 to repair the damage. But after the clean-up, a game warden estimated it would take ten to fifteen years for the creek to flush itself of silt and become usable again for spawning salmon and steelhead.

Until recent years, the State Forest Practices Act largely allowed the logging industry to police itself. In 1971, a state appeals court ruled that the Board of Forestry, established by the act, was unconstitutional because its regional boards were industry-dominated. Many conservationists feel that the make-up of the new board is still too heavily weighted in favor of the industry. However, some stricter regulations have been adopted. These include a provision that no logging activity may occur within one hundred feet of year-around streams or within fifty feet of seasonal flows.

The heavy siltation caused by improper logging is not only injurious to fish, but also aggravates flooding by raising the level of stream beds. On Highway 128, there are signs that show the depth of water over the road when the Navarro spilled its banks in the Christmas floods of 1964. Where towns lay in the path of the floodwaters, as on the lower Eel and Klamath Rivers, the destruction to life and property was calamitous. Hundreds of big trees were uprooted in Humboldt Redwoods State Park. The flooding was particularly severe here because logging and subsequent fires had altered the upper watershed of Bull Creek.

The rate of erosion in the Northern Coast Ranges is greatly accelerated by logging, road building, and stock grazing because these are young mountains with steep terrain and unstable soil formations.

In presenting its case to the public, the redwood industry tends to avoid the subject of erosion. However, Kramer Adams, a former public relations executive for the California Redwood Association, argues in

Winter steelheading on the Navarro River near Dimmick State Wayside Camp. These are drift fishermen working single salmon eggs and "Cherry bobber" type lures.

his book *The Redwoods* that "landslides . . . along with fire, flood, and high erosion rates, are as much a part of the redwood environment as fog. The tree has not only learned to live with these natural disturbances, but also, in the lowland forest, has come to depend on them." Adams neglects to point out that the frequency of such disturbances as "fire, flood, and high erosion rates" is enormously increased as the result of poor logging practice.

In 1966, Professor Clyde Wahrhaftig, a geologist at the University of California, told a state assembly committee that redwood forest soils were eroding at a pace thirty times the average geologic rate over the past million years. If logging practice was not carefully regulated, Professor Wahrhaftig warned, within one

hundred years as much as ten percent of the timberland would be unable to grow trees. He speculated that within a thousand years the entire North Coast might be as barren as the worst deserts in Egypt.

From the Dimmick State Wayside Camp, continue east on Highway 128 for six miles to the hamlet of Navarro, which bears the name of an old "doghole port" formerly located near the river mouth. Navarro (population 75) was once a booming company town with over a thousand employees. It boasted seven saloons before the mill closed during the depression of the 1930s. Subsequently most of the settlement was destroyed by fire. The Navarro Hotel, last landmark of the early days, burned to the ground in 1974.

The lone facility that keeps Navarro and scores of

other dying North Coast villages on the map is a United States Post Office. Where people are thinly scattered on ranches and isolated homesteads, the post office (often located on or near the premises of a general store) provides a community center and gives the settlement a sense of identity.

However, in 1975, faced with losses estimated at $7 million a day, the Postal Service launched a cost-cutting program which included the phasing out of nearly six thousand rural post offices across the country. As a result, on November 4, 1975, the postmistress at Navarro was given one day's notice that the station would cease to operate. Some communities have accepted such closings as inevitable, but the residents of Navarro organized a vigorous protest. One couple wrote their Congressman:

> We are willing to suffer a number of inconveniences—low voltage, antiquated telephone equipment that breaks down in every rain, undependable fire-fighting equipment, pot-holed roads, 50 to 70 mile trips to medical facilities or government offices—for the privilege of living and working in a relatively undisturbed beauty of the area. But there is a limit, which has just been passed.

After the residents pleaded their case to the district director of the Postal Service in San Francisco, the Navarro Post Office was reopened, but how long it will remain so is anyone's guess.

Near Navarro, the Masonite Corporation has a demonstration forest with a picnic area and self-guiding nature trail. The redwood industry has installed a number of such exhibits on the North Coast as part of an effort to convince the public that commercial timberlands are being properly managed.

Nine miles farther on Highway 128 is Philo. Philo was a lumber camp in the 1860s. Now a rural trading center and summer colony, the population swells to a thousand in August. At Philo is Indian Creek County Park, with its fifteen acres of prime redwoods. The only improvements here are trails and a picnic area. There's summer trout fishing in Indian Creek and nearby Rancheria Creek.

West of Philo on the Greenwood Road is Hendy Woods State Park, which has ninety-two campsites and redwood giants that crest above three hundred feet. The 605-acre park affords swimming and trout fishing on the South Branch of the Navarro.

From Philo, the highway follows Anderson Creek six miles to Boonville. This town lies at the head of the Anderson Valley, where thirty-nine varieties of apples are grown. The harvest is celebrated in late September at the Mendocino County Fair and Apple Show. This event features a particularly fine exhibit of arts and crafts.

The Woolgrowers' Meet at Boontown in July is highlighted by dog trials, sheep-shearing contests, and a lamb barbecue. It's apt to be a happy occasion because the North Coast is one of the finest areas in the world for sheep farming. The mild, wet winters afford year-round grazing. The cool, foggy summers promote the growth of a thick, long-stapled wool. The unstable soils of the uplands are highly productive of forage favored by sheep. This includes some plants with vicious spines, such as the star thistle (an emigrant from Europe), which cattle won't eat. However, most of the range is composed of perennial grasses, of which the mainstay is the California oatgrass (*Danthonia californica*).

Of course, the sheepmen have their troubles. These include competition from Australia and New Zealand, a shortage of trained herdsmen, the proliferation of synthetic fibers, and the rise in land taxes fostered by the second-home developments. Also, there is the sensitive issue of how to curb the depredations of the coyote. Some ranchers want to use poison (which would pose a hazard to other kinds of wildlife), but in 1972 the Federal government imposed severe restrictions on the use of poisons such as strychnine, and a complete ban on their use in Federal programs. "Eat American lamb: 100 million coyotes can't be wrong," read the bumper stickers on some ranchers' cars.

Perhaps more menacing than the coyote are packs of domestic dogs which have proliferated in rural areas with the rise in recreational subdivisions. Just overnight on one Sierra ranch in 1973, four dogs killed thirty sheep and injured twenty-five more. This was wanton slaughter, whereas coyotes kill for food and their diet consists mainly of rodents.

Nationwide this country's sheep herds have dwindled to the lowest point since the Civil War. But in 1974, after a thirteen-year decline, the numbers of sheep in California increased twenty-nine percent. Devaluation of the dollar helped. So did the sudden loss in popularity of men's double-knit suits, which are woven from synthetics. Most encouraging for the long term is increased demand by the apparel industry for fabrics made of wool-synthetic combinations.

Boonville was first known as Kendall City. The name was changed in the 1860s after W. W. Boone bought the general store from Levi and Strauss. The village has some restaurants and motels, but accommodations are scarce for miles around at county fair time and during the Woolgrowers' Meet.

Float Trips

As noted earlier, the opportunities for backpacking on the North Coast are limited to a few choice areas of federal land. However, those who place a premium on the beauty, solitude, and excitement of a wilderness adventure may find fulfillment on the navigable coastal rivers. Float trips by canoe, kayak, or rubber raft are feasible not only on such large waterways as the Klamath (190 miles) and the Eel (204 miles) but on numerous lesser streams, including the Bear, Mad, Mattole, and Gualala Rivers.

The Navarro, Noyo, and Garcia Rivers afford splendid scenery and easy navigation for canoe parties. White-water enthusiasts find roaring rapids on the forks of the Smith, Eel, and Klamath Rivers which range from "moderately difficult" to "impossible." Some rapids in the latter category involve very strenuous portages. Skilled kayakers steer a zig-zag, spray-flecked course down Redwood Creek where it cascades through groves of the world's tallest trees.

The longer rivers invite extended trips, lasting from several days to a week or more. Where the frontage is private, float parties may bivouac on wooded islands or, more commonly, on beaches and sand bars below the high-water mark.

The Smith, Russian, Eel, and forks of the Klamath sustain flows which permit float trips in summer. Most other streams are navigable only during winter and/or the spring run-off.

Old hands advise that the minimum requirements for river running include a knowledge of boating safety and the ability to swim. Also necessary are the skills requisite to steer a boat around obstacles and paddle in a straight line without excessive strokes. There seems to be consensus among authorities on river running that this is not a sport for loners. On the more difficult runs, a float party should include at least three persons, one of whom is an old hand with the ability to rescue another boat in trouble.

As is the case with backpacking, the successful float trip demands careful planning. You need to know the right time to go, the road which gives access to a launching site, the areas on the stream where you may anticipate a dam or waterfall, and the places downriver where you may return to a road. Also, you must make some provision for getting back to your automobile.

Two publications packed with information on floating North Coast streams are *Down the Wild Rivers* by Thomas Harris, and *River Touring* by Dick Schwind. Both books are profusely illustrated with detailed maps of the floatable streams.

Places other than the Russian (see Chapter 7) where canoes may be rented include the Catch-A-Canoe, located on Big River at 44900 Comptche-Ukiah Road, (707) 937-0273; and the Arcata Transit Authority, 650 Tenth Street, Arcata (707) 822-2204.

Among the organizations which provide instruction in canoeing and kayaking is the River Touring Section of the Sierra Club, 5608 College Avenue, Oakland, California 94804. For a complete list of California groups which sponsor river training classes, write for information from the California Department of Boating and Waterways, 1629 S Street, Sacramento, CA 95814.

Perhaps the best way to become acquainted with the joys of river running is to take one of the trips scheduled by white-water touring companies. Most such outfitters furnish meals, guides, boats, life jackets, and waterproof bags for your personal items. Some of the companies which feature floats down North Coast rivers are:

American River Touring Assn., 1307 Harrison St., Oakland, CA 94612

James Henry River Journeys, Box 708, Stinson Beach, CA 94970

O.A.R.S./Sobek, Box 67, Angels Camp, CA 95222

Outdoors Adventures, 3109 Fillmore St., San Francisco, CA 94123

Vic McLean's Wild River Tours, Box 500, Lotus, CA 95651

Watercourse Ways, 139 Sycamore Ave., Mill Valley, CA 94941

Wilderland, 930 Irving St., San Francisco, CA 94122

Zephyr River Expeditions, Box 2607, Sonora, CA 95370

*Private fish pond located off Main Street in Mendocino
City. Striking example of Gothic revival behind pond
is the McCallum House, built in 1855. It is now an inn.*

The Mendocino Headland

As you drive up the coast from bleak, windy Navarro Head, the first stream spanned by Highway 1 is Salmon Creek. A short way east of the bridge was the site of Whitesborough, where the lumber magnate L. E. White got his start before he shifted his operations to Greenwood.

Hardly a mile beyond Salmon Creek the highway crosses the bramble-filled gorge of the Albion River on a graceful arch which crests 120 feet above the water. Off the north end of the bridge, a side road drops down to the Albion Flat. Here the quiet estuary shelters a growing fleet of sport and commercial fishing boats. The settlement includes a seafood restaurant and two resorts with rental skiffs, launching ramps, and campsites for recreational vehicles. Despite the breadth of its estuary, the Albion is one of the shortest rivers on the North Coast. Fall-winter angling for steelhead and silver salmon is centered on the tidewater. The Albion River beach affords good perch fishing and skin diving. Access is by permission of the landowners.

The earliest lumber mills at Albion were built for William A. Richardson in 1851-53. Richardson was an English seafarer whose fortunes zoomed after he acquired Mexican citizenship and married a daughter of the Commandante at the San Francisco Presidio. In 1845, Richardson obtained a grant which stretched from the north bank of the Garcia River to Big River. This grant was not recognized by the U.S. Land Commission.

Richardson's first mill was powered by a water wheel placed in the sluice way of a low dam built across the estuary. The wheel turned when the tide was moving in or out. A second wheel located on a tributary stream kept the mill operating at slack tide.

Just a country mile beyond Albion is a lovely old inn with a sod roof. This is the Heritage House, built in 1877 as a home for James Pullen, who operated a mill on Salmon Creek eight miles upstream from Whitesborough. Before the Heritage House became an inn, it served as a hideout for the notorious gangster "Baby Face" Nelson.

On the three-mile drive to the village of Little River, there are some attractive inns of more recent vintage. Near the south edge of town, the Airport Road branches west to approach the Pygmy Forest which fills a remote corner of Van Damme State Park. Here thickets of gnarled and lichen-encrusted cypress trees, some as old as sixty years, grow just a few feet tall and less than half an inch in diameter. More widely scattered are the dwarf Bolander pines which range to fifteen feet. The Bolander is a coastal version of the lodgepole pine, which grows 150 feet tall in parts of the Sierra. The Bolander's small cones may take twenty years to open.

Beneath a thin overlay of highly acid black humus, the topsoil in the Pygmy Forest is nearly white. Centuries of rainfall have leached it of clay and iron compounds. These have precipitated into the subsoil to form a dense red hardpan that resists root penetration. The international name for this soil profile is the Russian term *podzol*. Large patches of it support islands of Pygmy Forest among the normal timber which grows on the coastal shelf between Salt Point and Fort Bragg. The area is known as the Mendocino White Plains. Scientists believe these flats were formed on beach sand when the present shelf was ocean shore.

The Little River Inn is a rose-covered mansion with gabled windows and eaves festooned with wooden scrollwork. It was built in 1853 for Silas Coombs, a native of Maine who ran a shipyard and lumber mill at the mouth of Little River. The inn includes a nine-hole golf course on its property.

From the Little River Post Office the highway dips down to the tiny beach at Van Damme State Park where Little River spills into a rocky cove. The gentle surf here becomes nearly warm enough for swimming in early autumn. Small boats may be launched from the beach. The cove is a rewarding place to skin dive or wade for abalone.

Van Damme's 1,831 acres fill a slender rectangle which points five miles into the highlands. The campground, in second-growth redwoods, has seventy-four sites. Facilities include hot showers and a laundry room. A new visitor center contains displays pertaining to the native wildlife, Coast Indians, and early days of lumbering.

The 2.5-mile scenic trail up Fern Canyon follows the route of an old skid road used by ox teams from 1864 until 1894. The trail is lined with numbered posts which identify plants, trees, and places of historical interest. Post Number 18 marks a massive redwood stump with salal and huckleberry bushes growing on top. About fifteen feet up one side of the stump is a slot used to support the spring board on which the tree fellers stood. High cuts were made by the early loggers to avoid the swelling base of a prime redwood.

The young redwoods in Fern Canyon are mixed with Pacific hemlock, lowland fir, and Douglas fir. These shade an under-story forest of red alder, tanbark oak, and bigleaf maple. The lush shrubbery includes the salmon berry, Oregon grape, and red elderberry which provides summer forage for flocks of migratory band-tail pigeons.

Everywhere the canyon walls are decked with ferns. The prolific sword ferns predominate over the lady licorice, toothed wood, birdsfoot, and the delicate five-fingered ferns whose black stems were used by the Indians to weave designs into their baskets.

The trail fords Little River nine times before it terminates at the start of a steep trail leading to the Pygmy Forest. Hardly more than a brook in summer, Little River's clear pools and gentle riffles are fringed with elephant ears and bridged in many places by mossy deadfalls. Growing on stream flats are masses of corn lilies and pagoda-like horsetails. The latter resemble plants that grew ninety feet tall in the age of dinosaurs.

The park is named for Charles F. Van Damme, a lumberman and boat builder born at Little River in 1880. The park originated on forty acres of river frontage which Van Damme willed to the state.

Just before the Shoreline Highway crosses Big River

Green canopy of red alder shades creek where it flows to sea from Russian Gulch State Park. The stream originates in the adjoining 52,000-acre Jackson State Forest.

Fishing Off the Rocks

A sturdy saltwater spinning outfit—seven to nine feet long, with monofilament line of thirty-pound breaking test—is recommended for rock fishing. Also, a standard boat rod may be used with a conventional star drag reel. Terminal tackle amounts to a short leader with a dropper for a snelled hook and snap swivel at the end for the sinker. Some fishermen prefer the two-hook rig, described for flounder in Chapter 4.

Size 1/0 hooks are good for blue, black, and sculpin rockfish as well as greenling and cabezon. A Number 6 hook is better for striped seaperch, while size 4/0 is not too large for lingcod. Shrimp, mussels, sandworms, and slices of anchovy are favorite baits.

At most locations, a lead sinker is too easily fouled on the rocks. It's better to use an inexpensive "break away" sinker, such as a cotton roll-your-own tobacco sack filled with sand. Tackle shops sell them without the tobacco.

A different approach to the problem of snagging is to fasten a two-inch bobber on the line so the sinker rides just off the bottom. This technique facilitates the use of a smaller sinker and fairly light spinning tackle. The disadvantages of light tackle are realized when it becomes necessary to reel in a big fish up a steep drop-off.

Rock fishing anywhere on the coast is apt to be most rewarding in the morning before the prevailing wind gathers strength. Slippery footing and the chance of being hit by an oversized wave are the main hazards. The danger is greatest when the fisherman is caught up in the excitement of landing his catch.

Scores of good places to rock fish on the North Coast are shown on two maps published by the state Fish and Game Department: "Ocean Fishing Map of Marin-Sonoma Counties" and "Ocean Fishing Map of Del Norte, Humboldt, and Mendocino Counties." Both publications include information on the kinds of fish caught, the best times of year to fish, and the gear and bait used.

---

it's joined by the Comptche Road, which spans the highlands to Ukiah. Fifteen miles up this road is the general store at Comptche, a former stage stop and logging center. The drive is a delight in spring when the rhododendrons and other shrubs which line the route are in flower.

From Comptche, it's another twenty miles or so to the Montgomery Woods State Reserve. This 1,100-acre preserve is located off the rough, unpaved Orrs Springs Road. It contains one of the most imposing stands of redwoods in the state. The only improvements are trails; the main trail winds through a moss-covered canyon where Woodwardia ferns grow seven feet tall.

On the same road about seven miles west of Ukiah is the Orrs Springs Resort, located on a ranch established in 1858.

Mendocino City lies across the mouth of Big River, perched on the projecting headland which girds the north shore of Mendocino Bay. This antique settlement was among the largest and most cosmopolitan of the old lumber ports. Nearly everything in Mendocino City is built of wood, including some of the sidewalks. Most of the houses have steep gabled roofs and siding of clapboard or rustic board and batten. There are false-front stores, plain New England salt boxes, and mansions in the early Victorian Gothic style with arched windows and edgings of fanciful scrollwork. The town resembles a coastal lumber village in Maine, the home state of many Mendocino pioneers.

A German sailor named William Kasten was the first settler on the headland. Kasten may have wandered in from the Northern Mines or been stranded by a shipwreck. In 1851, he sold his claim to Harry Meiggs, a San Francisco politician and wharf owner with a weakness for speculation. Soaring lumber prices at the outset of the Gold Rush encouraged Meiggs to buy Stephen Smith's sawmill at Rancho Bodega. The plant was too antiquated to suit Meiggs so he ordered new machinery from the East. Before it arrived, Meiggs found that Bodega was nearly logged out and decided to look for greener pastures. Meiggs may have heard about the magnificent redwoods at Big River from a salvage crew he sent to recover silk and tea from a ship wrecked off Point Cabrillo.

Mendocino City was first known as Meiggsville. Most likely, the name was changed in 1854 after Meiggs got himself into financial hot water and had to flee the country. He recouped by building the first railroad over the Andes but he left the mill at Big River

Once a booming lumber center, Caspar lives on its memories. Shown here is the aging white-frame school house which abuts the Four Square Lighthouse Church.

in sad shape. His former associates, J. B. Ford and E. C. Williams, experienced many setbacks. These included storm damage, labor shortages, bankruptcy proceedings, and machinery unfit to cope with the gargantuan redwood logs. A fire destroyed the mill in 1863. The plant was rebuilt and later sold to the Union Lumber Company at Fort Bragg which operated it until 1937.

At the turn of the century, Mendocino City was a thriving port visited by ships from all over the globe. On "Steamer Day," carriages from eight hotels met passengers at the wire chute. The town had twenty-one saloons. After six months in an isolated camp, a logger was prone to squander his wages in these places. He then had no option but to put in another stint in the woods. The lumber barons, often plagued by labor shortages, were torn by conscience and self-interest on the matter of liquor. Some company towns were "dry." In others, the mill owner profited by charging discounts as high as ten percent for pay checks cashed in the company saloon. Owing to the remoteness and company domination of the "doghole ports," strikes were rare and unions virtually unheard of.

The cliffs which rim Mendocino Bay are riddled with wave tunnels. One is known to be seven hundred feet deep. In the days of sail, a number of vessels were blown into these caves and never seen again. A publication of the Mendocino Historical Society relates how a small schooner was ripped from its moorings in heavy weather and dashed repeatedly against the mouth of a wave tunnel. When the masts were about to shatter, a young woman aboard tied her baby girl to a chopping bowl and dropped her into the surf. The vessel and everyone aboard were lost. The child drifted to a place where the townspeople were able to rescue her. The wave tunnel where the wreck occurred may be seen to best advantage from the Brewery Gulch Road, which leaves the highway south of Big River.

The mill was gone, the forest was logged out, and Mendocino City was fading fast in the 1950s when it suddenly blossomed as a cultural center. Artists were persuaded to move here for several reasons. Remote, half empty, and living on its memories, the town seemed secure from progress. The picturesque old houses could be had for a song. The natural setting was inspiring enough to invite the filming of such motion pictures as "Frenchman's Creek," "East of Eden," and "Johnny Belinda."

Prominent among the San Francisco painters who led an exodus of creative people to Mendocino were Dorr Bothwell, Emmy Lou Packard, Byron Randall, and William Zacha, who founded the Mendocino Art

Gray Whales

On a chill, blustery day in January 1976, the administration of the Point Reyes National Seashore was forced to take emergency measures to deal with a vast traffic jam that developed on the Sir Francis Drake Highway. Why so many autos in winter? Reporters hastily dispatched by Bay Area newspapers and TV stations found that the crush was caused by hundreds of whale watchers.

The overlook near Point Reyes Lighthouse is one of the better places on the North Coast to watch the California gray whales *(Eschrichtius gibbosus)* pass by on their yearly 6,000-mile migration from the Arctic to tropical lagoons in Baja California.

The California gray whale (which was recently designated the state's official marine, mammal) grows to fifty feet in length. Some specimens have weighed in at forty tons, but this is only "medium sized" as whales go. California grays rank first with whale watchers because they swim fairly close to shore at speeds which render them easily visible (six to seven miles an hour). Also, they indulge in a variety of subsurface acrobatics, sometimes rising straight up from the water to land on their backs with a tremendous splash.

Gray whales, like all baleen (toothless) whales, feed primarily on tiny zooplankton, such as waterfleas and sea butterflies. They mate and give birth to their young in warm lagoons before returning to the polar regions where zooplankton is most abundant.

The best time to view gray whales on the North Coast is from mid-December through January. They may be observed from most any seaside promontory with an overlook accessible by road or trail. Some favorite vista points are Bodega Head in Sonoma County; Salt Point, Point Arena, and the Mendocino Headland in Mendocino County; Shelter Cove and Trinidad Head in Humboldt County; and Point St. George near Crescent City in Del Norte County. (Grays may be seen returning to the Arctic from March through mid-May. But on this leg of their migration, they tend to travel farther from shore.)

Gray whales travel in small groups known as pods. Whale watchers spot them by the columns of water or spouts they send up. Grays must come to the surface every few minutes to take in air through nostrils located in the top of their heads. When they empty their lungs, the moisture in their breath condenses to form a spout of spray perhaps 20 feet high.

Gray whales native to the Atlantic were exterminated by whalers before the turn of the century. It was supposed the California gray whales were extinct before they were rediscovered by a Norwegian whaler in the 1920s. By international agreement, the gray whale was given complete protection in 1938. However, some conservationists, including persons with scientific credentials, claim that grays (along with other kinds of whales not protected) are still being hunted, principally by the modern whaling fleets of Japan and the Soviet Union.

However, since the 1930s, California gray whales have multiplied to a present population variously estimated at 11,000 to 12,000. According to a recent article in the state Fish and Game publication *Outdoor California*, this population has remained "relatively stable" in recent years, so it's not easy for the layman to discern the truth of the matter. The issue of whaling involves not only economic and political considerations but the strong emotions of those who feel that all mammals in the order Cetacea (which includes whales, porpoises, and dolphins) should be protected.

At Mendocino City, a group of residents meets regularly to discuss ways and means to frustrate the harvesting of whales. Among other projects, one example of their efforts occurred in 1975, when townspeople raised $2,000 to send artist Byrd Baker on a cross-country tour to enlist support for the save-the-whales movement.

Good source books on whales are *To Save a Whale: The Voyages of Greenpeace,* by Robert Hunter; *The Life and Death of Whales,* by Robert Burton; and *Wake of the Whale,* by Kenneth Brower.

A number of environmental organizations have come into being with special concern for whales. Some of these are the Greenpeace Foundation, Building 240, Fort Mason, San Francisco, CA 94123; The Whale Center, 3929 Piedmont Avenue, Oakland, CA 94611; and General Whale, P.O. Box Save-the-Whales, Alameda, CA 94501.

*This lovely vista point at Russian Gulch State Park
looks south on the marine terrace occupied by Mendocino City and the new Mendocino Headlands State Park.*

Center. The "natives," who included many retired people, viewed the rebirth of Mendocino City as a mixed blessing. The artists saved the town only to spark a boom which threatened to destroy its charm.

On the heels of the artists came "beatniks" and later "hippies," "flower children," and "freaks" who found themselves overwhelmed on weekends by throngs of "squares" numbering up to ten thousand. The crowds attracted small business and the Boise-Cascade Corporation, which proposed to build a modern subdivision on the 52-acre belt of land separating the town from the outer seashore of the headland. The price of local real estate skyrocketed. New stores and restaurants were built. The town's first neon signs threatened to sprout.

To prevent vacation-home development and preserve the rustic character of Mendocino City, a group of resident artists proposed that both the town and headland be established as a state "Historic District." This didn't work out, partly because many townspeople objected to the idea. But recently a Mendocino Headlands State Park was created. Most of the village is excluded, but the preserve takes in the meadows and sea cliffs which rim the town from the beach at Big River to the vicinity of Goat Island.

Mendocino City is best explored on foot, preferably on a weekday. A few of the structures at which visitors aim their cameras are the Joss House, built by Lee Hee in 1855; the Masonic Temple, built in 1866, and crowned by a redwood sculpture of "Father Time and the beautiful maiden"; the Mendocino Hotel, 1872, with its many antiques, including the town's first fire engine; and the white steeple of the Presbyterian Church, 1867, which supports a thousand-pound bell that sailed around the Horn.

Big River is one of the better streams on the North Coast to try for the elusive silver salmon. Beginning a week or so after the first heavy rain, trolling is apt to be good on the tidewater which reaches eight miles inland. Skiff fishermen go upriver on the incoming tide and return on the ebb tide. However, a singular hazard for both swimmers and small boats is the dangerous rip tide that occurs at the river mouth.

Canoes, kayaks, and fishing skiffs may be rented at

Bicycling

As yet, few trails expressly designed for bicyclists have been established on the North Coast. California's bicycle-trail program gives priority to areas adjacent to the major cities. Within a few years, the state hopes to complete the Cross-Marin Trail. This bikeway will run from the Larkspur Ferry Terminal on San Francisco Bay all the way to the Point Reyes National Seashore.

Highway 1 is not recommended for inexperienced riders or cyclists carrying small children. There are lightly traveled stretches with no grades to speak of, but the narrow roadway presents a hazard when an occasional logging truck or wind-tossed motor home is encountered. The steep mountain byways are to be avoided as are some lowland trails where the terrain is too sandy, rough, or otherwise unsuitable for bikes.

On the Marin Coast, the most popular bikeway for family groups is the Bear Valley Trail at Point Reyes National Seashore. Bicycles may be rented nearby at Olema Ranch.

In Sonoma County, the road which follows the Russian River from Guerneville to Mirabel affords a pleasant ride, especially in autumn after the vacation crowds have gone. The trip takes in the Korbel Champagne Cellars where visitors are welcome.

Bicycles may be rented at Mendocino City where the Heeser Drive invites a tour of the headlands. A few minutes away (by auto) are the interesting trails which run up stream gorges in Van Damme and Russian Gulch State Parks.

On the Humboldt Coast, cyclists may fill a weekend exploring the lush delta plain around the Victorian village of Ferndale. A rural road out of Arcata crosses farm-dotted bottomland to approach Mad River County Beach.

At Crescent City, the lovely Pebble Beach Drive and adjoining country lanes afford a scenic ride to Point St. George and a driftwood-covered beach at Pelican Bay.

In the spring of 1976, several state and federal agencies cooperated to implement California's "Bikecentennial '76" program. This involved establishing thirty-eight bicycle camps along a coast route posted with signs by CALTRANS (the state agency for transportation). For the most part, the thousand-mile route utilizes existing roads and is recommended only for hardy cycle buffs adept at negotiating fast-moving motor traffic and steep, twisting grades.

The "Bikecentennial" camps are primitive clearings which offer water, a place to put down a sleeping bag, and toilet facilities. The sites are open to hikers and cyclists (not motorized) on a first-come, first-served basis with a one-night fee of fifty cents per person and a maximum stay of two nights. Presently these camps are found in the following parks:

MARIN COUNTY

Samuel Taylor State Park
Tomales Bay State Park

MENDOCINO COUNTY

Manchester State Beach
Russian Gulch State Park
Standish Hickey State Recreation Area*

HUMBOLDT COUNTY

Benbow Lake State Recreation Area*
Humboldt Redwoods State Park*
Patricks Point State Park

DEL NORTE COUNTY

Del Norte Redwoods State Park
Jedediah Smith Redwoods State Park*

(*Not on the coast.)

Bicyclists can also stay at Youth Hostels, which are relatively new to Northern California. For more information on hosteling write to American Youth Hostels, Building 240, Fort Mason, San Francisco, CA 94123, or call (415) 771-4646. Among the hostels operating are these:

San Francisco International Youth Hostel, at Fort Mason in San Francisco (130 guests)

Golden Gate Youth Hostel, at Fort Barry near Rodeo Lagoon in the Golden Gate National Recreation Area (60 guests)

Point Reyes Youth Hostel, near Limantour Road in the Point Reyes National Seashore (45 guests)

The Mendocino Hotel used to dispatch carriages to pick up guests on "steamer day." Now, grandly refurbished, it caters to the "carriage trade" who arrive by auto.

a boat livery located on the south bank of the river off the Comptche Road.

The beach at the south end of the Mendocino Headlands State Park may be approached on a spur that leaves Highway 1 just north of the bridge. When the mill was operating here, the river was used to float logs down from the back country. The last "river drive" occurred in the late 1920s.

The Little Lake Road out of Mendocino approaches some prime steelhead water in the Mendocino Woodlands Recreation Area of the Jackson State Forest. About five miles up the road is the junction with Road No. 700, a dirt spur which runs three miles to Big River near the confluence with the Little North Fork.

The main river is open to fishing during the winter season upstream to Two Log Creek.

The west end of Little Lake Street connects with Heeser Drive, which curves out to the Heeser Fishing Access on the northwest side of the headland. The frontage was donated to the state by the late August Heeser, son of a Mendocino pioneer and for many years publisher of the weekly *Mendocino Beacon*.

The craggy headland is heavily indented with small coves. The surf is infested by jutting rocks and just offshore are several small islands. On a sunny day in spring clumps of vermilion paintbrush and other wildflowers on the bluffs stand out in vivid contrast against the turquoise and emerald hues of the sea.

Improvements by the State Wildlife Conservation Board have made the Heeser Access a mecca for rock fishermen. Some excellent places to wet a line may be approached on a trail hacked from solid rock and equipped with iron hand holds.

Heeser Drive loops around the headland to link with Highway 1 north of Mendocino City. About two miles north of town, across a high span, a side road drops to the checking station of Russian Gulch State Park. The fur hunters who were based at Fort Ross cached their otter skins in a number of coves along the coast. Historians speculate that Russian Gulch was the northernmost storehouse.

Russian Gulch State Park has thirty campsites. It's about the same size and shape as Van Damme Park and it offers the same attractions except there's more seashore here and the trail system is larger. One easy footpath runs up the forested gulch to a fern-fringed waterfall. Another trail crosses a meadow where the roof of a wave tunnel has collapsed to create a "blow hole." You may look into it and watch the breakers surge and ebb. Park wildlife includes a lively population of chipmunks, rabbits, and blue jays. Early risers may see deer.

The beach and rocky shore at Russian Gulch afford good shore fishing and skin diving for abalone. The Mendocino Area Headquarters and Information Center of the state parks system is located in the park.

From Russian Gulch, an old by-passed stretch of Highway 1 now known as Point Cabrillo Drive (or County Road 409) approaches two new undeveloped preserves—the Caspar Headlands State Reserve and Caspar Headlands State Beach. The latter is exposed only at low tide. On this drive, near the intersection with a spur that runs to the Point Cabrillo Lighthouse, a few dwellings mark the site of Pine Grove, settled in 1852 by Captain Peter Thompson. Once a busy trading center, Pine Grove boasted a hotel, brewery, dance hall, and race track. No trace of these or any conifers remains. The white octagonal tower of the Point Cabrillo Light rises on a lonely headland honeycombed with wave tunnels and "blow holes."

Before rejoining the main highway near Caspar Creek, there is a trailer park at Caspar Beach which has sites for tents as well as vehicles. This resort affords fresh water angling for black bass on a small impoundment of Caspar Creek.

West of the highway after it crosses the creek, the white spire of the Four Square Lighthouse Church marks the site of Caspar. A lumber mill operated almost continuously in this settlement from 1861 until 1955. The 52,000-acre Jackson State Forest is largely composed of cut-over land purchased from the Caspar Lumber Company in 1947. The mill and much of the town was razed in 1966. Very little remains of the original settlement besides the church, schoolhouse, some cottages, and a sleepy old inn.

Less than a mile from Caspar Creek, the highway spans Jug Handle Creek. This small stream is worth a second look because its watershed holds an "ecological staircase" that has attracted the interest of scientists all over the world. The "staircase" consists of five marine terraces formed over the centuries by wave action and then, one after the other, uplifted by the same forces which continue to this day to elevate the Coast Ranges.

Each step in the "staircase" is a hundred feet higher and a hundred thousand years older than the one below it. Each step holds a different ecosystem. The lowest terrace still lies partly underwater. The tide pools at this level are rich in such marine life as the Apollo octopus, cling fish, and red sea anemone. The second terrace supports native grasses and wildflowers with an occasional thicket of low-growing firs, pines, and sitka spruce. Redwoods and Douglas firs shade the incline to the third terrace, where there are spring-fed sphagnum bogs, sundew plants (which eat insects), and the beginnings of a pygmy forest. The upper terraces are dominated by dwarf pines and cypresses, along with such pygmy forest plants as salal, wax myrtle, and Labrador tea. Here a Bolander pine only three inches in diameter was found to be a hundred years old.

This "ecological stairway" is said to be of international significance for its potential as an outdoor laboratory where scientists may gain fresh insight into the processes of soil evolution. The portion of Jug Handle Creek which extends into the Jackson State Forest is protected, and extending downstream to the seashore one thousand acres of the watershed is contained within the newly designated Jug Handle State Reserve.

On weekends and some week days throughout the summer, state park rangers conduct interpretive tours of the five terraces in the Jug Handle Creek "ecological staircase." The four-mile hikes begin at 10 A.M. and 3 P.M. and last four to five hours. Visitors who wish to join one of these interpretive tours are advised to prepare for the terrain by wearing comfortable walking shoes and to bring a box lunch and rain gear. The meeting place for the tours is the parking area on the west side of the Coast Highway just south of the Jug Handle Creek bridge.

Also during the vacation season, "staircase" campfire programs are featured at MacKerricher and Van Damme state parks. For information on these programs and the interpretive tours phone (707) 937-5804.

*Noyo Harbor provides a safe haven for hundreds of com-
mercial fishing craft. Weather allowing, salmon sport
fishing party boats make two trips a day in summer.*

Highway 1 provides only a glimpse or two of the exciting Fort Bragg coast, which is heavily scalloped and peppered offshore with rocky islets. One way to see this coast is on a salmon partyboat excursion out of Noyo Harbor. Another way is to hike through the Mendocino Coast Botanical Gardens, a seaside nursery located three miles up the road from Caspar. The gardens encompass forty-seven acres of cultivated flowers interposed with natural areas of forest, shrubbery, and meadow. Hiking time on the trail system is about three hours.

A little way farther is the junction with State Highway 20, which cuts through the heart of the Jackson State Forest on its thirty-four-mile run to Willits. The forest on either side of the highway is laced with old logging roads. These afford access to numerous hunters' camps for which a use permit must be obtained from the Jackson Forest headquarters, in Fort Bragg. A map available at the headquarters shows the roads, camps, and areas open to hunting during the deer season.

Recreation is only a by-product of the Jackson Forest. Primarily it functions as a laboratory for the study of logging methods and their effect on water yield, erosion, stream sedimentation, and fish production. The forest was named for Jacob Green Jackson, founder of the Caspar Lumber Company.

One-half mile beyond the Highway 20 junction, the coast road spans the spectacular fjord of the Noyo River. One side of the bridge provides an aerial view of the ship channel leading into Noyo Bay. The other side overlooks the colorful fishing village at Noyo Flat. A side road north of the bridge drops down to the village. Strung out along the estuary are marine hardware stores, restaurants, partyboat landings, motels, and several fish-processing plants. In rough weather, the port is crowded with hundreds of fishing boats. The effect was even more picturesque before a boat basin built in 1968 relieved some of the congestion. The old harbor provided a setting for the film *The Russians Are Coming*.

The Noyo River takes its name from an Indian village that was situated at the mouth of Pudding Creek just north of Fort Bragg. Captain William A. Richardson, who operated the first lumber mill at Albion, attempted to establish a mill on the Noyo in 1852. It was plundered by Indians in 1853 and washed away by a flood the following year.

The Mendocino Indian Reservation was created in 1856. It stretched from the south bank of the Noyo nine miles up the coast as a crow flies to the vicinity of Ten Mile River. Living within its 24,000 acres were Coast Indians of many different tribes. Some came from villages as far south as Bodega.

In 1857, the ground was broken for Fort Bragg on the terrace north of the estuary. A detachment of soldiers commanded by First Lieutenant Horatio G. Gibson built a proper fort with sixteen buildings, a cemetery, and parade grounds. The fort's sole purpose was to oversee the Indians. It was named for Braxton Bragg, a hero of the Mexican-American War who later became a Confederate general and was roundly defeated by Grant in the Chattanooga Campaign.

Fort Bragg was abandoned in 1864. About this time, the Indians were removed to other reservations. Alexander McPherson had succeeded in building a mill on Noyo Flat in 1858. It was pressure from lumbermen who wanted the timber which caused the Mendocino Reservation to be terminated.

Noyo made the transition from lumber center to fishing port around the turn of the century. The settlement flourished when other ports were fading because it had had one of the safest harbors on the coast. Also, the fishermen were able to send their catch to market on the "Skunk Railroad."

In recent years, Noyo has grown as a sport fishing center. All the facilities are here, including skiff rentals, launch ramps, ice houses, custom canneries, and smoke houses. Partyboats make regularly scheduled trips in summer for ocean salmon. When the salmon are scarce, they turn to bottom fishing. Steelhead enter the river in winter, but the Noyo is more renowned for its autumn run of silver salmon.

Noyo lies inside the city limits of Fort Bragg. After the long drive from San Francisco through rustic hamlets and lonely pastures, this rural center of less than five thousand inhabitants may impress the traveler as a true metropolis. The impression is heightened by the profusion of motor lodges, trailer parks, restaurants, and various small business on the outskirts of town. Much of the sheep pasture around Fort Bragg has recently been subdivided for vacation homesites. But the hard core of the business district still retains the functional look of an old company town.

A couple blocks west of Main Street, the sprawling mill of the Union Lumber Company occupies the ocean frontage. It's one of the largest mills in northern California. Without this enterprise and several smaller mills, Fort Bragg would be reduced to a ghost town overnight.

Charles R. Johnson founded the town in 1885 and became the first mayor after it was incorporated in 1889. Son of a Wisconsin lumberman, Johnson gained experience as a working partner in a small redwood mill on Ten Mile River, which is nine miles north of Fort Bragg. In 1884, he convinced his associates that a larger mill was needed and went home to Wisconsin to raise capital for new machinery. Johnson obtained the funds with difficulty because his father refused to believe accounts of the redwoods' giant size. This skepticism was widespread in the East despite exhibits of redwood stumps at fairs and expositions.

One advantage of the old military post as a site for the new mill was Soldiers Cove. Here Johnson found it feasible to build a wharf where schooners could load directly without a wire chute. The Fort Bragg Lumber Company formed by Johnson and his partners absorbed the mill of McPherson and Weatherby on the Noyo River and gradually acquired other holdings to become the dominant enterprise on the Mendocino Coast.

When the forest on Pudding Creek was nearly exhausted, the company extended its railway to the Noyo River. This required boring a 1,129-foot tunnel through a ridge separating the two streams. The use of Chinese labor provoked a confrontation between the sheriff and white workers caught up in the hysteria of the "Yellow Peril."

To finance the work Johnson promoted another merger, which gave birth to the Union Lumber Company in 1891. As the logging crews inched up the rugged canyon of the Noyo, the railroad followed. It crossed gorges on rickety trestles, snaked around hogbacks, and switchbacked up grades in a dizzy succession of hairpin turns and double bow-knots.

The railroad was completed to Willits in 1911. At Willits the line was joined to the Northwestern Pacific Railroad, giving Fort Bragg a rail link with the San Francisco Bay Area. A night passenger train with a Pullman sleeping car operated from 1921 to 1929. In 1925, the first of several gasoline motor cars was put into service, replacing steam locomotives on the day runs. The fumes from these cars caused townspeople to refer to them as "Skunks."

Passenger service on the "Skunk Railway," otherwise known as the California Western Railroad, might have been discontinued years ago if it were not for the

One of many attractions in MacKerricher State Park is lovely Cleone Lake, a freshwater lagoon stocked with catfish and rainbow trout. Fishing is best in spring.

Pacific Salmon

Of the five kinds of Pacific salmon, the king and silver salmon comprise ninety-nine percent of the catch in North Coast waters. All Pacific salmon spend several years at sea before returning to their native streams for procreation. All die after spawning (unlike steelhead, which may survive to make as many as six spawning migrations in their lifetime). The record king salmon (*Oncorhynchus tshawytscha*), netted off British Columbia, weighed 126.5 pounds but a thirty-pounder is bragging size on the North Coast. Silver salmon (*Oncorhynchus kisutch*) run much smaller, averaging six to eight pounds.

The appeal of silvers is their propensity to make wild leaps above the surface when hooked on light tackle. Kings rarely jump, being more remarkable for their long runs and power dives.

Offshore trolling for kings and silvers is usually best from mid-June through early fall. Fairly heavy tackle is used, especially on partyboats where everyone must troll at the same depth to avoid entanglements. Also, a stout rod is needed because partyboat skippers won't let you take all day to land a salmon. The skipper has to give everyone on board a chance. The recommended tackle is a hefty boat rod five to seven feet in length with a star drag revolving spool reel that accommodates two hundred yards of thirty-pound test monofilament line. Such outfits may be rented from the skipper or partyboat operator for a modest fee.

Terminal tackle consists of a sinker release mechanism interposed between the end of the line and a four-to-nine foot leader to which a lure or bait harness is attached. Mostly one- to 3-pound "cannon ball" type sinkers are used, which is another reason the rod must have plenty of backbone. When a salmon strikes your offering, the sinker release allows the weight to become disengaged and fall to the bottom.

The heavier two to three pound weights are used by partyboats which work the Marin Coast out of San Francisco Bay. The boats based at Noyo Harbor and ports on the Humboldt-Del Norte Coast favor lighter weights, depending on the depth where a school of salmon is located. Commercial boats use metal lines to take salmon in water as deep as two hundred feet. Most partyboats troll closer to the surface in ten to sixty feet of water, at speeds of two to five miles an hour.

Small parties who rent a skiff or launch their own enjoy more freedom to try for salmon at various depths with lighter tackle. However, anglers not familiar with this coast would be well advised to make their first trip with a licensed navigator, either on a scheduled partyboat or private charter craft.

The grandest fishing for silver salmon begins in autumn where these fish congregate at the river mouths, preparatory to their upstream migration. At this time, silvers are caught in bays, lagoons, and estuaries by skiff fishermen trolling or mooching with the same light tackle used for winter steelhead.

Lines with ten to fifteen pound breaking strength are favored, with half-ounce sinker and 2/0 hook baited with a strip of anchovy or herring. Flashbaits, small plugs, and wet flies in steelhead patterns may produce when the fishing is "hot." Often the action is slow because silvers are not less tempermental than steelhead. For days in a row the tidewater may be alive with leaping silvers which refuse all offerings. The early settlers found the only way they could catch silvers was to spear them with pitchforks in the tributaries.

Silvers, kings, and steelhead all look alike when they first enter the rivers. One way to tell them apart is by examining the mouths. The king's mouth is black and the steelhead's is nearly white. The mouth of a silver is black except for a white crown on the gums.

The earliest runs of silvers occur in streams such as the Noyo, Albion, and Big River which are not closed by a sand bar during summer. The timing of a run is influenced by the pattern of rainfall. Silvers are important to the North Coast fishery because they migrate up the smaller rivers and creeks. The significant runs of king salmon occur in large rivers, such as the Smith, Eel, and Klamath.

A useful guide is the "Salmon and Steelhead Fishing Map" published by the California Fish and Game Department. This brochure contains information on inshore and offshore angling as well as river fishing. It lists the productive streams and places where fishing skiffs may be rented.

*Millpond of the mammoth Georgia-Pacific plant at Fort
Bragg. Visitors are invited to take a guided tour of
the mill and company museum on work days in summer.*

patronage of rail buffs. The present "Skunks" are diesel electrics that make daily round trips to Willits. The last steam locomotive, known as the "Super Skunk," was retired in 1981. The trains are so popular that advance reservations are needed.

Over a distance of 23 air miles, the double track travels 40 miles. Originally, there were 115 trestles and bridges, but relocations have reduced the number to 23. From near sea level, the rails climb to a maximum elevation of 1,740 feet in the highlands. The "Skunks" make frequent stops along the Noyo to let off or pick up campers and trout fishermen. Mail and supplies are delivered to isolated summer cabins and youth camps. This service is in the tradition of the early days when many mills operated holiday "picnic trains." Permits to camp on the river may be obtained from the depot at Fort Bragg. Information on train tickets, time tables, and charters may be obtained by writing the California Western Railroad, Box 907-B, Fort Bragg, California 95437.

The cut-over lands crossed by the "skunks" are lush with second-growth forest. C. R. Johnson pioneered selective cutting and reforestation before the term "tree farm" was invented. Other Johnson innovations were night shifts and the use of band saws. The company had its share of setbacks. The mill was damaged by several fires and nearly destroyed by the 1906 earthquake.

In 1901, the National Steamship Company was formed as a subsidiary to the Union Lumber Company. Over the years it operated a total of seven steam schooners, which carried both passengers and cargo. The last of these ships, the *Noyo III*, was sold to Thailand in 1940. The hardy skippers in the coastwise trade had colorful names, such as "Portwine" John Ellefsen and "Rainwater" Oscar Johnson. Captain "Saturday Night" Jack Bostrom always docked in time for the weekly dance at the Fort Bragg Schoolhouse.

Charles R. Johnson died in 1940, shortly after his son succeeded him to the presidency of the company. In 1968, the firm became a division of the Boise-Cascade Corporation, an Idaho-based conglomerate

One of the more obscure byways which span the outer
Coast Range is the Sherwood Road out of Fort Bragg.
It crests near the summit of 3,200' Sherwood Peak.

*Typically on a summer evening the ocean fog reaches
deep into the canyons of the coastal rivers. As a rule
the mist retreats within a short time after sunrise.*

which was for a time the largest developer of vacation-home tracts in California.

Beginning in the late 1960s, Boise-Cascade was subject to a rash of private suits and six major class action suits charging the firm with misleading sales practices and failure to provide promised recreational facilities and other improvements. The class action suits were resolved with one of the largest out-of-court settlements in the state's history. The company agreed to refund up to $24 million to dissatisfied customers and spend another $34 million for completion and/or maintenance of various projects. One of the assets sold by Boise-Cascade to improve its supply of cash was the Union Lumber Company.

In response to an antitrust complaint made by the Federal Trade Commission, the new owner, the mighty Georgia-Pacific Corporation, divested itself of part of the Union Lumber Company's enormous holdings. But it retained ownership of the mill at Fort Bragg. Guided tours of the mill are held at 2:00 P.M. on workdays in the off-season and several times a day in summer. The tours begin at the company museum, a low wooden building which is all that remains of the old military fort.

First stop is the Bellingham debarker. This enormous machine operates on the principle of a mechanized potato peeler with the added refinement of hot water jetted in under 1,400 pounds pressure. It strips bark up to a foot thick from a prime log in three minutes flat. An overhead ramp allows visitors to watch the logs which are being sawed into four-sided timbers known as cants. The ramp runs up the "green line" where the cants are cut into lumber. Grouped outside the mill are exhibits of early logging equipment.

A Rhododendron Festival is held in May but Fort Bragg really lets its hair down for the Paul Bunyan Days, which span the Labor Day weekend. Assorted high jinks and a grand parade are followed by logging events, such as axe throwing and pole climbing, and an old-time fiddlers' contest.

The pavement on the Sherwood Road out of Fort Bragg ends a few miles east of town. On its tortuous journey across the highlands this rugged byway touches a remote Indian rancheria.

Off the Shoreline Highway on the north side of town is Pudding Creek State Beach, a day-use area where swimming is possible. About three miles farther, a few dwellings occupy the site of Cleone, a lumber center before the last mill shut down in 1918. One of the earliest railroads on the coast ran from Cleone to a schooner landing at Laguna Point. Flatcars loaded with lumber were run by gravity to the wire chute and hauled back to the mill by horses.

Passengers debark at Fort Bragg from the "Skunk," a diesel-powered rail car which makes a daily run to Willits. The round trip consumes about five hours.

A side road out of Cleone enters MacKerricher State Park. This marvelous preserve takes in about a thousand acres of forest, meadows, sand dunes, ocean beach, and rocky headlands. Cleone Beach stretches four miles to the mouth of Ten Mile River, where dip netting for surf smelt is often good. Steelhead and silver salmon enter the stream during winter. The rocky shore south of Cleone Beach is popular with rock fishermen and abalone hunters. Tide pools abound and there are tiny beaches which yield driftwood and agates.

A logging road of the Georgia-Pacific Corporation slices through the park on a high embankment which divides the beach from a trout-filled freshwater lagoon known as Cleone Lake. Small boats (without motors) may be launched here. A small concession at the lake rents bicycles as well as boats.

The park has 138 campsites shaded by tanbark oak, shore pine, and Bishop pine. Shore pine is a coastal form of Ponderosa pine. Quail and deer are often seen at MacKerricher, which is named for a family from Canada who homesteaded the land in 1864.

A recent addition to the park is a 160-acre parcel of dune land. This abuts Inglenook Fen, a wetland ecosystem with plant and animal life found nowhere else in the world. Some species of plants here are believed to have survived from the last Ice Age. The state hopes to acquire the entire area (including little Sandhill Lake) since this is the only fen on the California Coast.

A trail which leaves the picnic area at South Kibesilla affords access to this lonely shore on the Forgotten Coast. Abalone, mussles, and rockfish are taken here.

The Forgotten Coast

Once the Mendocino Coast north of Fort Bragg was dotted with ports and villages. Booming Westport, with its long wharves and fourteen saloons, nearly qualified as a city. Ships called here for lumber from mills on Wages, Dehaven, and Howard Creeks. There were active mills and schooner landings at Newport, Union Landing, Hardy Creek, Rockport, Usal, Bear Harbor, and Needle Rock.

Now there are only stock farms, a few resorts, summer homes, and one gasoline stop. Westport has the gas stop and not much else. Rockport is a ghost town. Next to nothing remains of the other ports.

What killed the towns were the technologically advanced methods of felling redwoods and moving them to market. Fort Bragg's "Skunk Railway" hastened the decline of Westport. The motor truck doomed other ports. Yet some settlements might have survived if the forests had been harvested on a more rational basis.

The first official "tree farm" was not established in the redwood region until 1947. By then over half the original two million acres of prime redwood forest had been logged. As of 1975, it was estimated that less than 100,000 acres of virgin redwood remained on private fee-owned timberland.

The earliest loggers, with their lethargic bull teams and corduroy skid roads, scarcely made a dent in the redwoods. But then came the railroads, followed in the 1880s by the adaptable donkey engine, which mechanized the work of yarding, skidding, and loading logs. The pace of cutting increased enormously in the 1940s with the advent of the bulldozer, tractor truck, and portable chainsaw. These innovations made it feasible to log the most remote areas of the highlands. As the loggers pushed inland, their bases of operations gradually shifted to the Redwood Highway. Many acres of cut-over land near the coast reverted to brush, hardwoods, or grassland.

Of the old-line waterfront enterprises, only the Pacific Lumber Company in Humboldt County survived, thanks to its size and the careful management of its holdings.

North from Cleone, the Shoreline Highway bends inland to avoid a mile-wide belt of sand dunes. It's two miles to the farm hamlet of Inglenook. A mill built here in 1885 manufactured wooden pipe for Fort Bragg's water system. About four miles beyond Inglenook is Ten Mile River. Across the estuary, the coast is cliff-edged and riddled with wave tunnels. From Ten

Mile Bluff to the junction with U.S. Highway 101 near Leggett traffic is apt to be very light, but the traveler must remain alert for fast-moving logging trucks.

A short distance beyond the Ten Mile bridge, the highway executes a ninety degree turn and drops almost to sea level hard by a small county beach at the mouth of Seaside Creek. There follows a hairpin turn up Lobadiah Gulch. At the completion of the turn, the road straightens alongside the South Kibesillah Fishing Access. Here is parking space and some picnic tables perched on a scenic overlook. Short, steep trails lead down to mini-beaches which afford rock fishing, poke poling, and skin diving for abalone.

On the mesa north of South Kibesillah, some weathered sheds mark the site of a "doghole port" known as Newport. During the 1870s and 1880s, Newport was the landing for a mill on Ten Mile River operated by Calvin Stewart and his brother-in-law. Presumably this was the same Stewart who settled Stewarts Point on the Sonoma Coast. Charles R. Johnson, the founder of the Union Lumber Company at Fort Bragg, sawed his first redwood planks at the Stewart and Hunter Mill.

About a mile up the highway from Newport, a ranch occupies the site of Kibesillah, which was settled in the 1860s. For a time, this town supported four hotels. Etymologists speculate that *kibesillah* is a Pomo word meaning "head of valley," or maybe "bare rock" or "flat rock."

Just north of Kibesillah off the headland known as Bruhel Point is a slender channel bound by two flat rocks known to the Indians as Lilem. The spot was neutral ground for various groups of Indians who came from miles around to gather mussels.

North of Bruhel Point, the highway climbs a shoulder of Bell Mountain. Just over the ridge lies lonely, brooding Westport with its unpaved streets and weather-beaten salt-box houses. Westport has a small cafe, motel, and general store with gas pumps where A-frame nets used to catch surf smelt may be purchased or rented. The town overlooks a rock-studded surf that is as treacherous as it is spectacular.

Founded in 1864, Westport was first known as Beal's Landing. The name was changed around 1878 when James T. Rogers of Eastport, Maine, built a wharf here that was 375 feet long. Among the town's more important exports were shingles, railroad ties, and the bark from tanbark oak trees. The latter was in demand by the leather industry. Some mills specialized in making shingles to the exclusion of all other wood products.

Redwood ties commanded a steady market until they were deemed inferior to Douglas fir ties soaked in creosote. "Tie whacking" provided many loggers with employment when depressions closed the mills. The ties were manufactured on the spot where a small redwood was felled. All that was needed was a hand saw, adze, sledge hammer, some wedges, and lots of endurance.

A mile north of town is Wages Creek. The resort here has one hundred sites for tents and recreation vehicles situated nearly level with the beach. Over the next ridge at Dehaven Creek the highway is joined by the unpaved Branscome Road, which snakes twenty-seven miles over the Coast Range to Laytonville. About halfway, on the South Fork of the Eel River, are forty-five acres of virgin redwoods in the Admiral William H. Standley State Recreation Area. Close by is the Nature Conservancy's 4,000-acre North Coast Range Preserve. For information on hiking and nature study there, phone (707) 984-6653.

North from Dehaven Creek, an old by-passed section of Highway 1 gives access to the 2.2-mile Westport Union Landing State Beach. This rocky preserve is undeveloped, often deserted, but highly productive of rockfish, perch, and surf smelt. Waders may take abalone on extreme minus tides.

Hardy Creek offers a last look at the ocean before

Westport dwellings reflect the New England ancestry of early settlers. Now hardly more than a ghost town, Westport was once the busiest port on the North Coast.

Mussels

Mussels (family Mytilidae) make excellent bait and many people enjoy them fried or steamed with butter, herbs, and white wine. Occasionally, the white or pale yellow flesh of a mussel cushions a pearl.

The best places to look for mussels are rocky areas on the outer sea coast, remote from built-up areas which might be a source of pollution. Mussels grow in dense colonies on the sides of rocks from which they may be removed with such devices as a screwdriver, pry bar, tire iron, or small pickaxe. It's important to take mussels only from rocks that remain underwater except at the lowest stages of the tide. Any mussels exposed to the air for long periods may not be safe to eat. These blue-black bivalves grow to nine inches in length. The best eating sizes are three to four inches. Mussels with broken or partially open shells should be rejected. Bag limits are specified in the state angling regulations.

Mussels are usually consumed the same day they are taken but may be kept alive and healthy for several days in a plastic tub of sea water. The water should be kept cool and changed at least once daily.

A word of caution: Mussels taken on the North Coast are dangerous to eat when the annual state quarantine is in effect. This period usually runs from May through October but may go into effect as early as March at some locations. The quarantine is implemented when a tiny red plankton, known as the *Gonyaulux catenella*, proliferates to cause "red tides." These single-cell plankton contain a chemical (saxitoxin) which doesn't harm the mussels or other bivalves which ingest them but is deadly to humans. Clams are less prone to accumulate harmful concentrations of the toxin in their flesh. However, only the white meat is recommended for consumption during the mussel quarantine.

The limpet, whose pretty ridged shell rarely exceeds an inch in diameter, is not a bivalve but a mini-version of the abalone. Limpets are a nuisance to gather but make a fine appetizer, steamed for ten minutes and served on toothpicks with a dash of hot sauce. A pen knife comes in handy for dislodging limpets from the smooth surfaces of rocks. Another mollusk with a colorful shell is the rock scallop. Mostly this bi-valve is found in water accessible only to skin divers.

the road bears inland to avoid the highest, most precipitous stretch of coast between Canada and Mexico. From Hardy Creek, the highway switchbacks to an elevation of 747 feet on the heavily timbered Cottoneva Ridge. This rise bulges seaward to form rugged Cape Vizcaino. The merchant-explorer Sebastian Vizcaino sailed by this point on an expedition in 1602-03 to find ports which could provide emergency shelter for the Manila Galleons.

Over the ridge on Cottoneva Creek, a few wooden dwellings still stand at Rockport. Rockport's history exemplifies the spotty careers of most "doghole ports." Settlement came in the late 1870s when W. R. Miller built a sawmill. He later built a 250-foot wire cable suspension bridge which stretched from the mouth of Cottoneva Creek to a rocky islet in the cove. Vessels were loaded here by wire chute.

In the depression year of 1887, the mill was bought by the Cottoneva Lumber Company. Three years later, a fire destroyed the mill. In 1907, the mill site and

timber holdings were purchased by the New York and Pennsylvania Lumber Company. This firm operated a mill on Hardy Creek which burned in 1912. The firm of Finkbine and Guild bought the property in 1924. They built an electric mill, logging railroad, and new suspension bridge to replace the old span which had been destroyed by a storm. Timber cants were carried by ship from Rockport to the company mill at Jackson, Mississippi.

The Southern Redwood Corporation took over in 1928. A year later, the mill shut down. Ralph M. Rounds of Kansas acquired the mill in 1938. He formed the Rockport Redwood Company, which installed a new wire chute. The chute was used only twice before the company decided it would be cheaper to ship by truck. The mill burned down in 1942. After logging was suspended in the 1950's, the property was acquired by the Georgia-Pacific Corporation. Now Rockport sleeps, perhaps forever, and its timber is managed as a tree farm.

A sand bar built by wave action impounds Usal Creek in summer. No trace of the town which stood here remains. It was razed by fire in the early 1900's.

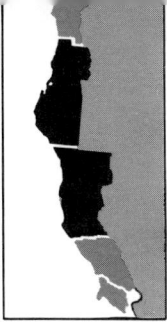

The Primitive Coast:
Mendocino and Humboldt Counties

Only small, isolated portions of the seashore on this 55-mile coast may be approached by road. There are no towns of any size for many miles inland. The largest settlement is Whitethorn, which serves a widely scattered population of 300. As many as sixteen hundred recreationists congregate at Shelter Cove in summer; in winter, this vacation development numbers less than one hundred people.

Hunting, fishing, backpacking, and beachcombing are the main attractions on this coast. All the main roads have steep grades and some are not paved. The amenities at Shelter Cove include a motel, trailer park, and seafood restaurant. There are a few rustic resorts off the road from Honeydew to Petrolia. Whitethorn, Honeydew, and Petrolia have general stores with gas pumps. Most other places shown on the AAA map, such as Capetown, Ettersburg, Usal, and Wheeler, are private ranches or ghost towns with no facilities for the traveler.

The federal Bureau of Land Management maintains several small campgrounds on roads which trace the east slopes of the King Range. Nine miles up the road from Honeydew, a county park affords camping on the Mattole River.

Usal

One mile up the Shoreline Highway from Rockport is a demonstration forest of the Louisiana-Pacific Corporation. The redwoods here shade a picnic area and self-guiding nature trail. Two miles farther on, the highway spans the North Fork of Cottoneva Creek.

Just across the bridge, look for a dim, unpaved forest lane (which may not be marked) turning off the left-hand side of the road and climbing steeply into the woods. This is the Usal Road. It substitutes for the Shoreline Highway on the northern twenty miles of the Mendocino Coast. The paved highway, which continues in a northeasterly direction from Rockport, is known as the Hollow Tree Road. It joins U.S. Highway 101 near Leggett.

The Usal Road isn't shown on some road maps. But this obscure byway was a vital link in the sketchy road system which joined Eureka with the San Francisco Bay Area before the Redwood Highway was completed in the 1920s. A proper road system was slow to develop on the North Coast, partly because the lumber kings found it more convenient to ship by schooner. Also, the sheep ranchers were fearful that roads would encourage settlement and force a rise in taxes.

Near the Mendocino-Humboldt County line, the Usal Road connects with other rural roads permitting the traveler to approach Eureka by way of the King Range, Mattole River, and lonely Cape Mendocino.

The Usal Road hasn't changed much since Jack London and his wife, Charmian, drove it in a horse-drawn carriage on a trip to Eureka in 1911. This road has some fierce grades and many twists and turns. The surface isn't half bad after the county works on it (which isn't often). It's never a good idea to attempt the Usal Road in a low-slung sports car or broad-beamed motor home. Hauling a trailer here is out of the question. An easier approach to the King Range and Shelter Cove is by way of an improved road which leaves U.S. 101 near Garberville. This road is being developed as an all-weather route and is suitable for hauling a small trailer in summer.

The gas stop closest to the southern terminus of the Usal Road is six miles up the Hollow Tree Road at Hales Grove. Here a small store is located near the intersection with a high-speed logging road of the Louisiana-Pacific Corporation. The truck drivers who stop here are apt to be informed about conditions on the Usal Road. There are no towns, stores, or settlements to speak of on the Usal Road. The nearest gas stop after you cross into Humboldt County is at Whitethorn on the Briceland Road.

Logging trucks may be encountered on the Usal Road but they won't be as large as those which travel the private high-speed logging road. These monster diesels carry up to 120,000 pounds of logs, which is far above the legal limit permitted on public thoroughfares.

From the main highway the Usal Road climbs with a minimum of switchbacks to a ridgetop that crests a thousand feet above the sea. There's a break in the forest here where sheep and cattle graze. This clearing and other openings along the route afford some spectacular views of the seashore when it isn't fogging. In spring the roadsides are edged with foxgloves, columbines, and yellow monkey flowers. Ferns and blackberry bushes grow thick in places.

On the five-mile drive to Usal, the road curves along the side of a ridge, passing through young stands of Douglas fir that may have signs on them reading "poison and bear traps." For centuries, the forest primeval withstood the depredations of chipmunks, squirrels, porcupines, deer, and "Smokey the Bear" without any help from man. But now the modern forester deems it necessary to wage war on these creatures to obtain the maximum yield of timber.

In a series of abrupt turns, the road drops to the meadows at Usal Creek where some decaying sheds and a horse barn are the only vestiges of the settlement. According to Alfred Kroeber, the name Usal is a Pomo word meaning "south." It was the name used by the settlers for the Sinkyone Indians who had a village at Usal. The ocean frontage is private now and access for rockfishing and smelt netting may be revoked at any time.

J. H. Wonderly built a redwood mill at Usal in 1889, together with a 1,600-foot wharf and three miles

View of the Primitive Coast from the Usal Road. White and purple foxgloves seen near the road are not native but spread here from the gardens of pioneer homesteads.

Shore Flowers

The purple foxgloves which fringe the Usal Road are not indigenous to the North Coast but originated from the gardens of early settlers. Other exotics, such as the sea fig (Africa), comfrey (Asia), and broom (Europe), may be seen growing near the seashore in company with some of the many different kinds of native shrubs and flowers.

One reason for the profusion of flora on the North Coast is the great diversity of habitats. These include ecological niches which support coastal forms of alpine and desert plants. On seaside bluffs are found the same colorful little succulents of the Stonecrop family that grow to timberline in the High Sierra.

The cool, temperate climate provides a growing season of 270 days along the shore of Del Norte County and over 330 days south of Eureka. Hardy natives, such as the bush monkey flower, begin to bloom as early as March and retain their yellow-orange blossoms well into the dry season. This longevity is due in part to the shore-side seepage of fresh water which emanates from high places in the Coast Ranges.

Heliotrope, fiddleneck, and other members of the Borage family are prone to flourish on the coast where the soil is slightly saline. Saltbush, saltgrass, and pickleweed rim the tidal marshes. Flowers that creep over beaches and dune areas include the peach primrose, beach pea, beach morning glory, and the sea rocket, an exotic of the Mustard family.

Some of the most vivid displays of spring color occur where lavender sea daisies, yellow wall-flowers, and vermilion paintbrush compete for living space on the edges of surf-battered cliffs. Lupines are ubiquitous on the North Coast. They range from the mountain tops to the tips of ocean sand spits. From late winter through May, you may see the delicate flowers of trillium, sorrel, and fairy lantern wherever redwoods grow. The shrubs that blossom in the redwoods include ocean spray, salal, Western huckleberry, and rhododendron.

Only two shrubs of the genus *Rhododendron* are native to the coast. These are the Western azalea and California rose bay. But scattered around Fort Bragg are numerous nurseries and private arboretums where rhododendrons from all over the world are grown. Many of the more than eight hundred species of rhododendrons that have been identified adapt well to the mild climate and acid soils of the Mendocino shore. Given loving care, some tropical species will flourish here. The North Coast is well represented at annual exhibits in the San Francisco Bay Area, where cuttings from thousands of different hybrids are shown.

All the larger towns on the coast feature festivals with displays of wild or cultivated flowers. The dates for these festivals may be obtained by writing the Redwood Empire Association, 360 Post Street, San Francisco, California 94108

Throughout this book are references to the local flora that may be seen to advantage from a trail. For motorists, it is mainly the unpaved back roads which afford more than a fleeting glimpse of color. These include the Usal Road and other byways that trace the Primitive Coast. On such drives, it behooves the person behind the wheel to keep his or her eyes glued straight ahead because there are logging trucks and no end of potholes to look out for.

A large variety of shrubs and flowers common on the North Coast are described in the guidebook *Shore Wildflowers of California, Oregon, and Washington* by Philip A. Munz. This small paperback includes ninety-six color photographs and over a hundred line drawings.

of logging railway. The mill and property were purchased by Captain Robert Dollar in 1894.

Usal was one of the most treacherous of the "dog-hole ports." The reluctance of shipping companies to permit their vessel to call here prompted Captain Dollar to acquire his own fleet. Dollar's first ship was the 218-ton steam schooner *Newsboy*, built to his order at San Francisco in 1888. The talented skipper who took command was Captain "Hoodlum" Bob Walvig, so-called because he was quick to denounce any crewman who questioned his orders as a "hoodlum."

The first steam schooners were conventional schooners with an engine and boiler added as an afterthought. Without this auxiliary power these little ships would have lacked the maneuverability to navigate the more difficult ports. Steam schooners were

Most of the ocean frontage off the Usal Road is private.
Permission from the landowner is required to use the
few dim trails and logging spurs that approach the sea.

first used on the North Coast in 1864. By 1880 they dominated the coastwise trade. Few of these vessels exceeded a thousand tons. Two well-preserved veterans of the lumber trade are permanently docked at San Francisco's National Maritime Museum, situated at the foot of Hyde Street near Fisherman's Wharf. These are the steam schooner *Wapama* and the *C. A. Thayer,* a conventional three-masted schooner.

Shortly after the Usal Mill closed in 1902, it was destroyed by fire. Most of the town burned with it. The schooner *Newsboy* sank in 1906 as the result of a collision with the *Wasp* on Humboldt Bay. By then Captain Dollar had acquired the steam schooner *Grace Dollar*, forerunner of the Dollar Line's globe-circling fleet of sixty freighters and passenger liners. In 1938

this fleet was taken over by the American President Lines.

From Usal the road runs four miles up Timber Ridge, climbing to 1,555 feet before it drops to a small wooded bench above Mistake Point. Here a rugged spur angles down the side of Anderson Cliff to an old mill site on Jackass Creek. Access for fishing and smelt netting is by permission of the land owner.

From the bench, it's a long, slow eleven miles to Four Corners by way of Jackass Ridge. The road ascends to a high of 1,864 feet on the ridge but touches few points where the timber allows a view of the coast. A topographical map comes in handy on this leg of the drive because of the numerous logging spurs. Some may easily be confused with the main road.

There's nothing at Four Corners except a junction. The Usal Road ends here. The Chemise Mountain Road, which is marked Route 431, continues north, crossing the Humboldt-Mendocino County line two miles north of the junction. This road passes two public campgrounds on the east slope of the King Range before it joins the Shelter Cove Road.

The road to the left of the junction angles south, losing 1,370 feet in elevation on its 5.5-mile descent to Bear Harbor. Settlement at this old doghole port dates back to 1868. A wire chute was built in 1892. Calvin Stewart, who helped C. R. Johnson establish the Union Lumber Company at Fort Bragg, moved to Bear Harbor in 1893. In this same year the Bear Harbor Lumber Company was incorporated. The company spent four years building a railway that ran nine miles by way of Indian Creek to the company wharf. But in 1899, just a few months after the railway was completed, a tidal wave destroyed the wharf and wire chute.

Bear Harbor has a spectacular black sand beach, which is inundated at high tide. It was recently acquired for the 3,500-acre Sinkyone Wilderness State Park, a new preserve not yet open to visitors.

On the right of the lonely junction at Four Corners is the turn-off to the Briceland Road, which is marked Route 435. It's a five-mile drive on this unpaved road to the general store at Whitethorn. Shown on some maps as Thorn or Thorn Junction, this sleepy hamlet was once a busy stage stop and later a roaring lumber camp with five sawmills. The town is situated on the upper Mattole River where it first rises as a small stream in the Whitethorn Valley. The road which leaves Whitethorn for Briceland and Garberville is paved.

Sheep and cattle may be seen grazing on the seaward side of the Usal Road wherever there is an opening in the forest. Winter rainfall here is apt to exceed 50 inches.

*Shortly after it leaves US Highway 101 near Garber-
ville, the Shelter Cove Road crosses the South Fork
of the Eel River on this sturdy steel truss bridge.*

From the vicinity of Four Corners, the mountains of the King Range stretch thirty-five miles up the coast, almost to the mouth of the Mattole River. These mountains are exceptionally rugged. Their foggy, wind-blown Pacific slopes rise directly from the ocean at angles of forty-five degrees or steeper. No improved roads challenge these grades except the Shelter Cove Road, which snakes down to the isolated marine terrace at Point Delgada. The highest mountain in the range is Kings Peak. It crests at 4,086 feet.

Roughly two-thirds of the King Range's 54,000 acres is federal land administered by the Bureau of Land Management. The summit and west slope is largely maintained as wilderness. Sheep grazing is permitted but the only improvements are trails and campsites. Some of the longer trails invite backpacking. The primitive camps scattered along the summit are most heavily used during the deer season. The King Range abounds with blacktail deer, but it's not easy country to hunt. A horse or mule is needed to pack out the kill. When the deer season opens, the legal bucks are apt to be concentrated in high places, such as Chemise Mountain, Queen Peak, and Kings Peak.

The densely forested east slope is managed for recreation and timber cutting. All the streams here are tributary to the Mattole River. Spreading north and east of the King Range is a rough hinterland which is penetrated by few roads other than jeep trails and logging spurs.

The resident Indians on the coast were the Sinkyone tribe of the Athabascans. They were ruthlessly hunted down by the early settlers and federal troops until virtually exterminated. The practice was to kill the men and send the women and children to remote reservations.

On February 20, 1864, this account appeared in the *Humboldt Times* at Eureka:

> Lt. Frazier, Co. E, C. M., with a detachment of twelve men stationed at Upper Mattole, started on a scout about the 1st. instant, and the night of the second succeeded in finding some Indians at Whitethorn Valley, on the Mattole River about 25 miles south of Upper Mattole. At this place, he captured thirteen squaws and killed four bucks—none escaping. The Indians offered no resistance, being completely surprised.

Among the older generation on the North Coast, some will defend the policy of genocide. A harsh assessment of the Coast tribes is found in the regional history *Lure of the Humboldt Bay Region*, by Chad L. Hoopes of Loleta. According to Hoopes, "Those Indians living along the Coast were an inferior civilization; they were thriftless, idle, and debased, usually provoking the unmerciful vengeance of the settlers by petty thievery."

Alfred Krober in his *Handbook of the Indians of California* allows that the Sinkyone were "backwoodsmen," culturally less advanced than the Pomos. But he suggests this was so because they lived a marginal existence in country less bountiful than the Pomo territory. The Sinkyone built their villages on the best land available, such as the meadow at Usal and the terrace at Shelter Cove. They resorted to stealing only after the settlers preempted this land.

The first European to visit the rugged interior of the Primitive Coast may have been the fur trapper Michel LaFramboise, "Captain of the California Trail." In 1838, LaFramboise passed through the Mattole River country on his way to rendezvous with a vessel of the Hudson's Bay Company at Trinidad Bay. A long, arduous march from the Central Valley brought LaFramboise and his party to an ocean cove located about a hundred miles south of Trinidad. Here the mountain man lingered until he realized something was wrong and set out on foot for Fort Vancouver. Historians speculate that the place where LaFramboise waited in "anxious suspense" for a ship that never came was Bear Harbor. There is no record that LaFramboise found anything of interest in the Mattole Country, which is not surprising. The entire North Coast proved a disappointment to the early mountain men because none of the streams contained beaver.

After the Sinkyone were evicted by loggers from their villages on the seashore, they tried to scratch a living in the back country. But soon every habitable valley was occupied by settlers. The pioneer families raised fruit, vegetables, a little grain, and livestock. They were nearly self-sufficient, but for money to buy tools and staples such as sugar and coffee they sold what produce they could spare to the lumber camps. This hard living would have been easier if the Indians had been willing to hire on as field hands.

But the way of the Sinkyone was to pick berries, gather acorns, dig edible roots, collect mussels and seaweed, trap fish, and hunt deer and elk. The women wove baskets, prepared acorn flour, and processed hides to be used for footwear, clothing, and blankets. Tools and eating utensils were carved from animal bones. Wedges made from elk horns were used to fell

*Some trails in the King Range climb high above the
mist which shrouds the coastline most days in summer.
Hiker is looking west from the summit of Chemise Mtn.*

trees. All this involved a lot of work, yet the Sinkyone
were deemed lazy and shiftless because they would not
forsake their traditional lifestyle to labor for the
settlers.

Now the scattered Mattole ranchers seem no less
tradition-bound than the Indians who preceded them.
They are disturbed by talk of Highway 1 being
extended from Rockport to link with the Redwood
Highway near Ferndale. Should this happen, they fear
the charm and quiet of their countryside would be
shattered by a flood of traffic and commercial development. Land values would soar but so would taxes.
Many of the old families here practice ranching more
as a way of life than as a business.

From the junction at Four Corners, it's five miles by

way of the unpaved Chemise Mountain Road to
Wailaki Camp on the east slope of the King Range.
Here are a picnic area and sixteen campsites on the
South Fork of Bear Creek. A short piece up the road is
Nadelos Camp with fourteen sites. These Bureau of
Land Management (BLM) camps have benches, ta-
bles, food lockers, piped water, stoves, and rest rooms.

From Wailaki Camp, a steep but well-engineered
trail switchbacks up Chemise Mountain. The first
quarter-mile is signed with BLM markers identifying
the native flora. These include many plants and
underlying trees associated with the redwoods but
virtually all the tall timber in the King Range is
Douglas fir. It's slightly more than a mile to the brushy
summit at 2,500 feet. From here, you obtain a dazzling

Beachcombing

You needn't be a collector to enjoy prospecting a lonely stretch of seashore, such as the beach which stretches north of Shelter Cove in the shadow of the King Range. It's enough to take delight in the discovery and contemplation of such objects as a pretty pebble, a sand dollar, or a lovely piece of weathered driftwood. Other treasures you might stray upon include antique bottles, petrified wood, various gem-stone material, and the colorful glass fishing floats which drift in from the Orient.

In this "plastic age," it may seem odd that floats of hand-blown glass still turn up on the beaches. In fact, most commercial fishermen have switched to using plastic or metal floats, but the Japanese long-line tuna fishery persists in using glass because it's cheaper. Even if the Japanese did turn to plastic, though, glass floats would continue to wash up on the North Coast for a long time to come. The reason for this has to do with the pattern of ocean currents.

The strongest current is the Kuroshio, or Japanese current, which flows east from the Philippine Sea by way of the Gulf of Alaska. As it approaches the Pacific Northwest, the Kuroshio forks. One branch, known as the Alaska current, veers north and then west to ultimately rejoin the Kuroshio. The other branch is the California current. This runs south to join the North Equatorial current which flows west to merge with the Kuroshio off the Philippines.

When the path of these currents is sketched on the map, they form a figure 8. Glass floats and other artifacts (including everything from cast-off light bulbs to derelict junks) may travel the figure-8 pattern for decades before a storm finally blows them ashore. The lower half of the figure-8 pattern was the "Great Circle" route navigated by the Manila Galleons.

The best time to look for glass floats off places such as the mouth of the Mattole River is directly following a spell of rough weather in spring. Beaches near towns are picked clean by local residents within hours after a storm.

Old bottles may turn up anywhere on the coast, but Indian artifacts are most likely to be seen near stream mouths where hunting parties made their camps. Beachcombers who work the more remote beaches with metal detectors may uncover hardware that originated in the lumber camps. Once in a while an old coin is found. The beach north of Shelter Cove contains many remnants of shipwrecks.

Driftwood tends to become more abundant on the beaches the farther north you drive. Most of the state parks permit the gathering of driftwood, but restrict individuals to fifty pounds a day. This regulation is directed mainly against entrepreneurs who take driftwood by the truckload and wholesale it to boutiques and gift shops.

The state parks open to rockhounding "within the wave action zone" are Pelican, Trinidad, Little River, Westport-Union Landing, and Manchester State Beaches. At last report it was still permissible to collect agates at Agate Beach in Patricks Point State Park. Most parks post local rules which should be consulted before any collecting is done. Some of the minerals prospected for along the beaches are jasper, carnelian, glaucophane, and jadeite (the true jade from which the gemstone is carved).

Amos Wood, in his book *Beachcombing the Pacific*, tells the story of a steelhead fisherman whose favorite water on a stream in British Columbia was marked by a large flat rock. Year after year, the man would return to fish off this rock until one season he found the rock was missing. Curious to know what became of it, the man made inquiries and was told that someone had discovered the boulder was a piece of jade and sold it for $60,000.

A pocket guide with hundreds of precise color illustrations is *Minerals of the World* by Charles A. Sorrel. Also recommended is the booklet *Rocks and Minerals of the San Francisco Bay Area* by Oliver E. Bowen, Jr. Amos Wood's *Beachcombing the Pacific* includes a survey of beachcombing possibilities along the Coast.

On the west slope of Chemise Mountain is a fir forest where the silence on calm summer days is broken only by the patter of condensed fog dripping from the trees.

view of the Primitive Coast if you're fortunate enough to make the hike on a fogless day in spring.

The trail down the west slope is less developed. It affords a rough 3.5-mile backpack to a wooded bench overlooking the seashore. About a third of the way down, you enter a Gothic belt of forest which drips with condensed fog most days in summer. Douglas firs grow differently here than on the east slope. They loom grotesquely in the mist; their massive trunks are twisted and foreshortened so the lower branches sweep the ground.

The trail grows ever more steep and tortuous as you lose elevation. On the lower edge of the forest where wild iris grow, there are oak-shaded flats suitable for an overnight bivouac. Chemise Creek runs in a ravine to the right of the trail. Some maps show a dim side trail leading to the stream, but it's good insurance to pack an extra canteen of water.

Before a landslide destroyed the last half-mile of the trail, it was possible to hike down to the seashore at the mouth of Chemise Creek. The rocky beach here is truly isolated. Shallow reefs make it difficult to approach by boat. Two miles north of Chemise Creek, the beach is cut off from Shelter Cove by Point No Pass. Another promontory, also known as Point No Pass, leans to sea three miles south of the creek.

From Wailaki Camp, the Chemise Mountain Road runs north 2.5 miles to a junction with the Shelter Cove Road. Turning west, it's a short climb to a pass at the

King Range Road at an elevation of 1,996 feet. The King Range Road is not recommended for trailers. It follows Bear Creek four miles north to Tolkan Camp, which has nine sites. About three miles farther is Horse Mountain Camp, also with nine sites. Near this camp, the Saddle Mountain Road takes off up the east slope to the start of Kings Crest Trail. This trail runs sixteen miles along the summit, climbing a thousand feet to Kings Peak before it terminates at a road on the north boundary of the BLM property. Several spurs branch off the main trail but none approach the seashore.

The limitations of the BLM trail system may be blamed on the checkerboard pattern of the private holdings in the King Range. In 1970, to afford better management of the area for grazing, timber, and recreation, Congress created the King Range Conservation Area. The boundaries of the new preserve encompassed 54,000 acres, of which 20,000 acres were privately owned. About $1.5 million was authorized for acquisition of private holdings and $3.5 million for the development of camps, trails, and access roads. In 1976, the BLM reported it had acquired an additional 7,000 acres through purchase or land exchange and was still negotiating for other properties. Only twenty miles of trails were maintained because inflation had caused the BLM to give priority to its acquisition program.

Permits are not required for overnight trips in the back country; however, the BLM requests that backpackers and horse parties sign the registers located near the trailheads. Also, hunters are reminded that permission is required to hunt on private holdings that remain inside the Conservation Area.

Information and a recreation map of the King Range may be obtained by writing the District Manager of the Bureau of Land Management at 555 Leslie Street, Ukiah, California 95482. The phone number is (707) 462-3873.

From the junction of the Shelter Cove and King Range Roads, it's four miles to Shelter Cove and the seashore at Point Delgada. When Shelter Cove was occupied by the Sinkyone, it was a major source of clam money for the Northern Pomo. The first white settlement sprang up around a landing where schooners called to pick up lumber, fish, and produce. Later, at Briceland (on the road to Garberville), a plant was built which extracted tannic acid from the bark of the tanbark oak. For a time, hundreds of men in the Mattole country made a living as "bark peelers." The hogsheads of extract were delivered by wagon to Shelter Cove for export to leather manufacturers in San Francisco and foreign countries.

Descending from the summit of the range, the

Casting for surfperch is apt to be rewarding off the beaches which stretch north and south of Shelter Cove. Skin diving is good at the cove when the ocean is flat.

Shelter Cove Road emerges from the timber to wind down a grassy mountainside laced with forty-three miles of paved streets. This maze of asphalt was built to serve a recreational subdivision with 4,700 lots. Most of the lots were sold in the 1960s but as of 1976 only a few dozen homes had been built.

Improvements other than roads at Shelter Cove include a nine-hole golf course. On the marine terrace fronting the ocean is Humboldt County's second largest air strip. In contrast with such developments as Sea Ranch, most of the seashore at Shelter Cove remains open to the public.

The bay at Shelter Cove is located on the lee side of Point Delgada. A restaurant, trailer park, bait shop, launching facility, and boat rentals operate here. Often fog-bound in summer, the main attractions at Shelter Cove are beachcombing, skin diving, and sport fishing. Some old hands insist that Shelter Cove is the finest salmon port on the North Coast. The trolling grounds lie close inshore on the shoals off Point Delgada. A fair number of king salmon are hooked but the bulk of the catch is silvers.

Bottom fishing is excellent for lingcod, cabezon, and black, blue, copper, and vermilion rockfish. Halibut in excess of fifty pounds have been caught here. The rocky shore around Point Delgada abounds with tide pools. The black sand beaches which stretch north and south of Shelter Cove yield driftwood, cockle clams, and a few agates. Perch and smelt are taken in the surf, which is normally too cold and rough for swimming.

Shelter Cove has a summer population of 1,600. A backpack trip to the cove from Punta Gorda lighthouse is described in the next chapter.

The hamlet of Petrolia lies nestled at the foot of
Appletree Ridge. The first oil wells in California
were drilled three miles east of town in the 1860's.

Cape Mendocino's primitive coast is not entirely roadless. Near the Eel River it's touched by the Centerville Road out of Ferndale. The Mattole Road skirts four miles of low, sandy seashore on the south side of the Cape.

To approach the Cape from Shelter Cove, the traveler may proceed north by way of the King Range or Ettersburg Roads. Neither of these steep, unpaved byways is recommended for trailers. Both run about eleven miles to connect with the Wilder Ridge Road at the foot of Kings Peak. Eight miles north of this junction, the Wilder Ridge Road meets the Mattole Road at Honeydew.

The Ettersburg Road branches off the Shelter Cove Road about midway between Garberville and Point Delgada. Logging trucks use this slender ridge route, which winds above the Mattole River across a patchwork quilt of forest and meadow. It's a six mile drive to Ettersburg where the road dips to span the river. Ettersburg is not a town but a private ranch with an air strip. It was settled in 1894 by Alfter F. Etter, who established an experimental fruit farm here. Apples grown on the ranch were delivered by horse and wagon to a schooner landing at the mouth of the Mattole River.

The Mattole River flows north from Ettersburg through wild country. The road bears west five miles to a junction with the King Range and Wilder Ridge Roads. At an elevation of 2,224 feet, this lonely crossroads affords a good overall view of the King Range and its loftiest peaks.

The Wilder Ridge Road contours through timber and open range, gradually losing altitude as it approaches the Mattole River at Honeydew. Honeydew (population 10) used to be a fair-sized town when it was an active lumber center. Now there's only a post office and general store with gas pumps. The paved Mattole Road, which is also known as the Wild Cat Road, crosses the river here and winds twenty-three miles northeast to join U.S. Highway 101 in Humboldt Redwoods State Park.

In winter, Honeydew is one of the dampest places in California. During the wet season of 1957-58, the Honeydew Weather Station recorded 174 inches of rain.

From Honeydew, it's fifteen miles to Petrolia. On this stretch, the road follows the Mattole River. At a few points, the pavement dips low and close enough to the stream to afford fishing access. Winter steelheaders

float this water with bait and lures beginning in late December. Both king and silver salmon enter the river after winter rains open the sand bar at the mouth. There's summer angling for pan-sized trout in some of the tributaries. But along most of its fifty-mile course, the Mattole is a private preserve. A state survey shows public access to be only one percent of the steelhead water. In recent years, the Mattole ranchers have been less disposed to grant strangers permission to hunt and fish on their property. They complain that too many recreationists are litterbugs and tend to be careless about such things as closing stock gates.

The Mattole is named for a tribe of Athabascan Indians who had several villages in the vicinity of Cape Mendocino. They shared the fate of the neighboring Sinkyone before scholars could learn much about them.

The hilly countryside off the river is a blend of hayfields, brushland, and second-growth forest. Time has softened the scars left by fire and clear cutting. Some logging continues but on a small scale.

On the drive to Petrolia, the road passes several rustic resorts and a small coffee shop. Nine miles up the road is the A. W. Way County Park, where wild iris bloom in spring. There's a campground on the river here with sites for tents and small trailers.

Petrolia (population 50) is a drowsy place which sprawls across the lower slopes of Apple Tree Ridge. A steepled church and wooden school house with a bell tower lend charm to the village. There is a single store with gas pump. Settlement came in 1861 when oil was discovered in the hills a few miles north of town. The first producing oil wells in California were drilled here. Of these, the most successful was the Union Well, drilled by the Mattole Petroleum Company of which Leland Stanford was president. It yielded about a hundred barrels of oil at the rate of one barrel a day.

In later years, derricks sprouted around Honeydew, Ettersburg, and Briceland. Little oil was found but now and then a wildcat outfit will do some exploratory drilling. A post office was established at Petrolia in 1865. It was during this year that the first shipment of oil was made. One hundred gallons in goatskin bags were packed out by mule train.

In 1871, a stage road from Ferndale was completed to Petrolia by the Petrolia and Centerville Plank and Turnpike Company. This road was gradually extended to Garberville along portions of the routes now followed by the Mattole, Wilder Ridge, Ettersburg, and

Shelter Cove Roads. From Garberville, a road climbed to link with the Mail Ridge Road in the Eastern Highlands. Before the Usal Road was built, the Mail Ridge Road provided the only overland approach to San Francisco.

The lagoon inside the mouth of the Mattole River is approached on a side road which forks off the Mattole Road near the bridge crossing east of Petrolia. This spur is known as the Lighthouse Road because it connects with a trail leading to the site of the Punta Gorda Light Station. After thirty-nine years of service, the light was abandoned in 1951 and replaced by a whistle buoy anchored at sea.

The lower end of the Lighthouse Road is unpaved and fit for travel only in a four-wheel drive vehicle. Fly fishing is sometimes excellent on the lagoon during the first half of the winter steelhead season. The outer beach affords netting for surf smelt as well as perch fishing. Driftwood is abundant and glass fishing floats occasionally turn up.

From the roadhead it's about a three-mile hike through the dunes to the old Punta Gorda Light Tower. The Bureau of Land Management (BLM) hopes to establish a campground here. After the station was closed, some former dwellings of the light keepers were occupied by a small commune, known as the "Belt Ministry." These young people tried to support themselves by making belts and other leather goods

View of the Sugarloaf from the Mattole Road. Opening to cave shows on left side. The rock rises off the tip of Cape Mendocino near an abandoned lighthouse.

Surfperch

Of several varieties of surfperch hooked in the breakers off North Coast beaches, the ubiquitous redtail surfperch provides the bulk of the catch. This silvery fish has a soup plate configuration with dark vertical bars on its sides and a touch of red in the tail fin.

The best fishing occurs from late winter through early summer when the large female perch move close inshore to give birth to their young. These perch average two to three pounds in weight. Being a "dry" fish, surfperch are best prepared for the table by dipping the fillets in batter and frying briefly at high heat.

Since most North Coast beaches have steep drop-offs, it's rarely necessary to make extra long casts to reach productive water. The rod and reel should be stout enough for use with 15 pound test line and pyramid sinkers to four ounces. The choice of sinker weight is dictated by the roughness of the surf.

The terminal rig consists of a three-foot leader with a snap on the end for a sinker and one or two droppers for size Number 4, 6, or 8 hooks. Good baits are sand crabs, shrimp, mussels, pileworms, and chunks of fish. Oval-shaped gray sand crabs (½ to 2 inches long) may be found at most beaches by digging along the water line with a garden trowel.

After the bait is cast, the sinker is allowed to rest on the bottom. The trick is to keep a taut line so strikes may be detected. Surfperch bite best on a running tide.

Accessories for surf fishing include a pair of fisherman's pliers, a cutting board with towel and knife (if you use cut bait), and a sand spike to which a bait can is attached. The purpose of the sand spike is to have some place to rest your rod while you bait up. A burlap sack or small plastic ice chest may serve as a creel. A wet suit or chest-high waders are recommended for winter fishing.

Some kinds of surfperch are caught mainly in the quiet waters of bays and estuaries. These are described in the Fish and Game booklet *Inshore Fishes*. Another state publication you may find useful is the *Marine Baits of California* by Turner and Sexsmith.

---

before they were evicted by representatives of the BLM and a deputy sheriff. This was necessary, according to the BLM, because the old buildings were too dangerous to live in. The District Manager told the press, "We had to get rid of them before someone got hurt." Subsequently, the homes were razed, but the light tower remains. The BLM plans to rehabilitate it as an historical monument.

Hardy, experienced "foot burners" might enjoy backpacking along the shore of the King Range from Punta Gorda all the way to Shelter Cove. At least five days should be allowed for the hike, during which seals and sea lions may be sighted. The round trip from the roadhead is sixty miles. A party with two cars could organize a shuttle trip. Advice should be sought from the BLM office at Ukiah concerning the areas of private frontage and places where the beach becomes inundated at high tide. Also, inquiry should be made as to the streams which provide drinking water. The U.S. Geological Survey topographical maps covering this shore are the Cape Mendocino and Point Delgada (15 minute) quadrangles.

Leaving Petrolia, the main road spans the North Fork of the Mattole. A private road follows this stream to approach the site of the first oil well drilled in California.

On the thirty-mile drive to Ferndale, there are no towns, resorts, or gas stops. It's four miles over a low grassy ridge to the sand dunes at the mouth of Domingo Creek. Here the road swings north and hugs the shoreline as far as Cape Mendocino. This windy stretch of coast is fog-bound most days in summer.

About halfway to the Cape is the Devil's Gate. The road skirts this outcropping on a low, wave-licked causeway which is hazardous to drive in stormy weather. A lone ranch dwelling, known as the Ocean House, looks out on Cape Mendocino where the road veers inland to climb Cape Ridge. On the tip of Cape Ridge is an automatic light. The original light was housed in a sixteen-sided pyramidal tower built in 1868. Sugarloaf Island is visible from the pavement here. It towers three hundred feet above the water just a stone's throw off the point.

Cape Mendocino, being the most westerly point on the Pacific Coast south of Alaska, has served as a landmark for navigators since the sixteenth century.

Ranch house near Honeydew. Families of pioneer stock in the Mattole country prize their isolation and practice ranching more as a way of life than as a business.

Cabrillo may have been the first European to see the Cape on his voyage of discovery in 1542. Drake, Cermeno, and Vizcaino reported sighting it. It was a landfall for many of the Manila Galleons which sailed the Great Circle Route back to New Spain with treasure from the Orient.

Fauntleroy Rock, Blunt's Reef, and The Great Break are among the shoals which accounted for more than two hundred shipwrecks off Cape Mendocino in the period from 1850 to 1950. On a foggy day in June of 1916, a 4,057-ton steamer, *Bear*, foundered near the Cape. The vessel carried 182 passengers and crew, of whom 155 were rescued. Attempts were made to salvage the *Bear* but it was a total loss. Captain

Dollar's little lumber schooner, the *Grace Dollar*, was among the ships which picked up survivors. And, on the calm and clear night of August 6, 1921, the steamer *Alaska* unaccountably plowed into Blunt's Reef three miles west of the Cape. Most of the passengers were gathered for a dance when the collision occurred. Forty-two persons were lost.

On the northern side of Cape Ridge, the road drops to Capetown, located a mile inland on the Bear River. A former stop on the old toll road, Capetown is headquarters for a sheep ranch. The last excitement here was in the 1860s when some oil wells were drilled in Bear Valley. For many years, the cook stove in a farmhouse at Capetown was operated on natural gas

*Old ranches which line the banks of the lower Mattole
River mostly grow hay and run sheep and cattle. Some
logging and wildcatting for oil goes on in the hills.*

obtained from seepage near the bridge crossing.

Bear Valley and the hills to the north have the look
of the Scottish Highlands. There are scattered stands of
timber, but mostly the rolling slopes support only
grass, low brush, and clumps of purple thistle. The
roadsides are edged with daisies. The unpaved Bear
River Road leaves Capetown to approach ranches in
the upper valley. Ultimately, this road connects with
the Bear Ridge Road which runs to Rio Dell.

King salmon, silver salmon, and steelhead rainbow
trout enter the Bear River after winter rains open the
bar. As with all the smaller rivers, the problem is to
arrive on the stream when a run of fish is at its peak. By
the time Eureka bait shops receive word of action, the
run may be scattered far upstream. Access for fishing
at Bear River is by permission of the landowner.

From Capetown, which is forty-five feet above the
sea, the Mattole Road winds to a junction at 1,877 feet
on Bunker Hill. The Bear Ridge Road leaves here for
Rio Dell. A trifle west of the junction is Oil Creek
where several wells were drilled in the 1860s. The
Mattole Road continues on across the northern tip of
the Mendocino Highlands, passing through ragged
stands of timber and fog-damp meadows that are green
with bracken. After six miles, the road comes to a
drop-off overlooking the flat, fertile plain of the Eel
River Delta. Nestled at the foot of the grade is the
quaint Victorian town of Ferndale.

*Driving the Mattole Road north on Wildcat Ridge, the
forest suddenly opens to afford this aerial view of
Ferndale and the green plain of the Eel River Delta.*

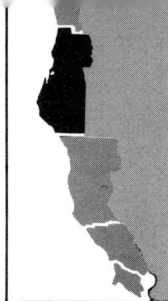

The Gold Coast: Humboldt County

The first settlements on this coast were ports established to supply the camps where gold was mined in remote canyons of the Klamath Mountains. Several years passed before the pioneers turned to logging the "red gold" of the virgin forest which rimmed Humboldt Bay.

The seashore of the Gold Coast extends from the mouth of the Eel River fifty miles northward to Redwood Creek. Humboldt Bay has thirty-five miles of protected shore. At present, most residents of Humboldt County dwell on the river-built plains that rim the bay. The traveler finds a good selection of restaurants, stores, and overnight accommodations at Fortuna, Eureka, and Arcata. There is swimming at Big Lagoon and overnight camping at Patrick's Point State Park.

Eel Delta

The coastal plain of the Eel River Delta invites a full day of road exploring. This bottomland spreads north of Ferndale almost to Humboldt Bay and east to Carlotta, where the Van Duzen River first emerges from its wooded canyon. The delta plain is dotted with dairy farms and laced with winding waterways, such as Hogpen Slough and the Salt River. The largest of the scattered towns are Ferndale, Loleta, Fortuna, and Rohnerville.

Ferndale is less a rural trading center than a sophisticated exurb of Eureka. As one of the best preserved of the pioneer settlements, the town is filled with homes and stores rendered in a modified version of the high Victorian style. Much in evidence are fans, niches, gables, bay windows, cornices, and bracketed eaves replete with elaborate fretwork.

The first settlement here was in 1852. At this time, much of the delta was forested with redwoods. Some trees were said to have stood more than four hundred feet tall. The timber was sufficiently cleared for dairy ranching by the 1870s when farmers from Denmark founded the town. Later came settlers of Portuguese and Italian descent.

Main Street is lined with antique shops and art galleries. Here a week-long arts and crafts show during May is highlighted by a colorful parade of "kinetic sculpture." Off Van Ness Avenue are the Humboldt County Fairgrounds. A rodeo is held here in late July. In August, the fair features thoroughbred racing with parimutuel betting.

The Centerville Road out of Ferndale runs west 4.5

miles to the Centerville County Park. This undeveloped area covers only four acres but provides access to ten miles of ocean beach between False Cape and the lagoon of the Eel River.

Some distance south of the parking area, an historical marker memorializes the wreck of the *Northerner* in the winter of 1860. This Panama Mail Line steamer was weathering a storm en route to the Columbia River when it ran aground on Blunt's Reef. The steamer began to sink the instant it was backed off the reef. With pumps removing twelve thousand gallons of water a minute, Captain W. L. Dall set a course for Humboldt Bay. But the pumps were not equal to their task. As the vessel was about to founder, the captain steered directly for the beach.

Attempts were made to ferry the 108 passengers ashore by lifeboat. The first boat made it through the breakers. The second boat capsized. Some survivors drifted to safety on sections of the deck. Others were landed by means of a line stretched to the beach. Thirty-eight persons were lost.

Driftwood collectors do well on the Centerville Beach and there's good smelt netting here in summer. Surf casting for redtail perch is apt to be most rewarding after New Year's Day through early summer.

From Ferndale, it's a short drive by way of Main Street to the Eel River crossing at Fernbridge, a small hamlet built around a creamery. On the east bank, turn left on Old Highway 101 and proceed two miles north to Loleta, another creamery town.

The lush bottomlands of the delta afford some of the

finest natural pasture in the world. The first California creamery was established here in 1888. Now most milk produced in the delta region is processed into butter and dried milk products. The big urban markets for the more profitable Grade A milk are too remote, but dairying accounts for almost fifty percent of farm income in Humboldt County.

The Copenhagen Road out of Loleta bears north through lush grazing land to approach Table Bluff, a low ridge which divides Humboldt Bay from the delta. At the junction with the Table Bluff Road, turn left and climb the ridge to obtain the first view of the bay.

About fourteen miles long and up to 3.5 miles wide, Humboldt Bay is the only major embayment left on the California Coast with miles of shoreline in their natural state. The bay remains sufficiently free of pollution to permit oyster farming. In 1971, the U.S. Bureau of Sport Fisheries and Wildlife was authorized to acquire

Ferndale abounds with well-preserved examples of East-lake and Victorian Gothic architecture. Built in 1894, this gingerbread mansion was once used as a hospital.

9,350 acres on the bay for creation of the Humboldt Bay National Wildlife Refuge. The new preserve takes in most of the South Bay plus some islands, mudflats, and salt marshes on the North Bay that are feeding areas for ducks and other migratory birds.

Money for acquisition of land in the refuge comes from the Migratory Bird Hunting Stamp Fund, created with the revenue from the sale of "duck stamps." The refuge affords fishing, clamming, and nature study, as well as duck hunting in season. More information on the refuge may be obtained by contacting the manager at Fifth and "H" Streets, P.O. Box 1386, Eureka, California 95501. The phone number is (707) 445-1352.

The Table Bluff Road winds by an Indian settlement and an old light station before it drops down onto the sandy South Spit. At the foot of the bluff, there's an undeveloped county beach known as Clam Park. The best clamming is on the bay side of the spit on tidal flats which yield softshell, littleneck, gaper, and Washington clams. The sticky mud here makes access difficult on foot. The productive clam beds are more easily approached by boat from landings and launching sites on the east shore of the bay.

The crude shelters seen spaced across the flats are used as blinds by duck hunters. Some of the best shooting comes in the season for the maritime goose known as the black brant.

Driftwood abounds on the ocean side of the spit, but the breakers here are almost too rough for fishing. The violence of the surf is explained by the sandy shoals offshore. Collectively, these are spoken of as the Humboldt Bar.

A gravel road runs the length of the spit, three miles to the South Jetty. This road is unsafe for travel in winter. In spring, the sand dunes which crown the spit are aglow with yellow lupines.

When you stand on the jetty to view the slender opening to Humboldt Bay, it may seem credible that this large body of water escaped notice by mariners until the nineteenth century. Jonathan Winship, a captain employed by the Russian-American Fur Company, entered the bay in 1806. Yet, for practical purposes, it remained undiscovered until Josiah Gregg's eight-man party came overland from the Trinity River in the winter of 1849. The goal of the Gregg expedition was to locate the mouth of the Trinity River, which is the largest tributary of the Klamath River. At the time, it was widely supposed that the Trinity came out somewhere on the coast.

Josiah Gregg died on the rugged trek to San Francisco. But soon after the emaciated survivors of his party straggled into town, there was a great rush to

Crabbing

Crabbing with a ring net is largely a matter of luck and patience. Ring nets may be purchased at tackle stores or rented at some boat landings. The nets are constructed so they will lie flush on the ocean bottom but assume the configuration of a basket when raised to the surface. Strips of fish are tied to the netting as bait.

When crabbing from a boat, you may not find a productive spot for hours. Crabs favor a clean sand or gravel bottom in shallow, protected areas of bays and estuaries. Low tide is best and the water should be fairly calm.

Lower the baited net to the bottom with a rope to which a buoy is attached. After waiting ten to fifteen minutes, haul in the ring net as quickly as possible, taking care not to jar the boat in a way that might spook the crabs.

The crabs most sought after by recreationists as well as commercial fishermen are white market crabs, commonly spoken of on the North Coast as Dungeness crabs. This species *(Cancer magister)* has white-tipped claws and is reddish-brown on the back. It ranges to nine inches in width. The open season generally runs from winter through early summer. Angling regulations should be consulted for the exact dates plus size and bag limits. There are limits but no closed season for red rock crabs *(Cancer antennarius)*. The latter are inferior to market crabs in that the edible meat is mostly concentrated in the claws.

The lower estuary of the Eel River in the vicinity of Crab Park probably affords the best inshore crabbing on the North Coast. Humboldt Bay and the shallows around Crescent Harbor are productive. Some crabbing is done from skiffs in sandy bottom areas of Tomales Bay and Drake's Estero.

Crabs may also be taken with ring nets from piers at Trinidad and Crescent Harbor. Accessories for crabbing include a measuring device and sack to creel the catch. To prepare for eating, plunge the live crabs into actively boiling salted water (2 tablespoons of salt for each quart of water). Cover the pot and boil the crabs rapidly for ten minutes and then gently for ten minutes more. Simple ways to serve crab meat are hot with melted butter, cold with mayonaise, or as a seafood cocktail with hot sauce.

---

establish trading posts on "Trinity Bay." Eleven ships and several overland expeditions were hastily outfitted by rival companies who believed the bay had a future as a port for the Northern Mines.

The bay made a satisfactory port except for the treacherous approach across the Humboldt Bar. Scores of ships foundered on the bar in winter storms. Many more came to grief in the pea-soup fogs which frequent this coast in summer. The most spectacular loss occurred in 1917 when a heavy cruiser, the *USS Milwaukee*, flagship of the Pacific Fleet, was sent to salvage a submarine grounded on the North Spit. When the *Milwaukee* attempted to winch the submarine off the spit, it was drawn by its own cable onto the beach. Here it remained until it was dismantled for scrap in World War II.

Captain "Midnight" Olson earned his nickname by crossing the bar on a stormy night when the channel was said to have been twenty feet deep on the crest of the waves and six inches deep in the troughs. The present channel is maintained at a depth of forty-five feet. Where it runs to sea between the North and South Jetties the channel is not safe for small boats on the outgoing tide. Most any day in summer when the tide is right the channel will be dotted with small cruisers and outboard-powered skiffs trolling for salmon. King salmon predominate over silvers in the catch here.

Fishing off the South Jetty is good for a variety of fish, including striped sea perch, kelp greenling, and starry flounder. White market crabs, locally known as Dungeness crabs, are taken with ring nets. Jetty fishing invites the use of lighter tackle than is customarily used for casting off the rocks.

Autos are not permitted, but pedestrians may walk nearly a mile out to sea on the South Jetty.

By returning to Loleta, one can leave Old Highway 101 on the Cannibal Road which runs 4.5 miles west to Mosley Island on the Eel River Lagoon. The road terminates at a county small boat launching area known as Crab Park. The lagoon and estuary afford trolling for king salmon in October and silver salmon in November or early December. Ring nets are used to trap market crabs during the season, normally best from late winter through spring.

Across McNulty Slough from Crab Park is a 168-acre state preserve known as the Eel River Wildlife Area. This consists of a long, slender strip of land which forms the north spit of the Eel River Lagoon. The black-tailed jack rabbit is believed to be the most abundant mammal here. A variety of shore birds and many kinds of ducks, such as pintail, widgeon, and teal, may be observed in the shallows of McNulty Slough. There is shooting for migratory waterfowl in season. Perch and flounder are caught by bank fishermen at Crab Park and dip netters work the ocean side of the wildlife area for surf smelt in summer.

The wildlife area may be approached by boat from Crab Park or on a two-mile hike through the dunes from Table Bluff. Information on the area may be obtained at the branch office of the Fish and Game Department located at 619 Second Street in Eureka.

The Eel River, which drains 3,480 square miles of mountain country, holds some of the choicest steelhead water in the West. Still, old hands may be heard to grumble that the fishing isn't anything like it used to be. State biologists can cite case after case of damage to the feeder streams by logging pollution. A study by the U.S. Geological Survey found that the Eel River Basin probably has "the highest recorded erosion rate in the United States." It was reported that, in the years 1957-67, some 320 million tons of soil and rock were stripped by winter rains from the Eel watershed. This incredible wastage originates on steep slopes of unstable soil where landslides occur as a result of frequent earthquakes, heavy rains, forest fires, overgrazing by sheep, and the construction of myriad logging roads.

The high erosion rate poses a threat not only to fish and wildlife but to the people who live on the river flats and delta plain. As the level of the river bed is raised by deposits of gravel, the area subject to flooding during years of exceptional rainfall becomes larger. In the great flood of 1964, the town of Pepperwood was destroyed and the mill at Scotia lost 23 million board feet of lumber. One farmer on the delta, trapped in his attic for three days, watched forty-five of his cows drown. His brother-in-law lost his house, barn, storm shed, and everything but the front lawn.

The building of giant flood-control dams has been proposed from time to time. It's the opinion of many scientists that these would not significantly ameliorate flooding or in any way compensate for their adverse effects on the native fish and wildlife . Dams would not only deny access of salmon and steelhead to their spawning gravels but inundate the winter graze of deer.

One of the recommendations of the Fish and Game Department following a recent survey of the delta is that federal, state, and local authorities prepare a joint plan to protect the watershed in order to reduce the inflow of sediments into the delta. Rehabilitation of the watershed would, of necessity, be a slow and massive undertaking, but the experts seem hard put to come up with a better solution. Conceivably, such a project could provide employment of the hundreds put out of work by automation and the fast dwindling supply of mature timber.

Despite the abuse to its watershed, the Eel is still a great fishing river. By recent estimate, it yields to anglers approximately 3,000 salmon and 13,000 steelhead each season. Steelhead may enter the Eel as early as July but the peak action occurs in winter beginning in late November. The river from Fernbridge to the mouth is open most of the year to trout fishing. On this stretch are such famous holes as Fulmore, Snag, and Singley Pools. These are mostly worked by skiff fishermen using bait, flashers, or wet streamer flies, such as the Carson, Shrimp, Mickey Finn, and Golden Demon. Upstream from Fernbridge are myriad pools and riffles suitable for wading. Some of the best water is found in the State Redwood Parks on the South Fork of the Eel.

East of Loleta is the interchange for the U.S. 101 freeway. The exit for Fortuna is three miles south. This residential town sprawls at the foot of a timbered slope on the eastern edge of the river plain. It was variously known as Springville, Slide, and Fortune when it was settled in the 1870s. Visitors are welcome to tour a cider works, cheese factory, and plywood plant. There are numerous motels and restaurants.

Right next door to Fortuna is an older settlement known as Rohnerville. It was founded in 1859 by Henry Rohner, a native of Switzerland.

The old Mail Ridge route, mentioned earlier, affords a fascinating drive. Starting from Fortuna, take the Rohnerville Road south to Hydesville. Here turn left on State Highway 36 and follow the Van Duzen River to a junction with the unpaved Alderpoint Road at Bridgeville. The Alderpoint Road links with other back roads to provide a 55-mile drive along the loosely forested crest of Mail Ridge. The drive ends on the Redwood Highway twelve miles north of Laytonville.

On the Van Duzen River is Grizzly Redwoods State Park, with thirty campsites handy to a good swimming hole, and Van Duzen County Park, with swimming, nature trails, and forty campsites. Reservations for Humboldt County Parks may be obtained by calling (707) 445-7553. Bridgeville, Strong's Station, Carlotta and Hydesville are old settlements on the river which hark back to stagecoach days on the Mail Ridge Route.

Of eleven vessels which left San Francisco in the spring of 1850 to pioneer a port for the Northern Mines, the first to sight Humboldt Bay was the schooner *Laura Virginia*, commanded by Douglas Ottinger. It was probably Ottinger who named the bay in honor of the naturalist-explorer Alexander von Humboldt. But when Ottinger's first mate, Hans Henry Buhne, entered the harbor in a small boat, the great race had only begun. There were years of fierce competition between rival ports before the winner was declared.

Driving north on U.S. 101, the first town on the bay is Fields Landing, which didn't appear on the map until the 1890s. The settlement is clustered around the Pacific Lumber Company docks. There's a small boat launching ramp at the foot of Railroad Avenue. The last whaling station on the North Coast operated at Fields Landing until 1951.

Just north of Fields Landing a side road runs to Buhne Point. This drive approaches California's first privately financed atomic power plant. Before the facility was built, Eureka obtained much of its power and light from the *Donbass III*, a salvaged Russian tanker which was towed into the bay and beached in 1946.

After the nuclear plant opened in 1963, it enjoyed

The busy Port of Humboldt is the only harbor of refuge for large deep-draft vessels on the North Coast. Over 450 commercial fishing craft operate from the port.

several years of trouble-free operation. Public tours of the installation were conducted in summer. There was a brief hiatus in 1971 when the Atomic Energy Commission charged the Pacific Gas and Electric Company with violating certain requirements relating to the safety of employees at the Humboldt facility. The company took issue with the charges while it implemented stricter monitoring requirements. Then, in May of 1976, the plant was temporarily forced to suspend power generation because of a water leak in the reactor's purification system.

The spillage was safely contained within the plant. But some weeks later, a geologist petitioned the federal Nuclear Regulatory Commission to close the plant because he had determined it was situated on top of an active earthquake fault. Subsequently the Commission ordered the plant shut down pending an investigation of the safety factor.

On the tip of Buhne Point is a development known as King Salmon. Here are several fishing resorts with trailer space, skiff rentals, and launching facilities. Charter boats and scheduled partyboats operate from here in summer. The partyboats troll a short distance outside the bay for king and silver salmon. Usually, it's no more than a twenty-minute trip to the fishing grounds. Tackle may be rented at the boat landing.

Both king and silver salmon are taken in quantity by sport fishing party boats based in Humboldt Bay. This catch may be identified as a king by its black mouth.

Cannonball sinkers up to 1.5 pounds are used with a device which releases the weight when a salmon strikes the bait. Torpedo sinkers as light as three ounces may suffice in late summer when the salmon begin to bunch up off the river mouths. At this time, the fish are more prone to forage near the surface.

The frontage north of Buhne Point to the Eureka city limit was the site of Humboldt City, the earliest settlement on the bay. It was founded by Douglas Ottinger on April 14, 1850. The town faded quickly because it was located too far south to compete in the trade with the Klamath mines. Ottinger's associate, Hans Henry Buhne, eventually settled on Buhne Point after experience as a miner, merchant, harbor pilot, whaling master, and professional deer hunter. He made his fortune as part owner of the largest sawmill on the bay.

Three miles north of Fields Landing the highway spans the Elk River, named by the Gregg party after it enjoyed a dinner of elk near the stream. Two spurs leading off the Elk River Road span the creek on wooden Howe-Truss covered bridges. Roosevelt elk still roam the wild country at the headwaters.

A mile farther on is the beginning of Eureka on Broadway. This corner of the city was formerly the town of Bucksport. It was founded in the summer of 1850 by David Buck, a survivor of the Gregg expedition. On a bluff overlooking the Bucksport district is the Fort Humboldt State Historical Monument. It is approached from Broadway by way of Highland Avenue. An old commissary building still stands. There's a museum and exhibit of early logging apparatus.

Fort Humboldt was garrisoned from 1853 until 1870 to protect the settlers from the Indians. There were many minor skirmishes here, one of the last taking place at Chalk Mountain near Bridgeville on the Van Duzen River. The fort is chiefly remembered because Ulysses S. Grant was stationed at it. Grant, depressed by his assignment, drank heavily. After six months, he resigned his commission and rejoined his family at St. Louis where he briefly tried his hand at farming.

U.S. 101 follows Broadway through "Motel Row" to approach the waterfront in the northwest corner of the city. At the foot of Commercial Street is a basin where most of Eureka's fleet of 450 commercial fishing boats is based. There's a small boat launching ramp here.

Visitors are welcome to tour the plants of the Coast Oyster Company at the foot of "A" Street and the

*Japanese freighter loads lumber at Samoa Docks of the
Georgia-Pacific Corporation. Near here visitors may dine
family style at the corporation's lumber camp cookhouse.*

Lazio Fish Cannery at the foot of "C" Street. There's
a popular seafood restaurant at Lazio's near the landing
of the old ferry *Madaket*. The *Madaket* makes scheduled thirty-minute tours of Humboldt Bay.

The *Madaket* used to ferry commuters to pulp and
lumber mills on the North Spit of the bay before the
Samoa Bridge was completed in 1971. One leg of the
new span stands on Indian Island, formerly known as
Gunther Island for a settler who diked its banks in
order to grow hay. Hans Henry Buhne built a lumber
mill on Indian Island in 1865. Since then, the island
has reverted to its natural state, almost deserted except
for the herons, egrets, and Western clapper rails which
frequent its marshy shoreline.

Artifacts have been unearthed at the island which
suggest Indian occupation for more than a thousand
years. In 1860, after a party of settlers raided a Wiyot

village here and slaughtered a hundred women and
children, Bret Harte wrote a scathing editorial in the
Arcata newspaper, *The Northern Californian*. Harte
was then a "printer's devil" who had temporarily taken
charge while the editor was absent. For siding with the
Indians, he was hounded out of town.

In 1973, seven Indians who claimed to be descendants of Wiyots killed in the massacre filed suit against
the City of Eureka to regain ownership of Indian
Island. The Far West Indian Historical Association
proposes to build a museum and Indian cultural center
on the 270-acre island. Some civic groups are eager to
develop the isle as a marina, while others prefer to see
it remain in the National Wildlife Refuge.

In 1885, when there were few Indians left, Eureka
citizens found occasion to vent their wrath against the
city's Chinese population. All the Chinese were

The redwood palace built by the lumber baron, William Carson, is widely recognized as the most extraordinary example of Victorian architecture ever seen in the US.

evacuated and their property confiscated following the accidental shooting of a city councilman in a *tong* war.

U.S. 101 North leaves Broadway at Fifth Street to run east through the business district. Here a facade of modern store fronts and new public buildings give Eureka the look it should have as the principal trading center for Humboldt and Del Norte Counties. Until recent years, the shame of the city was a decaying waterfront "skid row" packed with sleazy bars and cheap flophouses. (The term "skid row" is said to have originated on the North Coast: It referred to the shanty towns which sprang up alongside the early skid roads where they terminated at a coastal mill.) Now, due to an ambitious urban renewal program funded in part by the federal Department of Housing and Urban Development (HUD) and a $3 million bond issue, only remnants of the old slum remain. Some of the wooden buildings dating back to the 1880s have been razed, while others have been restored for offices, boutiques, and art galleries. Old Town Square, a new mini-park, has cobblestone walks, old-fashioned light stands, and

a gazebo which serves as a visitor information center during summer.

A Boston contractor named James T. Ryan was the prime mover of the Mendocino Company which founded Eureka in May of 1850. Some accounts have Ryan leaping ashore from a whale boat to shout, "Eureka!"—Greek for "I have found it." Ryan went on to become a wealthy lumberman, state senator, and general of the Northern California militia.

For a time, Eureka lagged behind neighboring Arcata, which was better situated on the trail to the Northern Mines. Eureka was positioned at the head of deep-water navigation on the bay. This advantage proved decisive when lumber exports became more important than trade with the mines. In 1856, the county seat shifted from Arcata to Eureka.

William Carson drifted in from the gold fields and leased a mill on the bay in 1856. Carson was probably the first to fell and saw the redwood giants which shaded Eureka down to the waterfront. "The most photographed house in the nation" is the Carson

Boating Off the Coast

Venturing out on the open sea in an outboard-powered skiff or small cruiser is fraught with hazard on the North Coast. Summer affords the best water conditions, but this is also when fog is most common. Typically, in the early hours of a summer morning the fog is so thick that navigation is impossible without local knowledge and a good compass. By mid-morning the fog will begin to lift, and there may be an hour or two of sunshine before the fog suddenly closes in again. The fog is capricious, but most days you can count on the prevailing northwest wind to whip up a choppy sea in the afternoon.

Smallcraft warnings (for winds to 33 knots) may be on display at marinas and Coast Guard stations for days on end. Winds of hurricane force are not unknown in summer—witness the "freak storm" of August 1972 that caused dozens of boats to be ripped from their moorings at Trinidad and Crescent City. The latter port and Bodega Bay remain accessible and provide good shelter under most sea conditions.

It is impossible for small boats to enter Humboldt Bay on an ebb tide or any time the sea is rough. Breaking waves block the approach to Noyo Harbor during storms and the harbor at Albion may be difficult to enter even when the weather is fair.

Shelter from northwest winds (but no place to land) may be found at such "doghole ports" as Shelter Cove and Fort Ross. Shelter Cove is one of the places where a small party might be seen trolling for salmon in a dinghy-size car-top boat. These are apt to be persons who lack experience or who are bored with life. For inshore fishing, old salts recommend a deep-draft boat no less than sixteen feet in length. Preferably, the boat should be fitted with two motors. Minimum equipment (required by law) includes flotation devices, fire extinguisher, and a whistle audible for at least half a mile. To avoid drifting into the surf in event of a breakdown, it's a good idea to take an anchor with three hundred feet of line.

Special attention is required when passing through the "bar" area of an estuary, bay, or harbor. River and/or tidal currents rushing to sea may collide with wind-driven waves to create a "rip" which is extremely hazardous for small boats. It's best to cross this area on a slack or flood tide. Boats caught outside a harbor when the tide is ebbing are advised to remain at sea until the tide changes. More than a few fishermen have drowned attempting to enter Humboldt Bay at the wrong stage of the tide.

It's never wise to leave a harbor without local advice on the tides and a last-minute check of the weather forecast. Open skiffs are recommended only for fishing inshore within a short distance of a port or landing. Two types of open craft noted for their seaworthiness are the Boston whaler and Oregon surf dory.

For longer excursions in a cabin cruiser, the common occurrence of fog demands a compass, charts, and radar reflector. A marine radio telephone and such electronic positioning equipment as a depth sounder and radio direction finder are highly recommended.

Before an excursion on open sea, it's wise to leave a "float plan" with someone who will notify the authorities if necessary. Printed float plans and several publications relating to the North Coast may be obtained by writing to the California Department of Boating and Waterways. Write to the Department at 1629 S Street, Sacramento, California 95814.

An illustrated handbook packed with information of interest to anyone who goes boating on the North Coast is the Northern California edition of the *Sea Boating Almanac,* edited by Captain William Berssen. This annual includes tide tables, radio, telephone and navigational data, aerial photographs of harbors, the locations of launch ramps, marinas, and repair facilities. Also included are a complete listing of the U.S. Coast Pilot No. 7, updated. This book may be obtained by writing to Sea Boating Almanac, Box Q, Ventura, California 93002. The 1976 softcover edition was priced at $4.95 plus 75 cents for delivery. Be sure to specify you want the *Northern* California edition.

Happy group of sports writers at Buhne Point landing display catch made trolling bait and flashers a short distance outside Humboldt Bay on a day in mid-August.

Mansion, located at the foot of "M" Street. Built in 1884, this three-story palace of redwood displays the ultimate in carpenter's Gothic. It's now a headquarters for the exclusive all-male Ingomar Club, which was recently sued by the state Attorney General's office for discrimination against women guests. The proceedings were occasioned by refusal of the club to permit Ellen Stern Harris of the California Coastal Commission to accompany other members of the agency on a tour of the mansion.

The earliest mill was the little "Taupoos," founded in 1850 by Jim Eddy and Martin White just four months after James Ryan founded the town. In 1852, Ryan went into partnership with James Duff to build a large mill. The machinery they ordered from San Francisco was swept off the deck of the *Santa Clara* in a storm. So Ryan ordered the vessel beached at a place between "D" and "E" Streets. Here the ship's engines were removed and used to power the new mill. The first shipments of lumber from the Ryan and Duff Mill were lost when the brig *Clifford* and the bark *Cornwallis* foundered on the Humboldt Bar.

William Carson suffered reverses before he went into partnership with William Dolbeer, inventor of the donkey engine, which revolutionized logging on the North Coast. The Carson Mansion memorializes the

feudal reign of the lumber barons. Now most of the old firms are gone. They have been replaced by a handful of corporate giants which have their headquarters outside the state. One holdover is the Pacific Lumber Company. This firm traces its beginnings to a small mill built by McPherson and Wetherby on the Albion River in 1869. Now listed on the New York Exchange, the company owns about 25 percent of the old-growth redwood that remains in private hands.

Lumber is still king in Eureka. It generates about 78 percent of local revenues. But there's been a steady decline since production reached an all-time high in 1959. Employment county-wide has dropped from 13,000 to less than 8,000. Lately, people have been laid off because of the slump in home building and a fall-off in exports to Japan. This may be temporary, but the industry faces further retrenchment as the last prime commercial stands of redwood are logged and production becomes dependent on the yield of Douglas fir and inferior second-growth redwood from tree farms.

In a favorable growing area, redwoods may be harvested in as few as forty years for manufacture of such products as pulp, veneer, and particle board. However, scientists estimate it takes five hundred years for redwoods to attain the fine grain and richness of color which make this timber so desirable for fencing, patio furniture, and house siding.

Efforts to lure other industry to Eureka have largely been frustrated by the city's isolation from the major centers of population. The local fisheries generate about $24 million in revenues, but there's not much hope of rapid expansion here or in the dairy industry. So the trend has been to encourage more visitors to come for conventions, sightseeing, and outdoor recreation.

Sequoia Park's forty-six acres, located at "W" and Manzanita Streets in the southeast corner of the city, hold a remnant of the virgin forest that once ringed Humboldt Bay. The park has a small zoo and a duck pond. It is the setting for Peter B. Kyne's novel *Valley of the Giants*, a saga of violence and double dealing in the redwood industry. The novel is based on the conflicts which erupted after rival interests had acquired huge tracts of public land at bargain-basement prices in violation of the Homestead Act of 1862.

A landmark in the city is the Eureka Inn built in the 1920s with a facade of beams and stucco in the Elizabethan style. The Clarke Museum at Third and "E" Streets is filled with Indian artifacts, old guns, antiques, stuffed birds, and other memorabilia of the early days.

Eureka is probably best known outside the Redwood

Log Cabin Living

The current penchant for nostalgia in this nation seems rooted in the tradition that cities are the fount of vice and social inequity, whereas the simple rural life represents the best of America. Yet for many rural youths the cities hold excitement and the promise of economic advancement. This dichotomy is reflected on the North Coast by two conflicting demographic trends, which make it difficult to forecast whether the next census will show a loss or a gain.

One trend finds the sons and daughters of loggers, millhands, and the old ranch families emigrating to the San Francisco Bay Area and other metropolitan regions. But local estimates and motor vehicle registrations suggest the exodus is being offset by a back-to-the-land movement that began in the 1960's.

Through the 1970's a preponderance of the newcomers were young, middle-class persons fleeing affluent suburbia in search of a more satisfying life. The influx included business and professional people endowed with the capital to renovate an aging seaside ranch or transform a Victorian relic into a charming country inn. Many artists and craftspersons were drawn to such picturesque villages as Mendocino City, where galleries and boutiques provided an outlet for their work. And more than a few individuals came to find spiritual fulfillment in a rustic seminary or formal monastic order, such as the Zen Buddhist group that operates an organic farm near Muir Beach.

Removed from the main roads, the most extreme manifestations of the back-to-the-land movement occurred in such raw subdivisions and logged-over lands as those in the rugged backcountry of Cape Mendocino. Here scores of young homesteaders tried to wrest a living from soil considered agriculturally worthless, by applying the principles of organic farming. The farmers included former civil rights activists, anti-war protestors, and one-time hippies who had turned to religious meditation in place of psychedelic "trips." Some were loosely organized in what Thoreau and other early-day advocates of Utopian socialism might have had difficulty recognizing as rural communes. In fact, few of these "new pioneers" professed any formal ideology, although some defended their life-style as a "political statement." Most commune members eschewed social activism for a passive humanism that embraced mysticism, hedonism, and some kind of nature worship or religious fundamentalism.

By conservative estimate, less than 4 percent of the population of the United States earns a living at farming. In 1976 an astute dairy farmer with a hundred head of cattle in the green hills of Marin would have done well to clear $12,000. How then could young novices with just a few cows and chickens and no cash crop hope to support themselves in the hinterland of Cape Mendocino? As it turned out, many couldn't, even with the help of welfare, food stamps, and handouts from their parents.

The homesteaders who managed a tolerable living did so by taking odd jobs, catching fish for the market, or operating a cottage industry. Ironically, the most successful farmers were those who grew "grass" beyond easy reach of the law. By unofficial estimate, the 1980 marijuana crop in Mendocino County was worth more than $100 million, second in value only to the timber harvest.

The back-to-the-land movement has subsided but by no means ended on the North Coast. Now, however, the newcomers tend to be older, with fewer illusions about country living. The Eureka area is popular with retired people. Individuals drawn to the more remote areas include "survivalists" preparing for a day when the economy collapses and the masses run riot in the streets.

In his work *Edges,* author Ray Raphael (who emigrated to the Cape Mendocino area in the 1960's) relates how the homesteaders drew fire from county officials because their rustic cabins did not conform to local building codes. The issue has abated somewhat since the state provided new guidelines for self-built rural housing. But this is just one of many problems a prospective homesteader may anticipate on the North Coast.

Most of the pitfalls are listed in *Finding and Buying Your Place in the Country,* by Les Schur, an attorney who owns 80 acres near Garberville. Another guide is *The Complete Handbook of Homesteading,* by David Robinson, who remarks in the opening chapter that "Country life *can* be idyllic, of course, but it can also be depressing, exhausting, and boring. Whatever it is, life in the country is rarely what it seems from a city standpoint."

Empire as the "coolest city in the nation." This tag only applies in summer; the average temperatures in July are 52 degrees minimum and 60.7 degrees maximum. In January, the range is 41.1 minimum and 53.6 maximum. Average rainfall is 38.43 inches. It's a rare day in summer when the coastal fog lifts to provide an hour or two of sunshine.

To approach the new Samoa Bridge, turn north off U.S. 101 on "R" Street. Across the bay, the Samoa Road runs south along the flat, sandy North Spit to Samoa, an old company town. Here sprawls a vast complex of veneer, saw, and planing mills which adjoin the docks and lumber yards of the Georgia-Pacific Corporation. The corporation's Samoa Cookhouse is open to the public. Samoa was founded by John Vance, who built a mill and steamer landing here in the 1890s. The name Samoa was inspired by the resemblance of Humboldt Bay to the harbor at Pago Pago.

Farther down the road is Fairhaven, where Hans Bendixsen started a shipyard in 1865. More than a hundred vessels were launched here, including barks, barkentines, and many steam schooners. At present, Fairhaven is occupied by the towering pulp mills of the Louisiana-Pacific and Crown Simpson companies. Some of the larger pulp and saw mills in the area provide guided tours in summer. Information on these may be obtained from the Greater Eureka Chamber of Commerce located at 2112 Broadway in Eureka, (707) 442-3738.

Beyond Fairhaven is a county fishing access with parking, rest rooms, and launching ramps. The tip of the peninsula is occupied by the U.S. Coast Guard and the Eureka City Airport.

North of Eureka on the Samoa Road is Arcata, known as Uniontown when it was founded on April 17, 1850. The business district is centered on "The Plaza," where pack trains assembled to load supplies for the gold mines. L. K. Wood, who logged the hardships suffered by the Gregg expedition, headed the thirty-man group which settled the town.

Arcata's pride is Humboldt State University, perched on the steep slopes of a timbered ridge known as Fickle Hill. Some of the nation's first pollution bioanalysts were educated here. The university has degree programs in nursing and chemistry but the major emphasis is on fisheries, forestry, and oceanography. Adjoining the university is the 600-acre Community Forest, laced with foot trails built by students. This preserve and a twenty-acre enclave known as Redwood Park are approached on Park Drive.

The university operates an experimental fish hatchery where the public is invited. Currently students are attempting to establish a run of silver salmon in Jolly Giant Creek from fish reared in recycled waste water. Another project involves rearing of trout and salmon in salt and brackish water. Such applied research contributes to the state Fish and Game Department's program to upgrade runs of salmon for the benefit of both sport and commercial fishermen.

On the Arcata Bottoms west of town, the Mad River Slough affords duck hunting in season. The fishing access and beach at Mad River County Park may be approached from "K" Street by way of the Alliance Road. Turn left when you come to Spear Avenue and left again on the Upper Bay Road which connects with the Mad River Road. Smelt netting is often good at the beach.

The Mad River owes its name to an argument which broke out when the Gregg expedition forded the stream. Josiah Gregg wanted to stop for an instrument reading while others in the party were anxious to push ahead.

Steelhead and king salmon migrate up the Mad River after winter rains open the sand bar at the mouth. There's good summer trout fishing upstream off State Highway 36 and at Ruth Lake. A new state hatchery near the town of Blue Lake rears thousands of salmon and steelhead. This production is augmented by the rearing ponds of the Humboldt Fish Action Council, a private organization supported by local civic, fraternal, and business groups.

The lumber mills and other industries on the North Spit are served by the Northwestern Pacific Railroad, which runs south by way of the Eel River Valley to the San Francisco Bay Area. At Arcata, the line is joined by the tracks of the Arcata and Mad River Railroad. This is the oldest operating railway on the coast. It was founded in 1854 as the Union Wharf and Plank Company. The first rolling stock consisted of a four-wheel cart drawn by an old horse known as "Spanking Fury." The cart ran on wooden rails from Arcata to the waterfront. The name of the line was changed in 1881 a few years after it was extended along the Mad River with narrow-gauge steel rails. Affectionately known as the "Annie and Mary Railroad," the company operates a steam-powered excursion ride each summer on the first Sunday in August.

On State Highway 299, two miles east of the U.S. 101 interchange, is an exit to State Highway 200 (North Bank Road), which approaches Azalea State Reserve. This thirty-acre natural area has picnic tables and a mile and a half of self-guiding nature trails. May is the best time to see the azaleas in flower.

Trinidad

On the drive from Arcata to Trinidad and northward to Big Lagoon Park, the Redwood Highway rarely strays far from the ocean or ventures close to any significant stand of redwoods. There are some stretches of new freeway which avoid the immediate shoreline. But where these occur, the old by-passed sections of U.S. 101 afford scenic side trips, free from the press of traffic.

After crossing the Mad River, the freeway slices through McKinleyville. During the 1950s, this residential community prided itself as the "fastest growing town on the Coast." In a decade, the population zoomed from 200 to 5,000 but has since declined to 2,000.

Twelve miles north of Arcata is the exit to Clam Beach County Park and neighboring Little River State

Beach. These undeveloped beaches afford fair digging for razor clams (*Siliqua patula*). However, the competition is keen when thousands of clam enthusiasts gather here on a minus tide in spring. The shovel recommended for razor clams is known as a "clam gun" in the Pacific Northwest. It has a long, thin blade, tilted at a 20 degree angle. Fish and Game regulations should be consulted for bag limits and special closures.

A slender, oval-shaped clam with a thin shell, the razor clam prefers beaches with fine sand. It's an elusive mollusk. You must dig rapidly because it takes only seconds for a razor clam to put itself out of reach.

Middle Clam Beach Lagoon contains cutthroat trout which seem to bite best in early spring.

Little River State Beach includes a half-mile of

Hunting agates on the beach north of Patrick's Point State Park. New rules ban rockhounding in many parks and limit the amount of driftwood that may be taken.

*Pleasure craft crowd Trinidad Harbor. The facilities
here include a fuel dock, restaurant and small marine
railway. Salmon partyboats operate daily in summer.*

Tide Pools

A superabundance of food and dissolved oxygen account for the immense variety of marine life normally found in tide pools. Along with clams, mussels, barnacles, crabs, the list includes starfish, periwinkles, sea urchins, sand dollars, jellyfish, sea lettuce, sponges, squids, sea anemones, and small octopi.

Tide pools used to be meccas for shell collectors as well as students of biology. However, during the 1960s, state biologists found the more accessible tide pool areas "were in danger of being studied to death." A Fish and Game warden reported that on one day he had seen thirty busloads of school children gathering specimens at the Duxbury Reef area near Bolinas.

After serious depletion by collectors, it may take from five to ten years for a tide pool to recover its normal quotient of marine life. Therefore California now forbids the taking of specimens other than game fish and certain tidal invertebrates listed in the sport-fishing regulations. The restriction applies from the high-tide mark to one thousand feet below the mean low-tide mark. The idea is that "tidepooling" should be approached as a purely visual experience.

This experience can be more rewarding if you take along a skin diver's face mask or box with a plastic window which allows a glare-free view of the life underwater. Any rocks turned over should be carefully replaced to avoid exposing fragile organisms to predators. A handy field guide is *Exploring Pacific Coast Tide Pools*, by Ernest Braun and Vinson Brown. The larger, more comprehensive *Between Pacific Tides*, by Edward Ricketts, Jack Calvin and Joel Hedgpeth is a classic in its field.

---

frontage on the estuary of Little River. The estuary marks the spot where the Gregg party first arrived on the coast after an arduous journey from Rich Bar on the Trinity River. North of Little River is Moonstone Beach where the frontage is private. Beyond Moonstone, the coast turns rocky and precipitous.

Across the Little River Bridge, take the Westhaven Drive exit and turn west to approach an old by-passed section of U.S. 101 which winds along the edge of sea cliffs to Trinidad. On this drive is Luffenholtz County Beach, an immensely scenic shore famed for its smelt runs and rocky tide pools.

At Trinidad, turn left on Main Street to approach the center of town, which includes a garage, market, and restaurant. The village (population 300) sits on a high bluff overlooking a small but spectacular harbor which is packed with sport and commercial fishing boats in summer. Linked to the bluff by a low neck of sand is the dome-like rock known as Trinidad Head. It rises 362 feet above the water.

Sebastian Cermeno sighted Trinidad Head in 1595, but didn't come ashore for fear of the rocks which infest the harbor. On June 9, 1775, Don Bruno de Heceta and Juan de la Bodega climbed to the top of the Head to erect a wooden cross on Trinity Sunday. Settlement came in May of 1850 when two of the eleven ships which came north from San Francisco following Gregg's discovery of Humboldt Bay elected to settle Trinidad as a port.

Trinidad was well situated for trade with the mines. For a year or so it was competitive with the towns on Humboldt Bay. Some estimates place the peak population at 3,000. People began leaving Trinidad after the shift was made to lumbering. The lack of a safe deep-water anchorage was chiefly to blame. The port enjoys no protection from winter storms which blow in from the southwest.

Incorporated in 1852, Trinidad is officially recognized as the oldest town on the North Coast. For some years, it was an important whaling station.

On the north side of the village is Trinidad State Beach. There's a picnic area and small beach which affords good fishing for perch and rockfish. Just a few yards offshore is picturesque Pewetole Island.

Humboldt State University has a marine laboratory in town that's open to the public. The aquarium here features exhibits of rockfish and the life in tide pools.

Edwards Street leads down to a pier and resort at the foot of Trinidad Head. The facilities here include a restaurant, skiff rentals, and a tramway for launching small boats. Commercial boats discharge fish at the pier in summer. There's a landing used by scheduled partyboats which troll for salmon just a few hundred yards outside the harbor.

Silvers predominate over king salmon in the local catch. When the salmon are scarce, the boats turn to drift fishing for black rock cod, lingcod, and other bottomfish. Anglers casting from the pier take cabezon, striped sea perch, and kelp greenling.

A steep, unpaved spur off the Harbor Road climbs to an automated light on Trinidad Head. The original light tower, built in 1871, was relocated to the village where it serves as a memorial to fishermen lost at sea.

Every spring, usually on a Sunday in late May or June, the Trinidad Chamber of Commerce sponsors a crab feed at the town hall on Trinity Street. Purchase of a modestly priced ticket entitles you to all the crab you can eat.

Returning to old U.S. 101 (not the freeway), it's six miles north to the state preserve at Patrick's Point. Several motels and rustic resorts are located on this drive.

Patrick's Point State Park takes in 425 acres of forest and meadow on a steepsided peninsula which was homesteaded by Patrick Begen in 1851. The "big trees" here, with trunks to ten feet in diameter, are Sitka spruce. A few Port Orford cedar are found. Winter rainfall in the neighborhood of sixty inches accounts for the extremely lush undergrowth of huckleberry, azalea, rhododendron, and other shrubs.

More than one hundred campsites are located in groves of red alders and shore pines. There's a small

Skin divers prepare to go spear fishing for rockfish and lingcod off Trinidad Head. In season, there is fair-to-middling abalone picking in the harbor area.

museum with Indian artifacts in the park. According to Yurok mythology, the spirit of the porpoises retired to Patrick's Point, known as Sumig, when the world was about to become populated with humans.

The "Ceremonial Rock" rises in the forest off the drive to the Agate Beach parking area. The summit is approached on eighty-eight stone steps. On a clear day, it affords a view of the coast from Cape Mendocino to the mouth of the Klamath River.

Patrick's Point has an elaborate trail system. The longest hike is on the Rim Trail which tunnels through dense undergrowth along the edge of the bluffs. Several spur trails lead down to rocky outcroppings which are productive spots for fishermen.

The most ambitious spur switchbacks to Agate Beach. This lovely sweep of dark sand stretches north to provide a surf-side approach to the parks at Big Lagoon. Agates are plentiful at Agate Beach. The best prospecting is along the edge of the surf on patches of coarse sand or gravel. The stones are not hard to recognize when wet, being a variety of quartz that is translucent or nearly transparent. Pieces of jade, jaspar, and other gem material occasionally turn up. The beach also yields some fine pieces of driftwood.

When you return to the U.S. 101 freeway from Patrick's Point, there follow nine miles of low brushy seaboard filled with shallow coastal lagoons. These are freshwater lakes which evolved over the centuries from saltwater bays similar to Humboldt Bay. They are diked from the sea by slender reefs of sand built up as a result of wave action and the drift of ocean currents. During winter storms, the lagoons are prone to overflow into the ocean. At such times, the lakes become stocked with a variety of fish, including surfperch, flounder, salmon, steelhead, and cutthroat trout. Angling is apt to be slow except for brief periods in the spring and fall.

About two miles north of Patrick's Park, a road leads off to Big Lagoon, which is nineteen feet deep, four miles long, and covers two thousand acres. Big Lagoon County Park is at the south end of the lake. Improvements include a picnic area, boat launching facility, and a safe swimming beach. The lagoon tends to fill with aquatic growth in summer. The coastal fog keeps water temperatures on the cool side. Fishing for steelhead and cutthroat is usually best at the extreme north end of the lake. There is shooting in season for black brant and other water fowl.

Due east of the county park across the Redwood Highway on Maple Creek is the Big Lagoon Camp of the Georgia-Pacific Corporation. During deer season, nimrods may obtain permits from the company office

This beacon for mariners is perched 196 feet above the sea on Trinidad Head. It replaces a light moved to the village to serve as a memorial to sailors lost at sea.

here to hunt in the hilly timberland which overlooks the lagoon area.

The low spit of sand which forms the west bank of Big Lagoon is part of Dry Lagoon State Park. This 927-acre preserve stretches north to the shores of Stone Lagoon. On Big Lagoon, the state beach duplicates the facilities of the county park. There is no camping here. Agates, driftwood, and perch fishing are main attractions on the ocean side of the spit.

Dry Lagoon is a small marshy basin crowded between Big and Stone Lagoons. Stone Lagoon is fifteen feet deep and covers 521 acres. Rainbow trout are most numerous in the lake.

From Stone Lagoon, the main highway veers across the Gyon bluffs to enter the Redwood National Park on a slender sand spit that dikes Freshwater Lagoon. This lake is less prone to spill its banks than Stone Lagoon. It is reported to contain rainbow, cutthroat, and Eastern brook trout.

The east shores of Big, Stone, and Freshwater Lagoons lie within The Three Lagoons Recreation Area of the Georgia-Pacific Corporation. It's open to the public for boating, swimming, and fishing. Just north of Freshwater Lagoon, the Redwood Highway bends inland to approach the village of Orick. Redwood National Park has an information center here.

Roosevelt elk are often seen at Prairie Creek State Park grazing on the "prairie" near park headquarters and in the meadows along the foot of the Gold Bluffs.

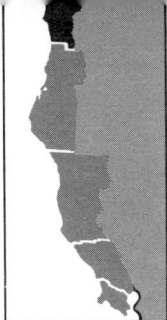

The Redwood Coast:
Humboldt and Del Norte Counties

This remarkable coast takes in seventy-five miles of seashore, of which more than thirty miles are fronted by the Redwood National Park, established October 2, 1968.

The new park amounts to a slender corridor of forest which links several state parks with a large block of forest on Redwood and Lost Man Creeks east of Orick. Presently, the state parks provide most of the developed trails, overnight camps, and other recreational facilities. The national park is not expected to function as a single administrative until such time as California and the federal government effect a land exchange. This is not likely to happen any time soon.

The Redwood Coast is blessed with two great angling waters—the Smith and Klamath rivers. On the lower estuaries of these streams and at Crescent City, the traveler will find an abundance of overnight accommodations.

Prairie Creek State Park

Until recently, the Redwood Highway faced the prospect of becoming a modern freeway where it rolls through Prairie Creek State Park. Many people were unhappy about this because they believed a freeway would destroy the park. Freeway construction in the Humboldt redwoods south of Eureka resulted in the removal of hundreds of trees, including redwoods over a thousand years old. The massive cuts and fills disrupted the natural pattern of drainage in a way that threatens the health of the big trees which line the Avenue of the Giants—a by-passed section of old U.S. 101 which winds through some of the most impressive redwood groves on the Eel River. Nowhere on this lovely drive is it possible to escape the sound of freeway traffic.

The U.S. 101 freeway was planned to pass through a number of the state-owned redwood parks because they provided the cheapest, most direct routing. Only a concerted stand by the Sierra Club, Save-the-Redwoods League, and other groups achieved a temporary moratorium on building a freeway through Prairie Creek State Park. Finally, the California Division of Highways agreed to reroute the proposed freeway so it would skirt the east boundary of the park.

Encompassing sixteen square miles of virgin forest, Prairie Creek is the crowning gem of the state preserves north of Eureka. Here the redwood giants march down to a spectacular seashore where Roosevelt elk roam. The dense summer fogs and up to one hundred inches of winter rain support a ground cover which approaches the lushness of the Olympic Rain Forest. The undergrowth includes a huge diversity of mosses, lichens, liverworts, ferns, and shrubs. Botanists have catalogued five hundred kinds of mushrooms and eight hundred varieties of flowers. Competing with the redwoods for space are lowland firs, Douglas firs, western hemlocks, and Sitka spruce.

Park headquarters and over one hundred campsites are located off U.S. 101 bordering a large meadow known as "The Prairie." Most of the park is primitive, in no way altered except for a network of trails with a combined length of forty-one miles. Aside from the Redwood Highway, there are two park drives. The East Ridge Road skirts the east boundary of the park. The Davidson-Ossagon Roads afford access to Gold Beach.

The park grew to its present size of 13,000 acres chiefly through contributions of land by the Save-the-Redwoods League. In 1980 the League pledged a million dollars to match state funds toward the purchase of Big Lagoon and adjoining redwoods from the Louisiana-Pacific Corporation. All donations to the Redwood Purchase Fund are tax-deductible and may be sent to the Save-the-Redwoods League, 114 Sansome Street, San Francisco, California 94104.

Approaching Prairie Creek on U.S. 101 from Freshwater Lagoon, one enters the valley of Redwood Creek. Here the scars left by logging are clearly

This is not the most efficient way to dig for razor clams but these youngsters are enjoying some success at Gold Beach. A long-bladed shovel is recommended.

evident on the hillsides. The next town is Orick, a small lumbering and ranching center which hopes to find prosperity as the "Southern Gateway" to the Redwood National Park. The town has motels, restaurants, and a trailer park.

A short way north of town, the Bald Hills Road heads east to wind twenty-three miles across rugged mountains to Martin's Ferry on the Klamath River. One-half mile up the road is the turnoff to the Redwood Creek Trail. This footpath runs 8.5 miles to a redwood grove where the world's tallest tree towers 367.8 feet. Primitive campsites for backpackers are situated within a mile of the grove.

Another 1.5 miles up the Bald Hills Road is the Lady Bird Johnson grove of redwoods, where there's a picnic ground and self-guiding nature trail. Logging trucks use the Bald Hills Road, which is almost too steep and rough for trailers.

The primeval forest on Redwood Creek and neighboring Lost Man Creek comprises the largest stand of virgin redwoods in the new Redwood National Park that did not previously enjoy the protection of a state park. The area is roadless except for a few dim spurs.

Information on access may be obtained at the park office in Orick.

Returning to the Redwood Highway, it's 1.5 miles from the Bald Hills junction to the Davidson Road, which runs four miles west to Gold Beach. A mile farther is the Humboldt County Fish Hatchery where visitors are welcome. From here, it's three miles to the headquarters and main campground of Prairie Creek State Park. If you're hauling a trailer, this is a good place to leave it while you visit Gold Beach.

The Davidson Road is a narrow, winding gravel drive which is subject to temporary closures in wet weather. It marks a boundary between the National Park and several huge tracts of privately owned redwoods in the Skunk Cabbage Creek watershed that are being logged at the rate of a thousand or more acres each year.

At one point on the drive, on the park side of the road, there is an ugly, bleak expanse of ragged ridges littered with burned stumps and a maze of skid roads. This area was clear cut by the Arcata Redwood Company before the Redwood Park was created in 1968. After logging, the company seeded the devastated acres and called them a "tree farm."

Most redwood tree farms on the North Coast are cut selectively in a way that minimizes damage to watershed and allows for "multiple use." Conservationists charged that Arcata Redwood elected to clear cut as part of a strategy aimed to defeat the campaign for a National Park. However, the company defended its action on the principle that, by removing all trees and competitive ground cover, the seedlings for a new forest would grow at a faster rate. Experiments suggest that, in some areas, this method achieves a superior yield of second-growth timber. The main argument against clear cutting is the terrible harm it does to the watershed. The total absence of ground cover, even though temporary, triggers landslides and otherwise accelerates the process of erosion.

The Davidson Road comes out on the seashore near a small lagoon. From here it's possible to hike south down the beach to the mouth of Redwood Creek. The beach road runs north through dunes and meadows in the shadow of the Gold Bluffs. These heights are crowned with magnificent firs and redwoods.

From the lagoon, it's 1.5 miles to the Gold Bluffs Picnic Area inside the boundaries of Prairie Creek State Park. One-half mile farther on is a new 25-site campground bordering the beach at Squashan Creek. The more exposed sites are sheltered from the sea breezes by improvised windbreaks of driftwood. There are benches, tables, piped water, fireplaces, and wash rooms.

The traveler is likely to see elk grazing alongside the

beach on the 1.5-mile drive from camp to Fern Canyon. Park rangers advise against approaching these animals too closely. The elk are in no way domesticated and roam the park at will. The original range of the Roosevelt, or Wapiti, elk was from British Columbia to San Francisco Bay. The bulls grow an imposing set of antlers and may attain weights in excess of seven hundred pounds. During the autumn rutting season, they are prone to lock horns in combat. The Prairie Creek elk herds number about four hundred. Elsewhere on the coast, there are herds on the upper reaches of Elk River and Little River and in Bear Valley of Del Norte County.

Over the centuries, Fern Canyon was cut through the Gold Bluffs by water erosion from Home Creek. The beach road affords access to this famed beauty spot.

A signed trail follows Home Creek into Fern Canyon. Although there are many beautiful "Fern Canyons" on the North Coast, this one is probably the most spectacular. The canyon walls are not high but they are sheer and completely covered with ferns. These include lady, sword, deer, chain, bracken, and five-fingered ferns, and the licorice ferns which were used by the early settlers to flavor tobacco.

The white pebbly floor of the canyon affords an easy walk. Here and there, the moss-covered trunk of a fallen giant leans across the creek. One-half mile from the road, the trail climbs out of the canyon to link with the James Irvine Trail. This popular footpath runs four

Battle for a Redwood National Park

The Gold Rush was hardly over before a movement began to save the redwoods of the Sierra *(Sequoiadendron giganteum)*. Some groves were set aside for posterity as early as 1864. But no stands of the Coast redwoods *(Sequoia sempervirens)* were given protection until 1902, when the Big Basin preserve was created in Santa Cruz County. By then, logging had become the most important industry in the state. Redwood was in huge demand for railway ties and telegraph poles, as well as boxes, bridges, buildings, and many other uses. The virgin forest for which the lumber barons paid a few dollars an acre was no longer cheap.

Numerous proposals for a Redwood National Park were gathering dust when several prominent scholars formed the Save-the-Redwoods League in 1918. This group had a new idea. Instead of lobbying Congress or tangling with the lumber barons, the League proposed to buy land for a national park (or its equivalent) with funds donated by the public.

The League found that buying a single redwood grove took a lot of nickels and dimes. Nevertheless, sufficient acreage was obtained by 1927 to require California to establish a parks system. Previously, the League's acquisitions had been managed by the Division of Forestry.

The Save-the-Redwoods League might have accumulated enough forest for a national park before 1960 if it had not been for World War II and the housing boom that followed. The League's acquisition program was helped enormously through contributions of land by the Georgia-Pacific Corporation, the Pacific Lumber Company, and other timber firms. But such was the pace of logging in the 1950s that the prospect for a national park seemed bleak without intervention by Congress.

A strong outcry from the public was needed to persuade Washington to act. The occasion for this came in 1964 when an expedition of the National Geographic Society exploring Redwood Creek discovered that the world's tallest tree lay in the path of a logging operation. About this time, the Sierra Club mounted a massive drive to create a redwood park of 90,000 acres.

The redwood industry responded with a campaign directed against establishment of a federal redwoods preserve of any size. The industry claimed that no amount of old-growth redwoods could be spared for a park without harm to the local economy. All the prime stands were needed to keep the mills going until tree farms could support operations on a "sustained yield" basis. Pro-park groups called this argument hogwash. They noted that few of the companies had shown much interest in tree farms before the campaign for a federal preserve had gathered momentum. It was charged that the redwoods were being cut at a rate 2.5 times that of renewal. The Sierra Club pointed out that a park of 90,000 acres would encompass less than 1.5 percent of the original forest.

Some residents of the North Coast opposed a

---

miles through the forest to park headquarters off the Redwood Highway.

The beach road fords a broad shallow crossing on Home Creek. From the creek, it's hardly a mile to Gold Dust Falls, a slender cascade which drops a hundred feet down the bluff. Three miles farther is Ossagon Creek. The road ends here. A short distance north of Ossagon Creek the shoreline becomes rocky and precipitous.

Gold Beach stretches eleven miles. Surf smelt, redtail perch, and driftwood are its main attractions. The dunes fronting the beach are carpeted with wild strawberries. Five miles offshore is Redding Rock, site of an abandoned lighthouse.

In 1851 a tent city sprang up on this lonely shore. The occasion was the discovery of gold by five prospectors who wandered down from the Klamath River in the Spring of national park on the grounds that it might reduce the revenue from property taxes. Yet the then current method of taxation was self-defeating in that it was partly to blame for the accelerated cutting of old-growth timber. Standing timber was taxed annually. But after it was harvested, the landowner was entitled to as much as forty years of tax relief. This encouraged the owners to cut their timber every thirty-nine years—long before the forest reached maximum productivity.

In 1976, the law was changed so that henceforth timber will not be taxed until it is cut. In addition, the new law provides for tax assessment of timberland on the basis of its use for growing trees—not for its potential as a recreational subdivision or other purposes.

As it was created by Congress in 1968, the 56,000-acre Redwood National Park represented a partial victory for the redwood industry. The park removed only 10,876 acres of old-growth redwoods from private holdings. About half the park consisted of state parks that had been in existence for many years. Perhaps the best thing that could be said about the new preserve was that it gave federal protection to over thirty miles of lovely seashore.

The largest acquisition was a tract of forest on the lower reaches of Redwood Creek where the world's tallest trees grow. Unhappily, these ancients were threatened by clear-cutting just outside the park on the upper watershed of Redwood Creek. Authorities such as Edward C. Stones, professor of forestry at the University of California, warned that these operations might trigger landslides into the creek and that water-borne logging debris might cause the stream banks to erode and thereby topple many park redwoods.

The legislation that created the Redwood Park authorized the Secretary of Interior to increase the size of the park if it was deemed necessary to protect the trees. But, despite urgent appeals and court action by conservationists, Washington was slow to act. Finally in 1978 Congress expanded the park by 48,000 acres and provided $40 million for retraining and income support of loggers whose jobs were ended by the designation of the park. A 30,000-acre "protection zone" was established on the upper watershed of Redwood Creek, and $33 million was authorized for rehabilitating the cutover lands.

The pun is lamentable, but it may seem that everyone concerned with the redwoods has some kind of "axe to grind." Use of lands is still an emotionally charged issue, which the traveler may find confusing to unravel. Some books that may be helpful include *Adventures in the Redwoods* by Harriett E. Weaver, the state's first woman park ranger. More specifically related to the North Coast is the beautifully illustrated Sierra Club publication *The Last Redwoods and the Parkland of Redwood Creek*. The logging industry explains its stand in a number of brochures and booklets. Some of these may be obtained by writing the California Redwood Association, 617 Montgomery Street, San Francisco, California 94111.

1850. A California Division of Mines publication describes how the gold was obtained:

The success of the operation was dependent on what was known as a "panning sea." Waves of a certain size and kind excavated natural riffles in the sand of the beach and gold concentrated in these. After the tide had receded, pack mules were taken to the beach, and the sand was packed in sacks. The gold was very finely divided and was recovered by means of the Oregon tom, ordinary tom, and amalgamating plates. Many thousands of dollars of gold was produced in this way; but the gold is no longer concentrated to the same extent. Perhaps the off-shore deposit that was feeding the beach has been exhausted.

Mouth of the Klamath River as seen from high point on the Klamath Beach Road. Seashore on both sides of the river is administered by the Redwood National Park.

The Klamath River

A long time ago, Wah-Pec-oo-May-ow, the Great Spirit, told the other spirits he was ready to shape the world. He would put people on it and provide water, rocks, trees, fish, and animals. The spirits were free to choose what they wanted to be. The spirit Oregos was friendly to people, so he became a high rock at the mouth of the Klamath River. It was the function of Oregos to tell the fish when they should enter the river and what route they should follow on their upstream migration. The fish did not always obey Oregos in every particular, but mainly they followed his direction. And so, each year in the period from February through April, the little smelt known as candlefish would swarm up the Klamath estuary. These fish contained so much oil that the Yurok people found they could use them as candles.

The sea-run cutthroat trout was loath to take orders. But usually he was present in May when the giant sturgeon was spawning in the estuary. The first runs of *napooie*, or king salmon, would arrive in July. The steelhead would begin to show in August, followed by the silver salmon in September. When none of these fish were present, the Yuroks could turn to the ocean for seaweed, crabs, mussels, razor clams, redtail perch, starry flounder, and a variety of rockfishes.

This abundance enabled the Yuroks to achieve a civilization that was remarkable for a Stone Age people. They built sturdy houses of redwood and sea-going canoes with sails. The leaders accumulated land, slaves, and other wealth. They used a thirteen-month calendar and a monetary system based on the tooth-shaped shells of a mollusk known as the dentalium. The shells originated from a particular area of Puget Sound and were acquired from other Indians through trade.

There were no tribes or clans in a formal sense. There were only families grouped in villages where leadership was provided by the wealthiest men. The slaves were poor Indians unable or unwilling to pay their debts. The Yuroks had an elaborate system of claims and compensation which covered marriages, births, and deaths, as well as injury to life or property. Wars amounted to occasional feuds between families, or villages. Illnesses were treated by women known as shamans.

Probably the first contact with the *waugie*, or white man, was in 1828 when Jedediah Strong Smith's ailing expedition camped near the mouth of the Klamath. The Yuroks provided food and other assistance. But all semblance of friendship ended shortly after five prospectors hiked down the coast from Point St. George to explore the river. This happened in 1850. In the same year, the Klamath was overrun by hordes of gold-crazed Forty-Niners who burned several villages, hunted the Indians for sport, and tore up the river bed in a way that halted the runs of fish.

Klamath City sprang up near the river mouth in 1851. The stores and dwellings were grouped around an iron house which served as a refuge when there was trouble with the Indians. The settlement lasted only a year because gold was scarce on the lower river and ships had difficulty navigating the slender entrance to the lagoon. Later, with the advent of the steam schooner, the old Indian village of Requa was developed as a lumber port.

Until 1963, logs were floated out of the Klamath back country in huge rafts guided by tug boats. Now the virgin forest is gone, but logging by fifty or so small contractors supports a mill of the Simpson Timber Company.

Despite hard use by the miners and loggers, the Klamath River survives as one of the great angling waters of the world. It is California's second largest river, 263 miles long and draining an area of 8,000 square miles. The source is Upper Klamath Lake in south central Oregon. Near the California-Oregon line, the stream is impounded by several power dams. But from Iron Gate Reservoir 188 miles to the mouth, there are no barriers to interfere with the runs of steelhead and salmon.

Of two hundred tributaries, the Salmon, Scott, and Trinity Rivers are the largest. These streams and 133 miles of the main river wind through beautiful canyons in the Klamath, Six Rivers, and Shasta-Trinity National Forests. They are closely followed by roads which afford access to hundreds of pools and riffles.

Commercial fishing was outlawed on the Klamath in 1934. But the Indians still work tribal salmon holes, employing the same style of net used by their ancestors for centuries. And from mid-summer through autumn, sport fishermen gather by the thousands on the lower river and lagoon. An estimated one-fourth of the turn-out are women.

Catering to the anglers are the villages of Requa, Camp Klamath, and Klamath Glen and resorts off the Klamath Beach Road. Every facility is to be found here including campgrounds, trailer parks, motels, lodges, restaurants, bait stores, smoke houses, freezing

Logging contests are a feature of the annual Salmon Festival. Following the axe throwing contest, woodsmen vie to saw a prime redwood log in record time.

plants, custom canneries, guide service, skiff rentals, and small boat launching ramps.

Several jet boats based on the lagoon feature scenic cruises on the river. One boat makes a daily run in summer thirty-two miles upstream to China Creek, with a stopover for lunch at Pecwan in the Hoopa Valley Indian Reservation.

If you're in a hurry to wet a line in the Klamath, the most direct approach from Prairie Creek State Park is by way of the U.S. 101 freeway, which resumes on the north boundary of the park.

The by-passed section of U.S. 101, known as the Alder Camp Road, affords a more interesting drive. It leaves the main highway just inside the park to skirt the edge of redwood-forested bluffs which crest five hundred feet above the sea. About three miles from the park, the road passes within sight of a leaning promontory known as Split Rock. According to Yurok mythology, the great fracture which divides the rock was caused when an Indian anchored his net there and the Spirit of the West Wind filled it with an enormous catch of salmon.

The drive links with the scenic Klamath Beach Road, which is too steep and rough for trailers. This road curves around Flint Ridge overlooking the great gorge where the Klamath River meets the Pacific.

A spur off the Klamath Beach Road leads down to the sand spit which encloses the lagoon. Here the excitement is huge after the salmon runs begin in mid-July. Spin fishermen stand shoulder-to-shoulder on the spit casting spoons, spinners, and bait. Just out of range are the skiff fishermen who troll or "anchor fish" in a manner that permits the current to give action to a fresh anchovy bait. Occasionally, there are scenes of

After years of neglect, this traditional Yurok Indian family home was restored by the Del Norte Historical Society. It may be the oldest dwelling in California.

DEL NORTE COUNTY
HISTORICAL SITE

wild confusion as lines tangle, boats collide, and tempers rise.

A Coast Guard vessel is posted near the entrance of the lagoon to keep boats away from "Suicide Row." Skiff fishermen used to anchor gunwale-to-gunwale here within a short distance of the pounding surf. Such is the force of the river current combined with the outgoing tide that a small boat caught up in it is powerless to resist being swept into the breakers.

In recent years, the annual run of king salmon on the Klamath has averaged 168,000 fish. Perch, flounder, and sturgeon to two hundred pounds are also caught in the lagoon. Candlefish are taken with dip nets. Runs of American shad occur from May through July.

The Klamath Beach Road rejoins the Alder Camp Road near the Klamath River Bridge, where there is an exit to the U.S. 101 freeway. Statues of golden bears guard the portals of the freeway bridge as they did on the old span which was destroyed by the terrible winter flood of 1964. The deluge destroyed several river resorts including the town of Klamath.

Just across the bridge, an exit leads to a junction of the Starwein, Vista Point, and Klamath Village Roads. The Vista Point Road runs to the site of Old Klamath, of which nothing remains. The Starwein road winds three miles upriver to Klamath Glen. Here several resorts occupy a flat below the Terwar Valley where Fort Terwar was garrisoned in 1855 to oversee the Indians. After the fort was damaged by a flood in 1862, the soldiers moved to a post on the Smith River.

A mile or so upstream from Klamath Glen, the Starwein Road peters out at Starwein Flat. For thirteen miles, no road follows either bank of the Klamath. A highway is planned but there is much opposition to it, especially among the Indians. Timm Williams, a Yurok leader, claims it would disturb the ecology and

The sandbar at the mouth of the Klamath always draws a crowd when the salmon arrive in July. The trick here is to cast without fouling another man's line.

Klamath River Fishing

Some steelhead leave the sea to enter the Klamath every month of the year. However, the fish are rarely numerous enough to afford good angling on the lower river before late August or September. At this time, the runs are largely composed of "half-pounders," the local name for steelhead in the one- to three-pound category. These are very sporty trout, prone, when hooked on light tackle, to leap high above the water. As the season wears on, succeeding runs of steelhead tend to come in bigger sizes. After December rains raise and roil the river, the best fishing is found upstream off State Highway 96.

A fifteen-horsepower motor will suffice for trips upriver, whereas twenty-five horsepower is not too much if you plan to fish anywhere on the lower estuary. Many anglers use boats solely as a means of transportation to shore-fishing areas not accessible by road. No one without experience on fast water should attempt to navigate the Klamath above Blue Creek. For wading, a wading staff and bootfoot waders with felt soles are recommended because the stream bottom is very slippery.

The first steelhead of the summer season are liable to be caught by both bank and boat fishermen working the Old Bridge Pool downstream from the site of the present bridge. Upstream, such riffles as Turwar, Glen, Blake, and Tarup are apt to be productive when the early runs begin. The slicks are drifted with bait, spoons, spinners, and small plugs, as well as wet streamer flies. Favorite fly patterns include the Royal Coachman, Silver Hilton, Thor, Mickey Finn, Umpqua, and Green Drake.

Late summer fly fishing on the big water of the Klamath calls for the same tackle described in Chapter 10 for winter fishing. For spinning bait and lures, a nine-foot outfit with twelve-pound monofilament is recommended except on the sand bar near the mouth where heavy surf tackle is used. Boat fishermen who troll or anchor fish the lagoon for salmon prefer a husky six- to eight-foot boat rod and star drag reel spooled with line of at least thirty-pound breaking strength.

The little paperback *Klamath River Fishing* by Jim Freeman is worth its weight in gold for anglers new to the river. This "tackle box" guide includes maps which pinpoint the pools and riffles. Much valuable information is contained in the Fish and Game brochure and map entitled "The Angler's Guide to the Klamath River." For purists, there is the classic treatise *Steelhead to a Fly*, by Clark V. Van Fleet. Sport fishing regulations should be consulted for creel limits and special closures.

run through Indian villages and burial grounds. In 1973, the *San Francisco Chronicle* reported there was a "thriving black market" in Indian skulls, some bringing fifty dollars or more. Traffickers in skulls were said to be especially active in San Francisco and Los Angeles, where the demand seems to come from white middle-class cults that practice magical rites or "Satan worship."

Returning downriver, turn right on the Klamath Village Road. Off this drive is a lumber mill where visitors are welcome. Next door is the depot of the Klamath & Hoppaw Valley Railroad. The line operates a summer excursion train on four miles of track salvaged from a logging operation.

The new Klamath Village includes a motel, post office, and small shopping center. After the 1964 flood, it was developed with federal aid on a site that is four feet higher than the river has ever been known to rise. From Klamath Village, it's a short drive north by way of U.S. 101 to the exit for Requa. The Requa Road forks near the picturesque old Requa Inn. From here, the Mouth of the Klamath Road winds down to a resort and boat launching area on the estuary.

The Patrick Murphy Memorial Drive climbs the steep headland that abuts the north bank of the lagoon. Off this drive .6 mile from the Requa Inn, a side road approaches a redwood dwelling known as "Lye-eck." This is an old family home of the Yurok which has been restored by the Del Norte Historical Society. The rough boards and planks were hewn with an adze of elk horn driven by a stone hammer. There were twenty-four family homes and thirteen sweathouses here before Requa was raided in the 1870s by some Tolowa Indians from Crescent City. The Tolowas attacked

A pleasant alternative to the freeway that approaches the Klamath is the Alder Camp Road. It winds 9 miles through virgin forest in the Redwood National Park.

because they believed a Yurok shaman at Requa had worked magic to stop salmon from entering the Smith River.

Off the Patrick Murphy Drive 1.5 miles from the Requa Inn is a vista point of the Redwood National Park known as the Klamath Overlook. From here, a scenic foot trail runs four miles up the coast to Lagoon Creek.

The Klamath Overlook commands an aerial view of the estuary and the rock which holds the spirit of Oregos. When the Klamath Indian Reservation was created in 1855, it stretched from Oregos forty miles upriver to the confluence of the Klamath with the Trinity River. However, in 1891, President Harrison annexed the Klamath Reservation to the Hoopa Valley Reservation on the lower Trinity. Later, twenty miles of frontage on the Klamath estuary and lower river was detached from the reservation and allotted to the Yurok families who occupied it. Some of this frontage (including the sand spit at the river mouth) is still Indian-owned, but much of the land was acquired by white settlers and timber interests. At present, the Hoopa Reservation takes in 87,500 acres on the Klamath and Trinity with a population estimated at 3,300 Yuroks, 1,500 Hupas, plus smaller representation from perhaps a dozen other groups.

By the standards of the small coast rancherias described earlier, the residents of the Hoopa Reservation are relatively well off. Some obtain an income from timber receipts. Some are college-educated and operate resorts, sawmills, and other businesses. Yet employment opportunities are limited and more than a few families live in poverty, with little or no aid from local agencies.

Travelers can hear the songs of the Klamath people and see the ancient ceremonial dances during the Salmon Festival held in late June at the Klamath townsite. The festival is an informal blend of country fair, Indian culture, and Chamber of Commerce hokum. The attendance is mostly local, with a big turnout from Eureka and Crescent City. There are pony rides, "games of skill," "art-in-action," and booths which sell cakes, pies, paintings, and Indian beadwork. There are displays of beautiful Indian baskets which can't be had for any price.

After the local notables make their speeches, the Princess of the Salmon Festival is crowned. The princess is an Indian maiden selected from several contestants dressed in ancient finery. Then the sacred songs and dances begin. The first dance is not genuine because the men wear bonnets of turkey feathers—an innovation of the Plains Indians. A spokesman explains this is done to convince skeptics in the audience

Yurok maidens wait to hear who will be named princess of Salmon Festival. Ceremonial dress is authentic except for feather bonnet worn by man on the left.

that they are true American Indians. But then the bonnets are exchanged for the authentic red headbands of the Coast peoples. The bands are decorated with the scalps of woodpeckers. There follow the Brush Dance, the World Renewal Dance, and perhaps the Dance of the White Deer Skin. Only the men dance, but at times the women sing. Afterwards, a salmon barbeque is held on benches spread out in a meadow. Then the crowd divides to watch boat races, motorcycle acrobatics, logging contests, and the rough and tumble Indian stick game.

For centuries the spirit of Oregos has prevailed over all adversity for the Klamath people. But the day may come when the great runs of salmon and steelhead up the river are halted forever. This will happen if the California Water Plan is carried to completion. The plan calls for a chain of high dams which would impound the major tributaries of the Klamath and the main river down to the sea. Attempts to include the Klamath in the National Wild and Scenic Rivers system have thus far been unsuccessful. However, in 1973 a massive campaign by outdoor sports and conservationist groups persuaded the California legislature to pass a state wild rivers bill. This legislation outlaws dam building on both the Klamath and Trinity Rivers. The act also bans further impoundment of the Eel River for a period of twelve years.

*Pebble Beach Drive at Crescent City affords some of
the most beautiful seascapes on the North Coast.
Numerous paths and stairways approach the beach.*

Crescent City and the Smith River

On his trail-blazing expedition up the Redwood Coast, the mountain man Jedediah Smith camped near the present site of Crescent City and logged the low coastal plain in his journal. Smith's discoveries on this journey of 1828 were largely ignored by the outside world. The only interest was on the part of fur trappers anxious to find an overland route to California from the Pacific Northwest.

Settlement, when it came to Crescent Bay in the 1850s, was sparked by a colorful legend. There were many versions of the legend but, in substance, it told of a solitary prospector who trekked over the Coast Range and found a rich vein of gold near the seashore. The miner built a cabin and worked the strike for some time, taking care to hide the treasure he accumulated in a cleverly concealed place. Then, one day, he was attacked by Indians who burned the cabin and left him for dead. Half out of his mind, the gravely injured man somehow managed to make his way back to civilization. Here he told a few close friends where his gold was buried before he died of his wounds.

The tale as it was circulated in the Forty-Niner camps apparently contained some details which pointed to the Smith River area as the probable location. It was on a search for the "lost cabin" that a party of prospectors sighted Crescent Bay in the spring of 1851. This discovery was investigated by a party that came down from Althouse, Oregon. The group decided the bay had possibilities as a port and dispatched a delegate to San Francisco to find a backer. In the fall of 1852, the schooner *Pomona* arrived with supplies and a band of settlers headed by J. H. Wendell.

The townsite for Crescent City was laid out in February 1853. Within a year, three hundred buildings had been erected. For some years, Crescent City flourished as a shipping point for the diggings in southwest Oregon. It also vied with Trinidad and the ports on Humboldt Bay for the trade of the Klamath mines. Optimism for the town's future knew no bounds when it took over the county seat from Trinidad in 1854.

The price of city lots was driven out of sight by speculators. A furious campaign was launched to make Crescent City the capital of California. Families from the East were lured to emigrate here on the promise the town would soon overtake San Francisco. The bubble burst in 1855 when the county seat was shifted to Orleans Bar. But there was fresh excitement the following year when gold was discovered only six miles outside the city limits. The last big strikes in the Smith River watershed were made in the 1870s. By then, lumbering was nearly established as the dominant enterprise of Crescent City.

On the drive to Crescent City from the Klamath River, the road dips low to a patch of sandy seashore and then goes through the virgin forest of the 6,375-acre Del Norte Redwoods State Park. Three miles up the highway from Klamath Village is a resort known as "Trees of Mystery." The main interest here is some deformed redwoods and a display of Indian artifacts.

A mile farther along is the seashore at False Klamath Cove. Here is the Lagoon Creek Picnic Area of the Redwood National Park. The lagoon is an old millpond filled with water lilies and rainbow trout. There are benches, tables, stoves, and rest rooms. The ocean beach abounds with driftwood. Two trails leave the picnic area. The Yurok Loop Trail is a short self-guiding nature path. The other trail runs four miles south along a precipitous shore to the Klamath Overlook.

A short walk up the beach is the Wilson Creek Picnic Area of the Del Norte Redwoods State Park. Jedediah Smith's party paused here to feast on elk steaks. It's a popular place to dip net for surf smelt.

The Redwood Highway climbs to 1,200 feet above sea level on its nine-mile run through the Del Norte Redwoods. From Wilson Creek, it's 4.5 miles to the start of the Damnation Creek Trail in the Henry Solon Memorial Grove. This steep trail winds 2.5 miles through giant ferns and lush thickets of rhododendron in a semi-rain forest. The hike ends at a small rocky beach where there are tide pools. It's a good idea to allow plenty of time for this walk because of the rough climb back to the highway.

Four miles farther up the road is the turn-off to park headquarters and the 145-site Mill Creek Campground. Shaded by second-growth redwoods, the camp lies some distance inland from the fog belt. Park wildlife includes ruffed grouse, foxes, wildcats, bears, and Columbia blacktail deer. There is trout fishing in Mill Creek and sixteen miles of trails.

Shortly after U.S. 101 crosses the north boundary of the Del Norte Redwoods, the forest opens to expose the long, graceful sweep of Crescent Beach. In the fever of the Gold Rush, every square foot of this beach was staked out with mining claims.

Approximately 2.5 miles from the Mill Creek turn-off is a vista point of the Redwood National Park. A

Campground in the redwoods at Jedediah Smith State
Park fronts this swimming beach on the Smith River.
Anglers come here in winter to cast for steelhead.

mile farther, the Bluff Road branches south to approach Crescent Beach. The Bluff Road ends at a picnic area of the national park known as the Crescent Beach Overlook. From here, the Nickle Trail runs half a mile to primitive campsites on Nickle Creek. Close by is Enderts Beach which affords clamming, rock fishing, smelt netting, and surf casting for redtail perch.

Back on U.S. 101, it's two miles to the Citizens Dock on Crescent Bay. The dock is a public wharf built entirely with private donations of money, equipment, and materials. Crescent City has always been strong on community effort. When gold mining petered out in the 1870s, civic leaders organized a cooperative sawmill. It operated on Lake Earl until destroyed by fire in the 1890s.

Young people gather at the Citizens Dock after school to fish for perch and jack smelt; older people come here to launch their boats. Light- to medium-weight spinning tackle may be used for pier fishing. All a small child needs to catch perch is some bait and a hand line with one or two clamp-on sinkers and a Number 8 hook. An angling license is not required in California for saltwater fishing off a public pier.

Several fish companies have stations on the Citizens Dock where visitors may watch commercial boats unload shrimp, crab, rockfish, and salmon. Activity is brisk most evenings in summer, but here as at other ports on the North Coast the fishing industry has its woes. Competition from the modern fleets from Japan and the Soviet Union may become less an issue now that the sea limit for fisheries has been extended to 200 miles. Foreign vessels must obtain a permit to fish within this economic zone. However, there's mounting concern about ocean pollution, a decline in crab and

Built in 1856, the Battery Point Lighthouse is maintained as a museum which visitors may walk to at low tide. Pebble Beach runs from here to Pt. St. George.

salmon catches, and the possibility that the Department of Interior may authorize oil exploration off the Humboldt-Del Norte Coast.

West of the Citizens Dock are piers where freighters take on lumber. Crescent Harbor is one of the safest ports of refuge on the North Coast. It's protected by rock jetties that are reinforced on the seaward side with 1,975 concrete tetrapods. The latter resemble giant playing jacks. A French invention, each tetrapod weighs twenty-five tons. However, the harbor is not invulnerable to freak storms such as occurred in August of 1972. Packing eighty-mile-an-hour winds, the disturbance caused a number of boats to capsize or wash ashore. It also knocked down power poles in the city and blew the roofs off several homes.

Crescent City lies near the south end of the Smith River plain, which is eight miles deep and twenty-five miles long. The plain is cool and foggy, with a summer temperature that averages 61 degrees. A warmer, sunnier summer climate is found just a few miles inland where the mountains begin. About two-thirds of Del Norte County's 15,000 population lives on the plain. Next to lumbering, the important industries are recreation, dairy farming, commercial fishing, and the growing of Easter lily bulbs. A small enterprise is the packaging of decorative greenery, such as ferns, huckleberry, and redwood boughs for Eastern markets.

With its new shops and park-like waterfront, Crescent City has a contemporary look that belies its romantic past. This impression largely results from the tsunami which destroyed the old business district on March 28, 1964. Commonly spoken of as a "tidal wave," a tsunami is more accurately described as a seismic sea wave. A recent study by Army Engineer physicists found that most seismic waves originate far out on the Pacific when earthquakes occur in the eastern half of the Aleutian Trench. The waves are only a foot or so high on the open sea. But traveling at speeds up to five hundred miles an hour, they can wreak enormous havoc where they impact on the coast. Scientists seem to agree that the entire Pacific Coast north from San Francisco is vulnerable to damage from seismic waves. The 1964 tsunami, which took eleven lives at Crescent City, killed 107 persons in Alaska.

Among the few remnants of the early days on the Crescent City waterfront is the Battery Point Light-house, which is perched on a rocky isle off the foot of "A" Street. Built in 1856, the station is maintained as a public museum. It's a 200-yard walk from the beach at low tide.

The museum of the Del Norte Historical Society, at 577 "H" Street, contains Indian artifacts and relics of the pioneer settlements. Antiques fill the McNulty Museum, located a block away at Fifth and "H" Streets. The handsome new headquarters of the Redwood National Park is situated at 1111 "K" Street near the shopping mall.

Pebble Beach is fronted by a scenic drive from

Picnic ground at Lagoon Creek area of the Redwood National Park adjoins an old millpond filled with trout and water lilies. Close by is Wilson Beach.

Weather

At Crescent City the temperature in January, the coldest month, averages only thirteen degrees cooler than August, the warmest month. At Eureka the variation is only nine degrees. The temperature at Fort Bragg has never risen above ninety degrees or fallen below twenty-four degrees. By contrast with areas a few miles inland, the diurnal range is slight. For example, at Point Reyes, the average variation of temperature from day to night is less than ten degrees.

Precipitation is minimal everywhere on the North Coast in July and August. The first moderate-to-heavy rain is apt to occur in October on the Marin-Sonoma Coast and in September from Fort Bragg north. Winds in winter often blow in from the west or southwest. Storms usually follow southwesterly winds. No protection from these storms is provided by the coves where mariners seek shelter from the prevailing northwest winds of summer.

Rock slides and occasional washouts occur on Highway 1 and less frequently on U.S. 101 during storms. River roads are subject to flooding.

National Weather Service reports may be obtained by calling (415) 877-3400, San Francisco, or (707) 443-7062, Eureka. Or on VHF radio by tuning 162.55 mHz San Francisco or 162.40 mHz Eureka and Point Arena.

The following local commercial stations provide frequent weather reports:

City	Station	kHz	Antenna Location
Arcata	KATA	1340	40° 51′ 12″ N 124° 05′ 00″ W
Crescent City	KPOD	1310	41° 45′ 34″ N 124° 09′ 49″ W
Eureka	KINS	+980	40° 48′ 05″ N 124° 07′ 31″ W
Fort Bragg	KDAC	1230	39° 26′ 30″ N 123° 47′ 30″ W

which numerous trails and stairways approach the shore. The beach is popular with fishermen, driftwood collectors, and also rockhounds who seek agates, jade, and fragments of petrified wood. The charm of Pebble Beach is enhanced by a number of rocky islets with pines and Sitka spruce growing on them.

At the intersection of Pebble Beach Drive with Ninth Street, an historical marker memorializes the loss of the *Brother Jonathan*. On a stormy day in the summer of 1865, this coastwise steamer foundered on the rocks as it was attempting to enter Crescent Harbor. Of 232 passengers and crew, only nineteen persons survived. Off and on for years, local divers have attempted to locate the wreckage of the *Brother Jonathan*. Besides 346 hogsheads of whiskey, the ship was said to have been carrying a $200,000 payroll for soldiers stationed in the Northwest.

The St. George Light, located seven miles off Pebble Beach, has provided a beacon for mariners since 1891. The rock tower, which is 146 feet tall, required four years to build.

Point St. George, where there's rock fishing and skin diving, may be approached by way of Pebble Beach Drive and Washington Boulevard. The latter road ends at a trailhead which gives access to Pelican Bay north of the point. Here, miles of driftwood-littered beach stretch north to the mouth of the Smith River. There's perch fishing, smelt netting, and beds of littleneck, razor, and Washington clams.

A few miles northeast of the business district at Crescent City, the Redwood Highway forks. U.S. 101 swings north to approach the estuary of the Smith River. U.S. Highway 199 bears east to enter the redwoods of Jedediah Smith State Park.

If you're not towing a trailer, the more interesting approach to the Jedediah Smith Redwoods is by way of the Howland Hill Road. This is a remnant of the old stage road which ran to Sailor Diggings and other mining camps in southwest Oregon. It was known as the "Crescent City and Yreka Plank Turnpike Road" when it was built in 1858. On this drive, we leave U.S. 101 southeast of town on the Elk Valley Road. It's about a mile to the junction with the Howland Hill Road.

Another mile brings us to the steep grade which crests on Howland Summit. It was here Crescent

City's first lumber mill, built by F. E. Weston in 1853, obtained timber. The logs were hauled to town on a wagon with wheels twelve feet in diameter. From Howland Summit, the narrow, unpaved road inclines gently through the heart of the Jedediah Smith Redwoods. The road joins Highway 199 just outside the northeast corner of the park in the Six Rivers National Forest.

Proceeding west on U.S. 199, it's a short run to the developed area of the park. There's a large campground where raccoons raid food left out at night and an attractive swimming beach on the Smith River. A number of trails leave the area for nature walks. One approaches the Stout Grove, said to contain the heaviest stand of timber on the coast. The largest redwood here measures twenty feet in diameter and 340 feet tall.

On a stroll along the banks of the Smith, you may see otters playing in the riffles. Summer fishing is good for rainbow and cutthroat trout. In winter, there's steelhead fishing on the main river and the Middle Fork upstream to Patrick Creek in the National Forest.

The Smith River estuary may be approached on the North Bank Road, an eight-mile scenic drive which leaves U.S. 199 near park headquarters.

The sparsely populated plain north of Crescent City may be explored on the Lake Earl Drive. This bypassed section of the original Redwood Highway may be approached from the junction of Highways 101 and 199 by way of Northcrest Drive. It's a 5.5-mile drive to Buzzini Road, which leads to a small boat-launching site on Lake Earl, a 2,000-acre freshwater lagoon fringed with tule marsh and logged-over forest. This ecosystem supports 15 kinds of fish, 58 kinds of mammals, and over 250 species of birds. Presently the state is in the process of acquiring the Lake Earl area as part of a program to save what is left of California's wetlands, two-thirds of which have been preempted for industry and housing. When the entire area has been purchased, state ownership will include six miles of ocean frontage.

The Lake Earl Drive runs north through dreary cutover land to Fort Dick, which has a cheese plant. The hamlet was named for a nearby farm, known as Dick's Fort, where the settlers took refuge from the Indians. A trifle north of Fort Dick, the road joins U.S. 101 just before it crosses the Smith River on the Dr. Fine Bridge. On the north bank, the Fred Haight Drive leaves the highway to approach the Smith River Angling Access where there's boat launching.

Four miles up the highway is the village of Smith River on Rowdy Creek. This is a dairy and lumbering

center where an Easter Lily Festival is held in July. Most of the potted Easter lilies sold in this country come from bulbs grown in the Crescent City area and just across the state line at Harbor, Oregon. The industry got started after imports of bulbs from Japan ceased in World War II.

On the Sarina Road, which leaves the Redwood Highway 1.5 miles west of Smith River, is the large bulb farm of Dahlstrom and Watt. The lilies bloom in the fields here during July. Bulbs which produce flowers in time for Easter are "forced" by florists in hot houses. Lily bulbs are a high-risk crop which call for an investment of as much as $10,000 an acre. Two growing seasons are required before the bulbs may be harvested. The most popular strains are the Ace and Nellie White.

The Sarina Road terminates at a large fishing resort situated where Rowdy Creek enters the Smith River.

Returning to U.S. 101, it's two miles farther to the fishing resorts clustered near the river mouth in the vicinity of Salmon Harbor. Here the facilities found on the Klamath River lagoon are duplicated. A landmark is the Ship Ashore Restaurant. It's housed in the SS Castle Rock, a 480-ton steel ship which was used by the Navy in World War II.

The Smith is only a shade less renowned than the Klamath as an angling river. Each year it yields trophy steelhead to twenty pounds and king salmon to fifty pounds. The best fishing gets underway just when the action on the lower Klamath begins to slow. October is the peak month for king salmon. This is when skiff fishermen anchor gunwale-to-gunwale across the lower estuary in rows known as "hog lines." The fall migration of silver salmon arrives in November. The early run of steelhead known as "half-pounders" peaks in late October. The trophy fish show in December and January.

The Smith supports the best fishing for sea-run cutthroat trout in California. Spring and autumn afford the peak action. The services of a professional guide are recommended because the productive water is highly localized. The east end of Tillas Island is apt to be rewarding in May. Spoons, wet flies, and strip bait trolled on a Number 2 hook are the favorite offerings.

Just where U.S. 101 veers north from the river mouth, it passes the Smith River Indian Reservation. The last stop before Oregon is Pelican State Beach. An obscure, unsigned lane near the Nautical Inn approaches this undeveloped frontage. The beach is usually fog-bound and deserted, but it holds a treasure trove of driftwood.

Information Sources

Highway Conditions: Call the Department of Transportation, (415) 557-3755.

Visitor's Bureau, Redwood Empire Association, 360 Post Street, San Francisco, CA 94108; (415) 421-6554.

CALIFORNIA AGENCIES

Boating and Waterways Department, 1629 S Street, Sacramento, CA 95814; (916) 445-2615.

California Coastal Commission, 631 Howard Street, San Francisco, CA 94103; (415) 543-8555.

CALTRANS (Department of Transportation), 1120 N Street, Sacramento, CA 95814; (916) 445-4616.

Fish and Game Department, 1416 Ninth Street, Sacramento, CA 95814; (916) 445-3531.

Region I, Eureka Branch Office, (Humboldt—Del Norte counties), 619 Second Street, Eureka, CA 95501; (707) 443-6771.

Region III (Marin, Sonoma, and Mendocino counties), Yountville Veterans Facility, P.O. Box 47, Yountville, CA 94599; (707) 944-2443.

Parks and Recreation Department, 1416 9th Street, Sacramento, CA 95814.

For reservations call for location of nearest Ticketron office. San Francisco area; (415) 788-2828; Los Angeles area; (213) 670-1242; Sacramento area, (916) 445-8828.

District 1 Headquarters, 3431 Fort Street, Eureka, CA 95501; (707) 443-4588.

Mendocino Area Headquarters, Highway 1, Mendocino, CA 95460; (707) 937-5804.

FEDERAL AGENCIES

Bureau of Land Management, Ukiah District Office, 555 Leslie Street, Ukiah, CA 95482; (707) 462-3873.

Fish and Wildlife Service
Humboldt Bay National Wildlife Refuge, Fifth and H Streets, P.O. Box 1386, Eureka, CA 95501; (707) 445-1352.

National Forests
Six Rivers National Forest, 710 E Street, Eureka, CA 95501; (707) 442-1721.

National Parks
Visitor Information, National Park Service, 450 Golden Gate Avenue, San Francisco, CA 94102; (415) 556-4122.

Golden Gate National Recreation Area, Building 201, Fort Mason, San Francisco, CA 94123; (415) 556-0560.

Point Reyes National Seashore, Point Reyes, CA 94956; (415) 663-1092.

Redwood National Park, Second and K Streets, Crescent City, CA 95521; (707) 464-6101.

CONSERVATION GROUPS

Audubon Society, Marin Chapter, P.O. Box 441, Tiburon, CA 94920; (415) 383-1644.

California Trout, P.O. Box 2046, San Francisco, CA 94126; (415) 392-8887.

Friends of the Earth, 124 Spear Street, San Francisco, CA 94105; (415) 495-4770.

Greenpeace Foundation, Building 240, Fort Mason, San Francisco, CA 94123; (415) 474-6767.

Nature Conservancy, 425 Bush Street, San Francisco, CA 94108; (415) 391-0146.

Point Reyes Bird Observatory, 4990 State Route 1, Stinson Beach, CA 94970; (415) 868-1221.

Save-the-Redwoods League, 114 Sansome Street, San Francisco, CA 94104; (415) 362-2352.

Sierra Club, 530 Bush Street, San Francisco, CA 94108; (415) 981-8634.

Trust for Public Land, 82 Second Street, San Francisco, CA 94105; (415) 495-4014.

CHAMBERS OF COMMERCE

Arcata Area Chamber of Commerce, 780 7th Street, Arcata, CA 95521; (707) 822-3619.

Bodega Bay Area Chamber of Commerce, State Route 1, P.O. Box 146, Bodega Bay, CA 94923; (707) 875-3407.

Del Norte County Chamber of Commerce, P.O. Box 246, Front and K Streets, Crescent City, CA 95531; (707) 464-3174.

Eureka Chamber of Commerce, 2112 Broadway, Eureka, CA 95501; (707) 442-3738.

Fort Bragg-Mendocino Chamber of Commerce, 332 North Main Street, Fort Bragg, CA 95437; (707) 964-3153.

Fortuna Chamber of Commerce, 735 14th Street, Fortuna, CA 95540; (707) 725-3959.

Marin Coast Chamber of Commerce, Box 94 Olema, CA 94950; (415) 663-1244.

Russian River Region, Inc., P.O. Box 255, Guerneville, CA 95446; (707) 869-2584.

Bibliography

ACCOMMODATIONS AND CALENDAR OF EVENTS

Redwood Empire Visitor's Guide (Annual). Redwood Empire Association, 360 Post Street, San Francisco, California 94108. (Enclose $1.00 for delivery.)

ARCHITECTURE

Gebhard, Montgomery, Winter, and Woodbridge. *A Guide to Architecture in San Francisco and Northern California*. Santa Barbara, California: Peregine Smith, Inc., 1973.

Kirker, Harold. *California's Architectural Frontier*. San Marino, California: The Huntington Library, 1970.

BIRDS

Kozlik, Frank M. *Waterfowl of California*. Sacramento: California Department of Fish and Game, 1957.

Peterson, Rodger Tory. *A Field Guide to Western Birds*. Boston: Houghton Mifflin Company, 1961.

Pough, Richard H. *Audubon Western Bird Guide*. Garden City, New York: Doubleday and Company, 1957.

BOATING AND WATERSPORTS

Berssen, Captain William. *Sea Boating Almanac–Northern California and Nevada Edition 1976* (Annual). Sea Boating Almanac, Box Q, Ventura, California 93001.

Harris, Thomas. *Down the Wild Rivers*. San Francisco: Chronicle Books, 1972.

Schwind, Dick. *West Coast River Touring*. Beaverton, Oregon: The Touchstone Press, 1974.

West, Carolyn and Jack. *Cruising the Pacific Coast*. Miller Freeman Publications, Inc., 1970.

> *Safe Boating Hints for the Northern California Coast,*
> *Boating Safety Hints for Hunters and Fishermen,*
> *Boating Safety Hints for Tomales Bay,*

California Department of Boating and Waterways, 1629 S Street, Sacramento, California 95814.

CAMPING

California State Parks. Menlo Park, California: Lane Publishing Company, 1975.

Sunset Western Campsites 1976 (Annual). Lane Publishing Company, 85 Willow Road, Menlo Park, California 94025.

The California State Park System (map and brochure). California Department of Parks and Recreation.

Woodall's Campground Directory—1976 Western Edition (Annual). Woodall's, 500 Hyacinth Place, Highland Park, Illinois 60035.

Woodall's Campground Directory—1976 Western Edition (Annual). Woodall's, 500 Hyacinth Place, Highland Park, Illinois 60035.

FISH COOKERY

Lawrence, Barbara. *Fisherman's Wharf Cookbook*. Concord, California: Nitty-gritty Productions, 1971.

Miloradovich, Milo. *The Art of Fish Cookery*. New York: Doubleday, 1970.

Sunset Seafood Cookbook. Menlo Park, California: Lane Publishing Company, 1975.

FISH AND FISHING: ANADROMOUS

Fry, Donald H., Jr. *Anadromous Fishes*. Sacramento: California Department of Fish and Game, 1973.

Coast Cutthroat Trout

> Johnson, Les. *Fishing the Sea-Run Cutthroat Trout*. Portland, Oregon: Northwest Salmon Trout Steelheader Company, 1971.

Pacific Salmon

> Briggs, John C. *The Behavior and Reproduction of Salmonid Fishes in a Small Coastal Stream*. (Fish Bulletin No. 94—Redwood Creek.) Sacramento: California Department of Fish and Game, 1953.

> Hershey, Marvin C. and German, Eugene R. *The Silver Salmon of Muir Woods*. The Muir Woods-Point Reyes Natural History Association, 1973.

> McClane, A. J., Editor. *McClane's Standard Fishing Encyclopedia*. New York: Rinehart and Winston, 1965.

Salmon and Steelhead

> Leitritz, Earl. *Trout and Salmon Culture* (Fish Bulletin No. 107). Sacramento: California Fish and Game Department, 1963.

> Shapovalov, Leo and Taft, Alan C. *The Life Histories of the Steelhead Rainbow Trout and Silver Salmon*. Sacramento: California Department of Fish and Game, 1954.

An Environmental Tragedy. Sacramento: State of nia/Citizens Advisory Committee on Salmon and Steelhead Trout/Assembly Concurrent Resolution No. 64/1970 Session, 1971.

Shad

Radovich, John. *How to Catch, Bone, and Cook a Shad.* Sacramento: California Department of Fish and Game, 1970.

Steelhead Rainbow Trout

Combs, Trey. *The Steelhead Trout–Life History, Early Angling, Contemporary Steelheading.* Portland, Oregon: Northwest Salmon Trout Steelheader Company, 1971.

Freeman, Jim. *Klamath River Fishing.* San Francisco: Chronicle Books, 1971.

Freeman, Jim. *Practical Steelhead Fishing.* New York: A. S. Barnes and Company, Inc., 1966.

Krieder, Claude M. *Steelhead.* New York: G. P. Putnam's Sons, 1948.

FISH AND FISHING: SALT WATER

Baxter, John L. *Inshore Fishes of California.* Sacramento: California Department of Fish and Game, 1963.

Cannon, Raymond. *How to Fish the Pacific Coast.* Menlo Park, California: Lane Publishing Company, 1956.

Fitch, John E. *Offshore Fishes of California.* Sacramento: California Department of Fish and Game, 1965.

Miller, Daniel J. and Lea, Robert N. *Guide to the Coastal Marine Fishes of California* (Fish Bulletin No. 157). Sacramento: California Department of Fish and Game, 1972.

Orcutt, Harold George. *The Life History of the Starry Flounder* (Fish Bulletin No. 78). Sacramento: California Fish and Game Department, 1950.

Phillips, Julius B. *A Review of the Rockfishes of California* (Fish Bulletin No. 104). Sacramento: California Department of Fish and Game, 1957.

Roedel, Phil M. *Common Ocean Fishes of the California Coast* (Fish Bulletin No. 91). Sacramento: California Department of Fish and Game, 1953.

Turner, Charles H. and Sexsmith, Jeremy C. *Marine Baits of California.* Sacramento: California Department of Fish and Game, 1965.

The Commercial Fish Catch of California for the Year 1947 With an Historical Review 1916-1947 (Fish Bulletin No. 74). Sacramento: California Department of Fish and Game, 1949.

GEOLOGY

Alt, David D. and Hyndman, Donald W. *Roadside Geology of Northern California.* Missoula, Montana: Mountain Press Publishing Company, 1975.

Bailey, Edgar H., Editor. *Geology of Northern California.* Bulletin No. 190. San Francisco: Division of Mines and Geology, 1966.

Bowen, Oliver E., Jr. *Rock and Minerals of the San Francisco Bay Region.* Berkeley: University of California Press, 1972.

Brown, Vinson and Allan, David. *Rocks and Minerals of California and Their Stories.* San Martin, California: Naturegraph Company, 1955.

Davis, William Morris. *The Lakes of California.* California Journal of Mines and Geology, Volume 44, No. 2. San Francisco: Division of Mines, April 1948.

Hinds, Norman E. *Evolution of the California Landscape.* Bulletin No. 158. San Francisco: Division of Mines, 1952.

Sorrel, Charles A. *Minerals of the World–A Guide to Field Identification.* New York: Golden Press, 1973.

GUIDEBOOKS: ROAD AND TRAIL

Bleything, Dennis and Hawkins, Susan. *Getting Off on 96–Drives and Hikes in the Trinity Alps, Redwoods, and Siskiyous.* Beaverton, Oregon: The Touchstone Press, 1975.

Doss, Margot Patterson. *Paths of Gold–In and About the Golden Gate National Recreation Area.* San Francisco: Chronicle Books, 1974.

Ferber, Richard. *Exploring Coastal Marin.* Stinson Beach, California: Curlew Press, 1969.

Miller, Jeanne Thurlow. *Seeing Historic Sonoma County Today.* Santa Rosa, California: The Miller Associates, 1967.

Mullen, Barbara Dorr. *The Mendocino Coast.* Fort Bragg, California: Privately printed, 1971.

Olmsted, Nancy. *To Walk With a Quiet Mind–Hikes in the Woodlands, Parks, and Beaches of the San Francisco Bay Area.* San Francisco: Sierra Club, 1975.

Spring, Ira L. and Manning, Harvey. *Wilderness Trails Northwest.* Beaverton, Oregon: The Touchstone Press, 1974.

Wood, Amos L. *Beachcombing the Pacific.* Chicago: Henry Regnery Company, 1975.

Del Norte County Vacation Guide (Annual). Crescent City, Del Norte Triplicate.

North Coast Tour Booklet. Fort Bragg, California: Mendocino County Historical Society, 1970.

Welcome to Humboldt (Annual). Eureka: Humboldt Council Chambers of Commerce.

Welcome to Mendocino County (Annual). Mendocino Chamber of Commerce.

HISTORY AND DESCRIPTION

North Coast: History and Description

Bronson, William. *How to Kill a Golden State.* Garden City, New York: Doubleday and Company, Inc., 1968.

Chase, J. Smeaton. *California Coast Trails.* Boston and New York: Houghton Mifflin Company, 1913.

Clark, William B. *Gold Districts of California.* San Francisco: California Division of Mines, 1970.

Dillon, Richard. *Siskiyou Trail.* New York: McGraw-Hill Company, 1975.

Ellison, William Henry. *A Self-Governing Dominion, California 1849-1860.* Berkeley: University of California Press, 1950.

Felton, Ernest L. *California's Many Climates.* Palo Alto, California: Pacific Books, 1965.

Gudde, Erwin G. *California Place Names.* Berkeley: University of California Press, 1965.

Hoover, Rensch, and Abeloe. *Historic Spots in California.* Stanford, California: Stanford University Press, 1966.

Lantis, Steiner, and Karinen. *California: Land of Contrast.* Belmont, California: Wadsworth Publishing Company, 1963.

Nixon, Stuart. *Redwood Empire.* New York: E. P. Dutton and Company, Inc., 1966.

Powers, Alfred. *Redwood Country*. New York: Duel, Sloan and Pearce, 1949.

Robertson, John W. *Francis Drake and Other Early Explorers Along the Pacific Coast*. San Francisco: Grabhorn Press, 1927.

Robinson, John. *The Redwood Highway*. California Highways and Public Works, May-June 1964 and September-October 1964.

Sullivan, Maurice S. *The Travels of Jedediah Strong Smith*. Santa Ana, California: Fine Arts Press, 1934.

Wagner, Henry R. *Spanish Voyages to the Northwest Coast of America in the Sixteenth Century*. San Francisco: California Historical Society, 1929.

Woods, Ruth Kedzie. *The Tourist's California*. New York: Dodd, Mead, 1914.

California Coastal Plan. Sacramento: California Coastal Zone Conservation Commission, 1975.

California Coastline Preservation and Recreation Plan. Sacramento: California Department of Parks and Recreation, 1971.

California's Historical Landmarks. State of California Resources Agency, Divisions of Beaches and Parks.

Marin County: History and Description

Gilliam, Harold. *Island in Time; The Point Reyes Peninsula*. San Francisco: Sierra Club, 1962.

Gilliam, Harold. *San Francisco Bay*. Garden City, New York: Doubleday and Company, 1957.

Mason, Jack. *Point Reyes; The Solemn Land*. Point Reyes Station, California: De Wolfe Printing, 1970.

Mason, Jack and Barfield, Thomas J. *Last Stage for Bolinas*. Inverness, California: North Shore Books, 1973.

Munro-Fraser, J. P. *History of Marin County*. San Francisco: Alley Bowen & Company, 1880.

Drake's Plate of Brass. San Francisco: California Historical Society, 1937.

Sonoma County: History and Description

Hansen and Miller. *Wild Oats in Eden*. Santa Rosa, California: Privately printed, 1962.

Kushner, Howard I. *Conflict on the Northwest Coast*. Westport, Connecticut: Greenwood Press, 1975.

Munro-Fraser, J. P. *History of Sonoma County*. San Francisco: Alley, Bowen, and Company, 1880. Republished Petaluma, California: Charmaine Burdell Veronda, 1973.

Thompson, R. A. *Fort Ross*. Oakland, California: Bio-books, 1951.

The Russians in California. San Francisco: California Historical Society, 1933.

Mendocino County: History and Description

Carpenter, A. O. *History of Mendocino and Lake Counties*. Los Angeles: Historic Record Company, 1914.

Menefee, C. A. *Historical and Descriptive Sketch Book of Napa, Sonoma, Lake and Mendocino County*. Napa, California: Reporter Publishing House, 1873.

Munro-Fraser, J. P. *History of Mendocino County*. San Francisco: Alley Bowen and Company, 1880.

Humboldt and Del Norte Counties: History and Description

Coy, Owen C. *The Humboldt Bay Region*. Los Angeles: The California State Historical Association, 1929.

Hoopes, Chad L. *Lure of Humboldt Bay Region*. Dubuque, Iowa: William C. Brown Co., 1966.

Palmquist, Peter E. *"Fine California Views–the photographs of A. W. Ericson."* Eureka, California: Interface California Corporation, 1975.

Raphael, Ray. *"An Everday History of Somewhere–Being the True Story of Indians, Deer, Homesteaders, Potatoes, Loggers, Trees, Fishermen, Salmon, and Other Living Things in the Backwoods of California."* New York: Alfred A. Knopf, 1974.

Raphael, Ray. *"Edges."* New York: Alfred A. Knopf, 1976.

Smith, Esther Ruth. *The History of Del Norte County*. Oakland, California: The Holmes Book Company, 1953.

History of Humboldt County, California. San Francisco: W. W. Elliot and Company, 1881.

INDIANS

Aginsky, B. W. and E. G. *Deep Valley*. New York: Stein and Day, 1967.

Forbes, Jack D. *Native Americans of California and Nevada*. Healdsburg, California: Naturegraph Publishers, 1969.

Heizer, R. F. and Whipple, M. A. *The California Indians*. Berkeley: California: University of California Press, 1971.

Heizer, Robert F. *The Destruction of California Indians*. Peregrine Smith, 1974.

Hoopes, Chad L. *Domesticate or Exterminate*. Loleta, California: Redwood Coast Publications, 1975.

Kroeber, A. L. *Handbook of the Indians of California*. Washington, D.C.: Smithsonian Institute, Bulletin No. 78, 1925.

Raymond, Lee and Rice, Ann. *Marin Indians*. Sausalito, California: Pages of History, 1957.

Warburton and Endert. *Indian Lore of the Northern California Coast*. Santa Clara, California: Pacific Pueblo Press, 1966.

Progress Report to the Governor and Legislature by State Advisory Commission on Indian Affairs. Senate Bill No. 1007 on Indians in Rural and Reservation Area, 1966.

MAMMALS

Daugherty, Anita E. *Marine Mammals of California*. Sacramento: California Department of Fish and Game, 1972.

Dasmann, William P. *Big Game of California*. Sacramento: California Department of Fish and Game, 1958.

Ingles, Lloyd Glenn. *Mammals of California and Its Coastal Waters*. Stanford, California: Stanford University Press, 1957.

Miller, Tom. *The World of the California Gray Whale*. Santa Ana, California: Baja Trail Publications, Inc., 1975.

Seymour, George. *Furbearers of California*. Sacramento, California: California Department of Fish and Game, 1968.

MAPS

California State Automobile Association
    North Bay Counties
    Northwestern California

C. E. Erickson & Associates, 337 Seventeenth Street, Oakland, California 94612
    Point Reyes National Seashore
    Mount Tamalpais
    Golden Gate National Recreation Area

Federal Bureau of Land Management Publications
King Range Recreation Guide

State of California, Department of Fish and Game Publications:
Angler's Guide to the Klamath River
Ocean Fishing Map of Marin and Sonoma Counties
Ocean Fishing Map of Del Norte, Humboldt, and Mendocino Counties
Salmon and Steelhead Fishing Map

NEWSPAPERS

Del Norte Triplicate (Crescent City)
Fort Bragg Advocate-News
Humboldt Beacon (Fortuna)
Humboldt Times-Standard (Eureka)
Independent Coast Observer (Gualala)
Mendocino Beacon (Mendocino City)
Mendocino Grapevine
Oakland Tribune
Point Reyes Light (Point Reyes Station)
Russian River News (Guerneville)
Sacramento Bee
San Francisco Chronicle
San Francisco Examiner
The Union (Arcata)

PERIODICALS

Pacifica—Magazine of the North Coast (Arcata)

RAILROADS

Abdill, George B. *This Was Railroading*. Seattle, Washington: Superior Publishing Company, 1975.

Crump, Spencer. *The Story of the Western Skunk Railroad*. Los Angeles: Trans-Anglo Books, 1963.

Dickinson, A. Bray. *Narrow Gauge to the Redwoods*. Los Angeles: Trans-Anglo Books, 1967.

Kneiss, Gilbert H. *Redwood Railways*. Berkeley, California: Howell-North, 1956.

REAL ESTATE

Robinson, David. *The Complete Homesteading Book*. Charlotte, Vermont: Garden Way Publishing, 1974.

Scher, Les. *Finding and Buying Your Place in the Country*. New York: Macmillan, 1976.

SHELLFISH

Carlisle, John G. *Red Tide in California* (Marine Resources Leaflet No. 2). Long Beach, California: California Department of Fish and Game, 1973.

Cox, Keith W. *Review of the Abalone in California*. Sacramento: California Fish and Game Department.

Fitch, John E. *Common Marine Bivalves of California*. (Fish Bulletin No. 90) Sacramento: California Fish and Game Department, 1953.

Phillips, J. B. *California Market Crab and Its Close Relatives* (Marine Resources Leaflet No. 5). Long Beach, California: California Department of Fish and Game, 1973.

SHIPPING

Gibbs, James A. *Shipwrecks of the Pacific Coast*. Portland, Oregon: Binforts and Mort, 1957.

Gibbs, Jim. *West Coast Lighthouses*. Seattle, Washington: Superior Publishing Co., 1972.

Kortum, Karl and Roger Olmsted. *Sailing Days on the Redwood Coast*. San Francisco: Published for the Pacific Lumber Company by the California Historical Society in cooperation with the San Francisco Maritime Museum, 1971.

McNairn, Jack and MacMullen, Jerry. *Ships of the Redwood Coast*. Stanford, California: Stanford University Press, 1945.

Newell, Gordon and Williamson, Joe. *Pacific Lumber Ships*. Seattle, Washington: Superior Publishing Co., 1960.

Putnam, George R. *Lights and Lightships of the United States*. Boston: Houghton Mifflin, 1917.

TIDE POOLS

Braun, Ernest and Brown, Vinson. *Exploring Pacific Coast Tide Pools*. Healdsburg, California: Naturegraph Publishing Company, 1966.

Ricketts, Edward F., Calvin, Jack, and Hedgpeth, Joel. *Between Pacific Tides*. Stanford, California: Stanford University Press, 1960.

Tierny, Robert J. *Exploring Tidal Life Along the Pacific Coast*. Tidepool Association, 1966.

Tucker, R. *Seashells of America–A Guide to Field Identification*. New York: Golden Press, New York, 1968.

TIMBER AND PARKLAND

Adams, Kramer. *The Redwoods*. New York: Popular Library.

Andrews, Ralph W. *Redwood Classic*. Seattle, Washington: Superior Publishing Co., 1958.

Leydet, Francois. *The Last Redwoods and the Parkland of Redwood Creek*. San Francisco: Sierra Club, 1969.

Moungovan and Escola. *Where There's a Will, There's a Way; Unusual Logging and Lumbering Methods on the Mendocino Coast*. Mendocino County Historical Society, 1968.

Weaver, Harriett E. *Adventures in the Redwoods*. San Francisco: Chronicle Books, 1975.

The California Coast Redwood. U.S. Department of Agriculture, Forest Service, October 1964.

TREES, SHRUBS, AND FLOWERS

Bowers, Nathan A. *Cone Bearing Trees of the Pacific Coast*. Palo Alto, California: Pacific Books, 1942.

Clements, Edith S. *Flowers of the Coast and Sierra*. New York: H. W. Wilson Company, 1928.

Crampton, Beecher. *Grasses in California*. Berkeley: University of California Press, 1974.

Dawson, E. Yale. *Seashore Plants of Northern California*. Berkeley: University of California Press, 1966.

Grillos, Steve J. *Ferns and Fern Allies of California*. Berkeley: University of California Press, 1966.

Jepsen, Willis L. *Trees, Shrubs, and Flowers of the Redwood Region*. San Francisco: Save-the-Redwoods League.

McMinn, Howard E. and Maino, Evelyn. *Pacific Coast Trees*. Berkeley: University of California Press, 1967.

Munz, Philip A. *Shore Wildflowers of California, Oregon, and Washington*. Berkeley, California: University of California Press, 1964.

Rowntree, Lester. *Flowering Shrubs of California*. Stanford, California: Stanford University Press, Second Edition 1948.

Index